THE TALE OF PRINCE SAMUTTAKOTE

T0355637

Thomas John Hudak teaches in the Department of Anthropology at the Arizona State University at Tempe, Arizona 85287.

THE TALE OF PRINCE SAMUTTAKOTE
A Buddhist Epic From Thailand

Translated, Annotated, and Introduced

by

Thomas John Hudak

Ohio University Center for International Studies
Monographs in International Studies

Southeast Asia Series Number 90
Athens, Ohio 1993

Printed in the United States of America
All rights reserved

97 96 95 94 93   5 4 3 2 1

The books in the Center for International Studies Monograph Series are printed
on acid-free paper ∞

Library of Congress Cataloging-in-Publication Data

Horathibodi, Phra, d. ca. 1680.
    [Samutthrakhot kamchan. English]
    The tale of Prince Samuttakote / translated, annotated, and introduced by
Thomas John Hudak.
        p. cm–(Monographs in international studies. Southeast Asia series; no. 90)
    Poem.
    Translation of: Samutthrakhot kamchan.
    Summary: Translation of an apocryphal birth-story about previous
incarnation of Lord Buddha as Prince Samudraghosa in Paññasajataka, Pali
Buddhist canon, as retold in Siamese chan-style verse by Horathibodi, Phra,
d. ca. 1680, augmented by Narai, King of Siam, 1632-1688, and finished by
Paramanuchit Chinorot, Prince, son of Phuttayotfa Chulalok, King of
Siam, Supreme Patriarch, 1790-1853.
    Includes bibliographical references.
    ISBN 0-89680-174-8
    I. Hudak, Thomas J.II. Narai, King of Siam,1632-1688. III.
Paramanuchit Chinorot, Prince, son of Phutthayotfa Chulalok, King of
Siam, Supreme Patriarch, 1790-1853. IV. Tipitaka. Suttapitaka.
Khuddakanikaya. Jataka. Paññasajataka. V. Title. VI. Series.
PL4209. H67A24   1993
895. 9'111–dc20   92-42731
                                              CIP

To my family

CONTENTS

ILLUSTRATIONS

ACKNOWLEDGMENTS

This translation project began under the auspices of a Fulbright Senior Research Grant that allowed me to spend ten months in Thailand. While in Thailand, I received valuable assistance from the National Research Council, the National Library, and the Department of Fine Arts. A number of individuals in Thailand were also especially helpful. Doris Wibunsin, former director of the Fulbright office in Bangkok, helped solve administrative problems and make important contacts. Kullasap Gesmankit from the Department of Fine Arts gave valuable time and encouragement to the project. Sidthorn Sangdhanoo provided help in translating difficult passages. Kongkaew Veeraprachak and Kasian Mapamo at the National Library lent their assistance in finding manuscripts and references. Sunee Chang photographed the paintings included in this volume, and Khun Pradit, the caretaker of the paintings, made arrangements for viewing the paintings. Ken and Jutharat Pas, good friends, always had time to show interest in the progress of the project. And Paladisai Inpim worked many hours as a valued research assistant. To all of these organizations and individuals, I would like to express my gratitude for their assistance and encouragement.

In the United States, another group of individuals lent their support and expertise. William J. Gedney first introduced me to classical Thai literature. Ann Hansen, Yui Hooncamlong, Ketkanda Jaturongkachoke, David Streckfuss, and Deborah Wong helped track down obscure references in the text. Fe Susan Go and Richard Richie provided library assistance. James Hudak, Juliane Schober, and Arthur Wrobel assisted in translating several German passages. Bonnie Brereton, Judy Chase, and Patricia Young contributed a number of different ideas about the translation. Marcia Schweitzer spent many hours entering and formatting the text. To all of these people, I would like to extend special acknowledgment and thanks.

A final note of thanks must be extended to James Cobban for his valuable editorial advice and to Hope Hendricks for her accuracy in completing the final manuscript.

INTRODUCTION

Since the thirteenth century, Thailand has had a rich and varied literature which, for the most part, has been little known in the West. Until the late nineteenth and early twentieth centuries when prose became a major literary force, most of this literature appeared in one of five classical verse forms: *raay, khlong, kaap, chan*, or *klon*. In fact, before prose, poetry and literature were regarded as one and the same thing. By far the oldest poetic forms are the indigenous raay and khlong meters which first rose to prominence when the Thai language had a system of three tones rather than the present-day five. During the Ayutthaya period (1351-1767), Cambodian kaap and Indic chan meters became the favorites of the court and the intelligentsia, the educated and the learned audiences for poetry. Eventually, these meters were replaced by the indigenous klon meter, which appeared in the early Ratanakosin period (1782-1851) or the late Thonburi period (1767-82) or even perhaps the late Ayutthaya period. Poetic masterpieces, some of them of great length, were produced in all five verse forms. The most common classical themes found in these poems include stories of the Buddha and elaborate Indic myths and legends that intermingle the human, natural, and supernatural worlds. In many cases, the same story appeared in a variety of different poetic meters. One of the most famous of these classical compositions is *Samutthakhoot kham chan* (The Tale of Samuttakote), begun during the reign of King Naray (1656-88).

King Naray and the Royal Composition Groups

The reign of King Naray produced dramatic developments in the areas of politics, economics, international relations, and literature. As for literature, critics frequently refer to this period as the Golden Age of Thai Literature. With the exception of klon, which had yet to appear on the literary scene, all of the classical verse forms functioned as vehicles for literary compositions during this time. While it seems certain that farmers and villagers also enjoyed poetry in a variety of forms, in songs and poetry contests, the classical meters were confined primarily to the court and the intelligentsia surrounding it.

For poets to survive, they had to be attached to a wealthy patron or to the court. Much, if not all, literary activity revolved around royal composition groups (*ratchaniphon* or *phraratchaniphon*) organized by the king. In these groups, the most adept and versatile poets, along with the king, created their poetic masterpieces. Over time, these literary salons, their participants, and the compositions they created gave rise to the assumption that literary talent "was part of the charisma, karmic status, and superior civility not only of the kings themselves but of the whole ambiance of the court" (Phillips 1987, 13). In a discussion of the ratchaniphon of Rama I (1782-1809), Prince Chula Chakrabongse describes activities probably common to all such literary groups (Chakrabongse 1967, 94). He relates that Rama I, an excellent poet himself, assigned particular passages of a lengthy poem to be written by specific individuals. Once completed, these partial compositions were distributed to all the members of the group for criticism and revision, and then combined to form the longer work. When serious composition was completed, the participants then engaged in rhyming bouts, poetry contests, and brilliant repartee for pure entertainment.

King Naray himself holds the reputation of being an eminent poet and the author of the second part of *Samutthakhoot kham chan*. Another prominent poet, Phra Maharatchakhru, contributed the first part, *Pongsawadan chabap luang prasert* (The Royal Chronicles), an early history of Ayutthaya, and *Suea khoo kham chan* (The Tale of the Tiger and the Cow), one of the first complete poetic compositions based on an indigenous jataka tale. Sri Prat composed *Anirut kham chan* (The Tale of Anirut), a masterpiece of punning and word play, and *Kamsuan* (A Mournful Journey), an account of his exile from court. Phra Sri Mahosot wrote *Khlong chalerm phrakiat somdet phra naray* (Stanzas in Praise of King Naray), a description of King Naray's reign from the court in Lopburi. Some critics also attribute the anonymous romantic epic *Phra Law* (The Tale of Phra Law) to this period, but others feel it was written much earlier in northern Thailand. Recognized masterpieces, these few extant works only can suggest the vast array of first-rate compositions that must have been produced in the literary circles and composition groups during that era.

The Author of Samutthakhoot kham chan

Samutthakhoot kham chan long has been regarded as a classic of Thai poetry.[1] Thai literary tradition claims that the poem was composed by three authors over a period of more than 150 years. Generally attributed to Phra Maharatchakhru, the first part of the poem (stanzas 1-1251) begins with the traditional salutation to the Buddha and the king and concludes with the marriage between Samuttakote and Phintumadi. The true identity of Phra Maharatchakhru remains in doubt, but he is reputed to have begun his royal service under Naray's father, King Prasat Thong (1629-56). Following that, he became the chief advisor/teacher to King Naray. Tradition further holds that he composed the poem as a text for a shadow puppet performance in celebration of Naray's twenty-fifth birthday.[2] He never completed the poem, probably due to his death. The second portion (stanzas 1252-1456), which follows the marriage between the hero and heroine and concludes with the defeat of the mythical deity, the phitthayathorn, is said to have been composed by King Naray himself. Again the poem was left unfinished, perhaps also because of Naray's death.

In 1846, the poem was brought to the attention of the patriarch-prince, Prince Paramanuchit Chinorot (1790-1853), a renowned scholar and Indic classicist. Prince Paramanuchit records the story of his involvement with the poem in a series of twenty-one stanzas at the conclusion of the poem. Krom Kraysorn Wichit, his younger brother, and a monk, named Phra Sombat Baan, first sought out the prince to complete the poem which had been left incomplete since the days of King Naray. The prince accepted the work and had only just begun the poem when his brother and Phra Sombat Baan died. Disheartened and depressed, he stopped work until two years later when he was persuaded to continue by Krom Luang Wongsathiratsanit (Krom Wongsasanit in the poem). He finally completed it in 1849 (stanzas 1457-2221).

Within the stanzas describing the completion of the poem, Prince Paramanuchit states that Maharat completed the first section of the poem. Here is recorded one of the only references to the original author, and much speculation has arisen over his identity. Many scholars feel that Phra Maharatchakhru (Maharat) and Phra Horathibodi, the court astrologer, are one and the same person. Others refer to evidence from the chronicles that the two titles indicate separate individuals and therefore separate authors. Still others cite oblique references to Maharat in other poems (*Phra Canthakinari* [The Tale of Canthakinari], *Khlong Kawi Boran* [The Ancient Tale of Kawi]) and contend that the reference is to a monk. (For a summary of these views, see Yuden 1984, 136-38). More recent research (Kieyakul 1982) claims that the poem was written sometime between the reign of King Boromatrailokanat (1448-88) and King Ramathibodi II (1491-1529). In addition, this research identifies Ramathibodi II as the probable poet who composed the parts attributed to Phra Maharatchakhru and King Naray. Among Western scholars, only Rosenburg (1976) has examined this issue; most others devote their efforts to critical editions of the Pali version of the original jataka (Terral 1956). While all of these theories have led to much hypothesizing and controversy, most critics and scholars still tend to support the three-author theory.

The Origin of Samutthakhoot

Originating in India and Ceylon, the jatakas, or Buddhist birth stories, have had a great influence upon the arts and literature of Thailand, particularly the last ten lives. But perhaps even more influential in Thailand, as well as the rest of Southeast Asia, has been a group of fifty stories known as the *pannyatsachadok*, or apocryphal jatakas. These extra-canonical tales appear most frequently in Thailand, Burma, Laos, and Cambodia. Tradition maintains that these stories were written in the Pali language in the Chiengmai area between 1457 and 1657. (For the Pali versions, see Jaini 1981, 1983; for an English translation, see Horner and Jaini 1985, Jaini 1986.) While most of the tales contain elements of local legends and beliefs, personal and place names seem to indicate that many of them ultimately had an Indic origin, although such an origin has yet to be traced.

The jatakas have a traditional framework that can be identified readily in all the stories. Based on Jones (1979, 7-26), this framework consists of seven components: number, title, quotation, introduction, jataka proper, verses, and identification. With each jataka appears a number that indicates the number of verses that make up each story. Besides a number, each story also has a title, an unreliable indicator since it may refer to a character or to a line, and not the story. In other cases, a single story may have several titles or several stories the same title. A quotation which usually serves to help identify the story comes immediately after the opening stanzas. The introduction then follows and places the story within the context of the Buddha's life, frequently delineating where the Buddha was when the story was told and the circumstances under which the story was told. After this section is the jataka proper, which is always told by the Buddha. Throughout the jataka proper appear Pali verses which are regarded as the canonical portions of the tales. Explaining and expanding these verses, prose sections link them into a whole story. For many of the tales, these verses take the form of proverbs or moralistic aphorisms. An identification section concludes each of these tales. In this section, the characters found in the tales are identified with important individuals in the Buddha's life.

The so-called apocryphal jatakas essentially follow the same framework as the jatakas, although the number of each tale reflects its order in a particular collection. *Samutthakhoot*, for example, is number 1 in the Thai collection, number 6 in the Burmese, number 1 in the Lao, and number 1 in the Cambodian. Two variations of the story are found in the Thai vernacular. The first, closely following the jataka framework, consists of a mixture of Pali and Thai. In this case, the original Pali verses and various Pali lines are retained and explicated with a Thai translation. The more common renditions of the jataka take the form of a simple folk tale, a retelling of the story in Thai. This is the form with which most people probably are familiar.

The pannyatsachadok tales have had an enormous influence in Thailand, providing the subject matter for other literary forms. While a number of the stories have formed the basis for the drama, most have been changed into major poetic compositions. This is the case for *Samutthakhoot*. The transformation of the jataka *Samutthakhoot* into the poem *Samutthakhoot* has involved a number of significant changes. The most obvious one has been the rendering of the verses and prose into specific classical meters. Concomitant with this change has been the addition of a variety of literary tropes and devices characteristic of classical Thai poetry. Central among these devices are the extended descriptions (*phannanaa* passages, see Hudak 1988), catalogues, formalized dialogues and summaries, and major similes and metaphors. Other transformations also have occurred both in the content of the story and in the traditional structure of the jataka.

The simplest of the content changes involves slight variations in a number of the characters' names. For example, in the jataka, Samuttakote's queen is named Wintumadi whereas in the poem she is Phintumadi. More important changes consist of additions to the original plot. In the poem, the following events and characters have been added: the lengthy elephant hunt that reputedly reflects Naray's hunting skills and prowess; Surasuda, Samuttakote's first wife; Phintumadi and her maid drawing pictures to guess the identity of Samuttakote; the test with the iron bow to win Phintumadi and the ensuing battle with the failed suitor kings; and Phintumadi's disguise as a nun after her separation from Samuttakote.

The second major change has been in the traditional framework of the jataka. While the poem retains the same title as the jataka, it no longer has the number, the quotation, or the introduction. Reputedly written for a shadow puppet performance, the poem now reads almost like a performance. As such, it can be divided into distinct sections. The first is the traditional invocation to the Buddha, Hindu deities, and the king (stanzas 1-11), the section that traditionally begins all literary compositions. The second describes the king's order to compose the poem (stanzas 12-66). The third part (stanzas 67-228) begins the shadow puppet performance with the poet's invocation to the gods and his request for a successful performance (stanzas 67-70). It continues with a description of the site of the story and the characters (stanzas 71-121) and the *boek rong*, the entertainments that precede the main story (stanzas 122-228). Most Thai scholars interpret these entertainments as performances with shadow puppets (Pluang 1964, 83). However, the descriptions are explicit enough to be real-life entertainments commonly seen in seventeenth-century Thailand (Reid 1988, 173-235).[3] The fourth part is the expanded story of Samutthakhoot (stanzas 229-2182). At the conclusion of the story, the poet appends the traditional jataka conclusion, the identification of the characters to form the fifth part (stanzas 2183-2196). The last part is a history of the poem's composition (stanzas 2197-2221).

The Format of the Poem

The title *Samutthakhoot kham chan* includes the term *kham chan* which defines the type of poetry used in the composition, a combination of kaap and chan meters. During the Ayutthaya period, kham chan poetry flourished. However, the compositions written during this period, such as *Samutthakhoot kham chan, Bunnoowaat kham chan* (Discourse by Bun), and *Anirut kham chan*, have more stanzas written in kaap than chan. In contrast, the poems composed during the revival of kham chan poetry in the early part of the twentieth century, such as *Phra non kham chan* (The Story of Phra Non), *Inlarat kham chan* (The Story of Inlarat), and *Saamakkhiipheet kham chan* (The Rending of Harmony), are almost totally written in the chan meters (Hudak 1990). In many cases, the poems conclude with several stanzas of a khlong meter that function as a type of coda to the entire composition. The subject matter of these works ranges from Buddhist birth stories and Indic myths and legends to descriptions of kings and their merit-making activities.

Probably borrowed from Cambodian (Gedney 1989, 512), kaap is a syllabic verse form which uses a set number of syllables per line coupled with end rhyme to establish rhythm. Three varieties of kaap appear in *Samutthakhoot kham chan*. The first, *kaap chabang 16*, has sixteen syllables arranged in a three-line stanza. (In the following schema, an O over a word indicates one syllable.)

Stanza 163

O	O	O	O	O	O
sɔ̌ɔŋ	fan	sɔ̌ɔŋ	kan	sɔ̌ɔŋ	theeŋ
two	slash	two	together	two	stab

O	O	O	O		
sɔ̌ɔŋ	thían	phɔɔ	reeŋ		
two	small	enough	strength		

O	O	O	O	O	O
lɛɛ	cay	mí	málaay	sàk	ʔan
and	heart	not	die	even	one

The two clashed, the two together, the two stabbed:
The two equal in strength,
Neither heart defeated at all.

The most favored of the kaap meters, chabang, is used for narrative purposes and plays a large role in the kham chan compositions of the Ayutthaya period.

The second variety of kaap, *kaap yaanii 11*, consists of eleven syllables per line arranged in a two-line stanza. Two hemistiches equal one line; here the hemistiches are written on separate lines.

Stanza 1196

0 0 0 kruŋromyá city of Romyaburi	0 0 tháaw rom- noble Romyaburi		

0 0 0 yábùrii	0 0 0 râatcháphuubaan Lord of the Realm		

0 tὲɛŋ prepare	0 sàp all	0 0 sămràp for	0 kaan task

0 cà will	0 0 0 0 sàwáyomphɔɔn ceremony	0 sĭi glorious	

Romyaburi, nobles of the city,
The Lord of the Realm
Arrayed and readied all
For the splendid ceremony.

With a slower rhythm, yaanii is used for descriptions of nature or beautiful items.

The last of the three forms used in Thai poetry, *kaap surangkhanang 28*, has seven four-syllable lines per stanza.

Stanza 141

0 kûu redeem	0 níi this	0 thay Thai	0 thĭi respect

0 tὲɛ from	0 0 chaawlûm farmers	0 lĭi spread about	

0 wâa say	0 kuu I	0 0 khamhĕɛŋ brave	

0 khăw they	0 khîn raise	0 chĭi name	0 kuu I

0	0	0	0
chîi	?åay	hǔa	khěɛŋ
name	(title)	head	hard

0	0	0	0
kuu	chon	klaaŋ	plɛɛŋ
I	fight	midst	field

0	0	0	0
bɔ̀	rúu	kìi	plaaŋ
not	know	how many	rounds

My name returned, the Thai respect,
Farmers spread my fame,
They say I'm daring
And give me the name
Ay Hua Khaeng.
I fight in fields
Not knowing the rounds.

The short lines create a quick rhythm, making it appropriate for describing emotions such as excitement or anger. In *Samutthakhoot kham chan*, these kaap meters dominate that portion attributed to Phra Maharatchakhru.

The chan meters had their origin in Pali forms which the Thai poets borrowed and adapted in accordance with the linguistic constraints of the Thai language and with the aesthetic principles dominant at the time of borrowing (Hudak 1990). These meters consist of two types of syllables designated as light and heavy. In Pali, light syllables end in a single consonant; heavy syllables, on the other hand, end in a long vowel or any vowel plus more than one consonant. Thai uses similar criteria in defining these syllables. Light syllables terminate in a short vowel, with the unwritten glottal stop that follows a final short vowel ignored. Heavy syllables end in a long vowel or any vowel plus a final consonant. Each of the 108 chan meters in the Pali corpus has a specific number of these syllables arranged in a prescribed order. From the 108 possible meters, the early Thai poets borrowed six meters that they used consistently in the kham chan compositions of the Ayutthaya period. They expanded this corpus to approximately eighteen meters during the chan revival of the early twentieth century. In the three parts of *Samutthakhoot kham chan*, the original six meters appear, dominating the parts attributed to King Naray and Prince Paramanuchit. These meters include *intharawichian chan 11*, *todokka chan 12*, *wasantadilok chan 14*, *maalinii chan 15*, *satthunlawikkiilit chan 19* or *sathun*, and *sattharaa chan 21*. With repeated use over time, each of these meters became associated with a particular subject matter or content.

One of the most popular of these meters, intharawichian chan 11, has two eleven-syllable lines per stanza with two hemistiches per line. Hemistiches appear on separate lines here. (Each O over a word represents a heavy syllable and each * a light one.)

Stanza 71

```
  0          0 * 0        0
bîaŋ       tháksìnaa    sǎan
side       south        wall


  * *        0          * 0         0
máhì       maan        bùrii       sǐi
great      have        city        glorious


  0  0                   * 0         0
cancòot                pràchaa     mii
spread by mouth        people      have


  *          * 0 *       0   0
phon       phíriiyá    chaanchom
forces     strong      elated
```

Towards the southern wall
Lies a splendid city.
Among the people it's said
Strong, skilled soldiers stay there.

The similarity of this meter to kaap yaanii 11 is so great that in the early kham chan compositions it is quite difficult to differentiate between the two, the final decision often being purely subjective. Gedney suggests that the Cambodian meter may have developed through an imitation of the Sanskrit variety of the intharawichian chan 11 meter (Gedney 1989, 524). Like its yaanii counterpart, intharawichian chan is used for elaborate descriptions of nature or beautiful items.

With a rapid rhythm dictated by the light syllables, todokka chan 12 has two twelve-syllable lines in the following stanzaic form:

Stanza 1993

```
  *          *          0          * *  0
cà         khɔ̌ɔ        khɨɨn      wárákhǎn-
will       beg         return     noble sword


  *          *          0          *        * 0
khá        coŋ         phlan      cà        thàwǎay
           must        quickly    will      offer
```

```
  *  *            0              *  *  0
bɔ̀mí            phían          ʔàphípraay
not             differ         intention
```

```
  *  *            0        *  *  0
sìthí           thammákàthǎa
power           discourse
```

I beg to return the sword,
I must quickly offer it.
I won't oppose you,
The power of your words.

Only occasionally appearing in the Ayutthayan compositions, this meter tends to be used for passages meant for light entertainment, although this does not seem to be consistent in all compositions. Considered the most aesthetically pleasing, wasantadilok chan 14 has two fourteen-syllable lines in the following stanzaic form:

Stanza 1406

```
    0             0        *       0        * * *      0
ʔòop            ʔûm       bɔ̀      ploŋ      bɔ̀wárá     oŋ-
embrace         carry     not      put down  noble     (classifier)
```

```
    *             *        0        *        0          0
khá             lɛ́       phîi     kɔ̂       phaa       tháyaan
                and       I        then      take       garden
```

```
    0             0  *              0    * * *  0
yaŋ             meerú             râatcháhìmáphaan-
at              Meru              Royal Himaphan
```

```
    *             * 0               * 0  0
tà              khìrii            phíromyaa
                mountain          pleasure-filled
```

I embraced you tightly, noble one,
And took you to the garden
At majestic Meru
And Himaphan, the mountain of pleasure.

In most compositions, this meter is used to describe the actions of the royal hero and heroine. It also appears with descriptions.

While used, the last three meters are generally considered difficult to fulfill both because of the number of syllables and because of the light syllable arrangements. The first of these three meters, maalinii chan 15, has a stanza of three hemistiches, the first of which consists of six light syllables.

Stanza 2121

* *	* *	* *	0 0
phóná	khóchá	khaná	săamâat
forces	elephant	group	capable

0	* 0 0
raan	rípuu plàat
fight	foe flee

*	0	0
kɔ̂	laan	thák
then	break	accost

Elephant forces, highly skilled
In shattering forces fleeing,
Breaking them.

A meter with a rapid rhythm, maalinii chan 15 tends to be restricted to descriptions of the ancient army with its four components: the elephants, the horses, the chariots, and the infantry. The longer meter of nineteen syllables, satthunlawikkiilit chan 19 is regarded as aesthetically pleasing because of its light-heavy syllable arrangement, but difficult to fill because of its large number of syllables. The stanza has the following shape:

Stanza 1413

0	0 0	* * 0	* 0	*	*	*	0
sàp	sàpaaŋkhásùraaŋ		khánaa	dàŋ	rí	cà	than
all	all+classifier		group	as	not	will	equal

0	0	*	0	0
thiam	ʔoŋkhá		ʔeew	wan
equal	(classifier)		waist	form

* 0
wílâat
charming

No heavenly nymph can match your alluring, your captivating form.

Because of the difficulties outlined, the meter is inappropriate for long narrative passages. However, it does appear in shorter passages that describe deities, praise royalty, or pay obeisance to the Buddha. The last of the chan meters used, sattharaa chan 21, has restrictions and uses similar to satthunlawikkiilit chan 19. It has the following schema:

Stanza 1979

0	0	0	0	* 0	0
chûay	ʔɔ̀op	ʔûm	càak	kràsɛ̌ɛ	sǎay
help	embrace	carry	from	current	(classifier)

* *	* * * * 0
chóná	chíwítantàraay
water	danger to life

0	*	0	0
rɔ̂ɔt	rí	mɔ̂ɔt	málaay
rescue	or	die	destroy

* 0	0
damroŋ	sàkon
sustain	all

Carry them from the currents,
Their life in danger.
Rescue or they die.
Sustain them all.

Although *Samutthakhoot kham chan* was composed by three separate authors, the use of the kaap and chan meters has been remarkably consistent throughout the poem. Narrative passages appear in kaap chabang 16, elegant descriptions in kaap yaanii 11 and intharawichian chan 11, and short, rapid, descriptive speeches in kaap surangkhanang 28. Descriptions and dialogues of the hero and heroine are almost always in wasantadilok chan 14, and the description of the ancient army in maalinii chan 15. Graceful praises and sorrowful laments associated with the royal characters form the content for satthunlawikkiilit chan 19. On the other hand, todokka chan 12 is recorded in two short descriptive passages. Sattharaa chan 21 is also used sparingly, only at two climactic points in the poem: when the magic sword is stolen and when Samuttakote is rescued from the sea. The consistent use of the meters by three authors over a period of more than 150 years suggests that the repertoire of the meters and their use remained a stable source for all poets. However, whether the Thai poets developed their own uses for these meters or followed prescribed Indic uses still remains to be determined.

The last of the meters used are the khlong forms, purely indigenous forms consisting of five-syllable lines arranged in stanzas of two, three, or four lines; additional syllables usually follow each of the five-syllable lines. In *Samutthakhoot kham chan,* the poem concludes in four stanzas of form known as *khlong 4 suphap.*

Stanza 2219

0	0	0	0	0	0	0
raŋ	săn	chăn	sèt	sîn	sùt	săan
adorn	create	poetry	finish	complete	end	message

0	0	0	0	0	0
sàmùtthákhôot	tɔ̀ɔ		tamnaan	nɔ̂ən	kháaŋ
Samuttakote	continue		legend	slow	remain

0	0	0	0	0	0	0	0	0
rácìt	rîaŋ	bɔ̀	phítsàdaan	ʔàdìit	hèt	sàdĕɛŋ	hǝǝy
beautiful	story	not	diffuse	past	reason	show	vocative

0	0	0	0	0	0	0	0	0
dooy	phúttháphócàná	rót	ʔâaŋ	ʔàt	cɛ̂ɛŋ	thàlĕɛŋ	tham
by	words of Buddha	flavor	designate	aim	clear	explain	Law

The created composition finished, the tale done,
Samuttakote continued, the story long unfinished,
An exemplary tale, a noble reason
To show the words of the Buddha, explain the Law.

In nearly all cases in the Ayutthayan compositions, the khlong stanzas form a type of coda to the entire composition, often stating that the poem is finished. Sometimes the date of completion and the author's name or title also appear, as in the case of *Samutthakhoot kham chan.*

Whatever meter is employed, Thai poetry is famous for its incomparable patterns of rhyme. Two types of rhyme play extremely important roles. External rhyme, the rhyme between end syllables of lines, marks ends of lines, organizes stanzas, and helps establish rhythms. External rhyme also links stanzas to one another throughout the poem. Internal rhyme, the rhyme between syllables within a line, also helps to establish rhythm. Thai poets identify a number of different types of internal rhyme: alliteration, intermittent alliteration, assonance, intermittent assonance, and end rhyme, to name a few (Hudak 1987). Contributing to the aesthetics of sound which dominates all of classical poetry, both types of rhyme can be found in the samples given above.

Manuscripts of the Poem

The original manuscripts of *Samutthakhoot kham chan* held by the National Library in Bangkok are made of accordion-folded *khoy* paper which unfolds to double-faced sides. Defined as a *lem*, each manuscript has a number that indicates its order in a particular collection. Thus a collection may consist of lem 1, lem 2, and lem 3, or any number of lem. In addition, the National Library has numbered all of the manuscripts consecutively. This numbering by the library does not seem to reflect any significant order or principle, although collections purchased or donated by a single patron are kept together. Thus, manuscripts numbered 1, 2, 3, and 4 by the library are lem 1, 2, 3, and 4 respectively and contain the complete narrative of *Samutthakhoot*. In contrast, manuscripts numbered 13, 14, 15, and 16 by the library are lem 1, 2, 3, and 4 respectively, but they record only a little more than half of the narrative. For this particular collection, the remaining lem that complete the narrative have been lost, if indeed they were ever completed by the scribes. Of the forty-seven manuscripts owned by the library and kept in the Aksornsaat Section, only one collection records the complete narrative: NL1, NL2, NL3, and NL4 (NL means National Library Number rather than lem number). In many cases, only a single lem of a collection exists, for example, NL25, NL26, NL31-47. All of the manuscripts appear to be from the nineteenth century.

Besides these numbers, each manuscript has a series of numbers which indicates the cabinet where it is located, its position on the shelf in the cabinet, and the bundle in which it is tied. Manuscripts are tied into bundles for storage, although this grouping seems haphazard. For example, NL13, NL14, NL15, and NL16, all donated in 1900, record a little more than half the narrative; however, NL13 and NL14 are in bundle 33 while NL15 and NL16 are in bundle 34 (Appendix A).

The revised edition of the poem, printed in 1979 and reprinted in 1980 by the Department of Fine Arts, was used for this translation. In the preface to this volume, the director of Fine Arts states that the National Library published the poem in 1924; this edition contained a large number of errors because of the haste with which it was printed (p. 5). In the second edition, by the Department of Fine Arts in 1960, the following changes were made: the poem was divided into its component parts; titles summarizing these parts were included; appendixes explaining historical information and characters were added; and pictures of the story from Wat Dusitaram in Thonburi were reproduced. The third edition in 1979 is identical to the second. As such, the third edition is not a critical edition since no critical apparatus has been used to solve textural problems. While spelling has been modernized in some cases, spelling errors still remain and frequently hinder comprehension. Moreover, there is no discussion of which manuscripts have been used for the printed edition; NL1, NL2, NL3, and NL4 appear to be the most likely. A comparison of the printed edition with each of these manuscripts reveals no missing stanzas. The revised edition can, therefore, be regarded as the complete story. In the translation, the stanzas have been numbered consecutively for ease of reference; this numbering system does not appear in the original Thai. Chapter headings have also been added, which at times coincide with those in the revised edition.

The different meters used in the poem are indicated at the right hand margin of the translation; where a decision must be made between yaanii and intharawichian, the most likely meter is italicized.

The Translation

Thai poetry poses a number of problems for the translator. Foremost is the rendition of foreign meters into English. The kaap meters, the syllabic meters determined by a set number of syllables, present the fewest problems. For these meters, I have attempted to keep the same number of syllables per line in English as occurs in the Thai. The chan meters with their light and heavy syllables are more difficult. The closest duplication of these meters in English is the contrast between stressed and unstressed syllables or between long and short vowels. However, such a system proved unworkable, particularly with meters such as maalinii chan 15 with its initial string of six light syllables. As a result, a syllabic translation was again selected. A similar solution was used for the final khlong stanzas. The reader will quickly discover, however, that an exact duplication of syllable number has never been completely achieved, although many stanzas approach the correct number.

As noted earlier, Thai poetry is famous for its repeated and incomparable use of external and internal rhyme. The external rhyme proved impossible to duplicate given the objective of producing a relatively literal, line-by-line, yet readable, translation. The internal rhyme patterns within a line were easier to imitate simply because of the wide variety of types. While the rhymes could not be matched syllable for syllable, enough of the patterns have been reproduced throughout the poem to give the reader a feeling for the original ones.

Another significant translation problem occurs with the catalogues, those descriptive passages that consist of long lists of birds, fish, trees, flowers, and the like. These catalogues generally appear at a point in the narrative when the hero or heroine experiences some emotion that has been generated from seeing one or more of these groups. For example, Samuttakote suffers pangs of loneliness for his wife when he sees birds and fish with their respective mates. The combined effect of seeing these animals and hearing the sounds of their names emphasizes the emotion for the prince. This sound play ideally produces the same emotion for the audience (or reader) of the poem. These names can be organized according to consonant or vowel rhyme in one of the many internal rhyme patterns. Other organizational patterns allow for punning and double punning. Since sound, and not meaning, is of prime importance in these catalogues, the Thai names have been retained, except in those cases where the item has a well-known equivalent in English. The English renditions of these names have been devised to duplicate the Thai sounds as closely as possible without using an elaborate and incomprehensible phonetic system. Translations of the names, along with their Latin equivalents, appear in the endnotes. At times, no identification of the item has been found other than "a kind of bird" or "a kind of tree." In these cases, the item is identified with those terms. For a number of items, no identification can be found at all, although the context suggests that the item is a bird or fish, for example. In these cases, the phrase "an unidentified species of bird," has been used. Many of the Thai terms are actually generic names that refer to several different animals with similar characteristics; for these, the most common equivalent, as noted in the McFarland Thai-English dictionary, has been used for identification purposes. Punning represented a more formidable problem, with no truly adequate solution reached. As a result, puns have been simply explained in the endnotes.

Because of metric requirements, names of characters and places often appear in different forms, Romyanakhorn or Romya for Romyaburi, for example. To simplify matters, these variations have been regularized. Epithets associated with the characters have been translated. Of course, all of these selections and modifications can never do justice to the original work. I hope, however, that this attempt will give the reader at least a flavor of the original.

A final note concerns the photographs included in the volume. These photos are from a series of paintings of the story found in Wat Dusitaram in Thonburi. Attributed to the nineteenth century, these paintings are in elaborate gilded frames behind glass and hung well above eye level. Because of the difficulty in reaching these paintings, the photographs are not always clear and sharp.

NOTES

1. Under King Vajiravudk (Rama VI, 1910-25), a literary committee selected the poem as the best example of chan poetry in Thai literature.

2. The traditional shadow puppet show was popular during the Ayutthaya period with references to performances appearing in a number of literary works. Unlike the shadow puppets in Java, the ones in Thailand were leather figures often as large as a man. In performances known as *nang yay* "giant shadow play," these figures were held in front of a screen rather than behind it. Although *Samutthakhoot* was written for a shadow puppet performance, no extant remains of the puppets exist. However, puppets of characters

from the *Ramakian* can be seen in a number of temples in southern Thailand and in Bangkok. The *Ramakian* has been the traditional story for the shadow puppet theater, and in the past on special occasions the complete story was presented over a period of ten nights (Kerdchouay and Smithies 1973, 50). During the twentieth century, with the advent of the cinema and television, the popularity of the shadow puppet theater has declined throughout Thailand with the exception of the south. Additional information can be found in Nicolas 1926; Dhaninivat 1948, 1959, 1965; Smithies and Kerdchouay 1972; Kerdchouay and Smithies 1973; and Posakritsana 1977.

3. Prior to the performances of the *Ramakian*, the entertainment consists of a battle between a black monkey, representing evil, and a white one, representing good. After the white monkey triumphs, he takes his defeated foe to a hermit who teaches the importance of following Buddhist precepts. This shadow puppet performance helps set the tone and mood for the following longer story. No entertainments such as those found in *Samutthakhoot* have been associated with the *Ramakian*.

The Tale of Prince Samuttakote

Invocation

1   Lord Buddha, Glorious Teacher[1]   chabang
With great understanding
Transcending all ascetic fires,[2]

2   Countless nagas, giants, kings[3]
Bow jeweled heads
Offering praise at your lotus feet.[4]

3   Render aid to all the world,
Descend to unawakened Brahma[5]
Who seeks refuge without leaving.

4   I raise my hands, my heart,[6]
Praising with reverence
Your lotus feet, O Blessed Sage.

5   I praise Lord Brahma and Siva,[7]
Lord Vishnu with his divine[8]
And majestic power.

6   I seek refuge, prosperity,
Success with penance.
May peace and calm fill the world.

7   King of Kingdoms, Lord of the Earth,
Ramathibodi,[9]
Victor with superior power and might,

8   His glory bends other kings
Through the three worlds,[10]
Fearing his authority.

9   Before his unsullied lotus feet,[11]
Nobles from every corner,
Pay homage and respect,

10   Knowing his royal duties,
Seeing his knowledge of the Dhamma,
Each and every aspect of the Way.

3

11   This knower of all stratagems
Debates all matters,
Dispels confusion and complexities.

The King's Command

12   This king recalled the fame[12]
Of the Glorious Master
As King Samuttakote, the incomparable,

13   When having ruled the heavens,
He placed himself
Midst mortals on this earth,

14   Showed his skill with bow and arrow
Battling kings
On battlefields, yearning

15   To win a princess named
Phintumadi,
Long thought pure and elegant.

16   This king ordered a composition,
Wondrous rhymes and craft,
A song praising the Master.[13]

17   Carve a shadow puppet of beauty,[14]
Replete and complete,
The royal order commanded,

18   Let skilled artists
Perform this work,
Their duty to entertain.

Summary of Samuttakote

19   Once, a noble resided on earth:[15]
King of the earthly realm,
Phintutat, the Earth-Bearing,

20   Ruled the royal capital
              Phromburi, diffused[16]
              With his fame and renown.

21   And then the Master ruling the heavenly realms
              Completed that life
              And returned to earth

22   As a royal child, innocent,
              Son to Phintutat,
              Ruler of the wealth-producing earth.

23   And then the Master received the royal name
              Samuttakote,
              The resplendent power.

24   And then Samuttakote
              Reached his jeweled palace
              Arrayed in splendor and wealth.

25   And then the woodsman roamed
              Deep forests and crags
              Discovering countless noble elephants.

26   Told this news, the prince
              Bid his royal father farewell,
              Revealing his intentions.

27   And then the Earth-Bearing prince set out
              To snare elephants,
              To admire and delight in the forest.

28   And then he halted his chariot and troops
              Near a forest tree,
              Broad and sprouting lovely leaves.

29   And then the Bho tree spirit[17]
              United the prince with a maiden,
              And the two dallied in games of love.

30   And then the Bho spirit returned
              The prince to the forest to sleep
              In the sparkling jeweled chariot.

31   And then the prince awoke in fear, with questions.
    And with longing and ten-thousand sorrows,
    He returned to the city.

32   And then Phintumadi, enamored,
    Amazed and puzzled,
    Her heart agitated with desire,

33   Ordered his picture drawn, each feature,
    A heavenly figure,
    None comparable to it.

34   And then she sent the servant Thari
    To report her sorrow,
    To welcome back the prince.

35   And then Indra, the resplendent power,[18]
    Sent Matuli
    To bestow a chariot.

36   And then in that splendid, shining chariot
    With divine steeds sparkling
    Like heavenly deities,

37   From the celestial domain,
    The prince crossed forests and mountains
    Into Romyaburi.[19]

38   And then he dallied in luscious love
    With Phintumadi, the maiden,
    The two reveling in pleasure.

39   And then to choose a mate,[20]
    From Chomputhawip,[21]
    All the noble lords came.

40   And then showing their skill
    These lords fought
    With countless arrows.

41   And then all readied for battle,
    Pounced forward
    Revealing their strength.

42   They readied ten battalions,
      Massed formidable forces,
      And dread echoed across the earth.

43   And then all the nobles fought,
      Leading soldiers out.
      And the defeated foes fled.

44   And then Narakup with happy heart
      Offered his daughter
      To the prince, the Earth's-Leader.

45   And then two phitthayathorns,[22]
      In haste, readied troops
      And fought in the firmament.

46   And then the Earth-Bearer in the forest
      Met the phitthayathorn
      Longing and seeped in sorrow.

47   A superior sword the phitthayathorn gave,
      And the prince swept it back and forth,
      Embracing his maiden beauty,

48   And flew off to the Himaphan forest,[23]
      Delighting in every
      Mountain, gorge, and cave.

49   And then heavenly kinnarees,[24]
      And the kinnaree king
      Welcomed them to their city.

50   And then they slept on a lustrous dais
      With golden ornaments glittering;
      And the two lay in peace and content.

51   And then the cruel and savage phitthayathorn
      Stole the royal sword,
      The mainstay of the Lord of Men.

52   And then the two nobles wandered the earth,
      And reached the sea
      Tormented by intense sorrow.

53   And then astride a log they crossed,
      Foam blowing them forward
      Till the log split in two.

54   Long separated, their hearts ached.
      And the sea foamed furiously
      Tormenting Samuttakote.

55   And then the waves dashed over her, unprotected.
      The current carried the princess
      Crying for the prince,

56   And washed her up at Mattharat,[25]
      Where her royal appearance
      She changed to a comely ascetic.

57   And then she built a pavilion,
      Where an artisan inscribed
      The tale of the two together.

58   And then Indra ordered the sword returned,
      And the prince
      Found the pavilion with its frieze.

59   And then he met the maiden beauty
      And washed away her sorrow
      With care and devotion.

60   They returned to Romyaburi,
      And Sri Narakup
      Crowned the prince ruler.

61   And then the royal father, long lonely,
      Sent a messenger
      Inviting the two to Phromburi.

62   And then, in sport, thousands of troops
      Went to the Earth Bearer,
      Phintutat, the King.

63   And then he crowned the noble two,
      Handed down Phromburi
      To rule with joy and perfection.

64   He taught rites and rituals;[26]
             He taught the ladies-in-waiting
             Moral precepts, and he taught the troops.

65   And he taught Sri Narakup[27]
             Living in the forest
             As a committed ascetic.

66   This, learned men tell,
             The honor and fame
             Of Prince Samuttakote of old.

The Poet Pays Obeisance

67   Here, I'll show the precepts,[28]   yaanii/*intharawichian*
             The story, the message,
             After those from before,
             Scholars who've taught it.

68   I pay obeisance to the gods[29]
             Who protect all directions.
             I ask for well-being, for blessings,
             For fulfillment, for the heart's desires.

69   The puppeteers who await
             Quickly follow. Torches illuminate
             Behind, shining brightly
             Over all directions, all parts.

70   Clearly create a picture[30]
             Surpassing all in design
             For all to see.
             For those who look, look well.

The Description of Romyaburi and Phromburi

71   Towards the southern wall[31]
             Lies a splendid city.
             Among the people it's said
             Strong, skilled soldiers stay there.

72   There, a great festival's held
            With fun and frolic.
            Romyaburi's splendid power
            Spreads far and wide.

73   Seven levels of seas,[32]
            Eternal shining circles,
            With crystal water spray,
            Splash and dash every spot,

74   Like seven rivers,[33]
            Pure as benign hearts.
            Five kinds of lotus mix[34]
            With gold and white ones.

75   Seven levels of unrivalled walls.
            Lines of jeweled mountains,
            Precipices winding around,
            Gird the space within.

76   Towering gates loom with arches
            Garnished in glowing gold;
            Ornate doors beneath appear
            Festooned with flawless jewels;

77   The royal residence radiates
            In jeweled coral, wondrous and pure.
            Glancing up it seems
            The sun has split asunder.

78   Beyond the level of lions[35]
            Runs a series of peaks
            In orderly arrangement,
            All flowing, joyful nagas,

79   Decorating each section,
            Reaching radiant levels:
            An auspicious palace
            With porticos of pure gold.[36]

80   A vast, sweeping city
            With thousands of powerful soldiers, it's said:
            Elephants, horses, armies,
            Jeweled chariots throughout.

81   Wondrous gardens exist[37]
      With countless golden deer.
      Trees as straight as tapers
      Sprout sprigs and shoots.

82   This jeweled palace
      Equals the sun and moon,
      Studded with wondrous stones
      That bid the world to stare.

83   Sparkling carved kinnarees,[38]
      Male and female, stand in rows.
      Columns and pillars
      Shine with the nine jewels.[39]

84   In the jeweled throne room,
      Hundreds of handmaidens
      And ladies-in-waiting
      Surpassing city women wander about.

85   All chosen for their elegance.
      To soothe the world with beauty
      And pleasure,they array themselves
      In raiments and adornments.

86   Exultant in that palace,
      A lustrous celestial site,
      They serve the king
      Who rules in pleasure.

87   His Majesty Narakup,
      The all powerful,
      Rules with content
      Over his radiant kingdom.

88   The ruling queen of that kingdom,   wasantadilok
      Queen Kanokphadi,
      Surpasses all ladies of the land,
      A woman of stately beauty.

89   Her most excellent daughter
      Is Phintumadi, youthful and lovely,
      An auspicious star,
      Fair, delicate, and innocent.

11

90   The King, Lord of Men;
The Queen, an elegant beauty;
Their love overflows; the two care
And deepen their love's flavor.

91   In the north lies a city,[40]   yaanii/*intharawichian*
One admirably pleasing,
Called Phromburi
In times long past.

92   Perhaps equal to Indra's capital[41]
Miraculously built by deities,
It's vast and sweeping,
Alluring to all the earth.

93   Ramparts and jeweled walls
Surround the splendid city.
Like a massive roadway,
The walls envelop and encircle.[42]

94   Massive doors are decorated
With arches over every one;
Guard towers bedecked with gold
Overlook the shimmering city.

95   The superior seas,
Deep and wide waters,
Hold wondrous blooming blossoms
Like the nine jewels mixed together.

96   Guard towers on the city walls
Line up row after row
With watchtowers like hills
And great towering mountains.

97   Roads tremble as, to and fro,
Go maidens and handsome soldiers.
Flags and banners arrayed in order
Are grouped in the evening light.

98   The royal parade ground's a golden mirror
Beaten smooth by heavenly beings.
Foreign nobles for royal audiences
Fill the roadways full.

99   It's a place to drill with elephants,
        To try out horses, to drill donkeys,
        A place to drill with weapons,
        To try out brave soldiers.

100   Far and wide in every place
        It's pure and spotless.
        Weighed down with offerings,
        One hundred noble lords come to pay obeisance.

101   The victory flags flutter
        And snap as hands sway.
        Before them swaying, others cower,
        As the king's fame extends over the land.

102   Eternal radiant light glows
        From the golden porticos
        Like Phaychayon palace[43]
        Built and hallowed by Indra.

103   This jeweled palace
        Glistens with gleaming rays,
        With glittering rays from gems
        Shimmering side to side.

104   Golden columns radiantly adorned,
        Together, one after another,
        Densely covered with gems,
        Gloriously glint and gleam.

105   Cut, carved, and incised
        Windows are strung together
        With the nine jewels catching rays,
        With elegant ornamention.

106   Joined in a mesh of gold,
        Shining with gleaming reflections,
        Pillars stand side by side,
        Lined in beauty one after the other.

107   Seven levels in this celestial city
        Please and delight,
        Seven patterned circuits,
        Peacefully calm, gleaming gold.

108   Seven adjacent walls encircle Phromburi
        Creating internal waterways,
        Seven vast levels
        Shining bright with moonbeams.

109   The palace is a golden circle
        Like earth's elegant form,
        Raised high and lofty,
        Seeming to support the sun.

110   The throne's roofed with shining jewels.
        A royal bed with cushions,
        Headrests, and pillows scattered
        Gives rise to restful sleep.

111   Arrayed in royal regalia,
        Various and sundry raiments;
        Arrayed in golden ornaments,
        Shining and resplendent;

112   Attended by royal hand-maidens,
        Nubile with golden circular faces,
        Chanting verses and dancing,
        Singing, strumming stringed instruments;

113   Attended by royal soldiers,
        Ministers, officers,
        High ministers of state,
        Noble deputy kings, all serving,

114   Noble Phintutat rules, his fame
        Spreading over the celestial city.
        Every king, every kingdom
        In the universe bows in obeisance.

115   He has a noble queen
        With a face like the full moon,[44]
        A comely beauty as wife
        Called Thepyatida.

116   His noble son, the excellent prince[45]
        With the wise countenance,
        Studied the bow and string
        Till his power reached perfection.

14

117   King Phintutat, Lord of the Land,
Ruled earth and universe,
And one-hundred kings bowed
To the dust at his royal feet.

118   The most excellent princess,
Surasuda her name,[46]
Chose the noble born to attend
Arrayed in their finery,

119   And she seemed like the full moon[47]
Appearing in the night
Surrounded by pleasing stars
Radiating shimmering rays.

120   Ten nobles, like the immortals,
Ten royal warriors,
And the prince like immortal Indra
Descending to earth to live,

121   They would sustain the world
If oppressed by force;
They would protect the righteous[48]
And maintain his fame throughout the land.

The Entertainments

122   First the screen drops,[49]   surangkhanang
Just as wished.
Soon it'll start
With puppets and puppeteers
Skilled and wondrous.
A show they'll make
With laughter and mirth.

123   All this made
For the great king.[50]
With special powers,
I'll create and show
Some fun, some beauty,
Something to gaze upon,
All things wondrous.

124   To present many ways,
     Various ways
     With many verses
     Humorous and fun
     For everyone.
     It'll be a model
     For all on earth.

125   May his honor
     And his fame spread,
     This Lord of the Land.
     May it increase
     In the royal capital,
     Glorious Ayutthaya,[51]
     Ruled in joy.

126   Preserve and protect
     His wondrous fame.
     With admirable skills
     I'll follow the old way
     With a performance of merit,
     An appropriate story
     To praise the king.

127   And then there'll be two bald heads,[52]
     Both village heads,
     With mountain brows,
     Forced to fight
     In an arena.
     Watch their heads!
     Who has the strength?

128   There'll be the Lao,
     Both rude and brash
     With teeth puncturing.
     Who's really good?
     We'll see their strength.
     Who's brave and strong?
     We'll see their skill.

129   There'll be many things.
Two from Java,
Terrible ones, the Thai say.
A wooden club upheld.
A spear in hand,
Sharp and pointed,
Waving back and forth.

130   There'll be rhinos
In close combat
Lowering strong, sharp horns.
There'll be oxcarts.
Those from farmers
Competing together
Echo and resound.

131   There'll be crocodiles,
Fearful, dreadful.
From before it's said
One's called Phanwang[53]
And one Ay Nakleng.
It'll be clamorous,
A really good show.

132   There'll be elegant boats
With fishermen paddlers,
And they'll paddle.
When they go astray,
The forces in the boat
Exhort together
To align them again.

133   They'll perform till done.[54]
Then, the time Prince Samut
Snared elephants;
The time the prince slept
In the great forest
And a spirit took him
To sleep with the maiden;

17

134   The time he fought
All ten warriors
On the earth's face;
The time he showed skill with a bow
To win a wife,
A comely maiden,
A budding flower.

135   There'll be the time
When he took her
To frolic in Himaphan;[55]
The time he fell
Midst the wide sea,
The sea which split
Those two apart.

136   There'll be the time
When he met her,
Embraced the beauty,
Returned to the city,
Returned to rule
Both capitals
In joy and delight.

137   There'll be this tale,[56]
An extraordinary one;
Not a popular one,
But a traditional one,
An ancient one,
An orderly presentation
For suspense and excitement.

The Bald-headed Men Fight

138   The two baldies refrained,[57]   chabang
Their fame apparent,
Back and forth they fanned fear.

139   "Fighting, I'll buy back my cow.
Together we're family,
Together, house and field."

140   The two sides fought fiercely.
         The two saw their heads,
         Incited with loathing.

141   "My name returned, the Thai respect,   surangkhanang
         Farmers spread my fame.[58]
         They say I'm daring
         And give me the name
         Ay Hua Khaeng.[59]
         I fight in fields
         Not knowing the rounds.

142   Don't think about that smooth head!
         I'll smack that water pot,
         Smash it and bash it.
         And all the farmers
         Will cry out in fear.
         You fight me,
         But I won't die."

143   "I'm a farmer.
         I lower my head
         And all bald heads,
         When I start a fight,
         Run and hide.
         They call me 'Sir,'
         Me, Ay Hua Tan.[60]

144   I left the house
         One day, and baldies,
         Four of them, conspired.
         When they found me,
         I began the fight.
         In fear and dread
         They fled to the melonfield."[61]

145   "Pity me, sir.
         I fear to lose my head.
         I come out, brave and strong,
         To make your head
         Crack and break.
         Your strength's inferior.
         You're only arrogant."

146   In a flash the two came out.   chabang
             Invulnerable bald heads,
             The two fought together:

147   Two arms, ready to pounce, teeth gritting,
             Eyebrows up, eyes protruding,
             Up and down, ready to fight.

148   Back and forth, fighting, enduring,
             Bald heads with thousands of tricks,
             Not knowing the other's wiles,

149   Whirling, whirling, two bright heads gleamed,
             Reflecting in each other's eyes.
             Striking, resisting, they moved.

150   No pain, no scraping, no weakening,
             Like elephants, the two
             Fought midst muddy fields.

151   Smack, smack: sounds of two strong heads.
             Blood spread out red.
             Both faces, both pairs of eyes still stood.

152   The lowland baldy weakened,[62]
             Staggered about drunk with blood,
             Met defeat in every spot, every part.

153   The baldy from the fields jabbed short,
             Came in close, pounced,
             Plowed the ground with the head.

The Lao and Thai Fight

154   Another show had   surangkhanang
             Lao and Thai volunteers[63]
             Who fought with swords.
             Whoever was good, won.
             Pushed together,
             They took the field,
             Both in haste.

155   "I'm a Lao
From Phayao.[64]
No one equals me.
They all call me
Famed Krayhan.
When I attack the city of giants,
The ruler flees in fear.

156   If you're brave,
Come out, don't delay.
We'll turn a bit,
Then I'll smash your head
Into flying pieces.
I'm the tough one
Feared by one and all."

157   "I'm a true Thai.
They talk of me
In Sukhothai.
Wherever I go,
Every time, a win.
Yea, I'm brave. My chief
Had me try out here.

158   He trusts me
And rewards me.
Whoever comes to fight
Must be good!
Don't pester me!
Rewarded many times,
I'm called Katay.[65]

159   If you're brave,
Come and meet me.
Again I say
Get up, come out!
Don't wait for orders.
If you fight me,
Your head'll fly."

160   Krayhan, so brave,
        When he heard,
        Came out, caught hold,
        Shouting, "I'm the one,
        Better than all men."
        Grasping sword and shield,
        He danced about the field.

161   Katay chased with his sword.   chabang
        Fighting fearlessly:
        The two in furious anger.

162   The two slashed back and forth,
        Two fierce ones,
        Striking close in the field.

163   The two clashed, the two together, the two stabbed:
        The two equal in strength,
        Neither heart defeated at all.

164   Slash, slash, swords resisted.
        The two strove on
        As crushed shields flew aloft.

165   Each knew sword fighting, shielding.
        And then Katay tried a trick,
        Insulted Krayhan, "You're a coward."

166   First slashing, the two taunted,
        One to the other,
        "Hey, you didn't come alone."

167   The two fought, turned, back and forth,
        "All your friends
        Will fight me as one?"

168   Krayhan flamed with fury.
        Katay turned slyly,
        And Krayhan fell flat up.

169   The Lao, with defeat on all sides,
        Scattered in fear,
        But found no refuge.

The Javanese Fight

170   "I'm Patimanoro[66]
       From Thomomasu,
       The Javanese.

171   With a spear I kill
       Many, it's true.
       With skill, I spear.

172   You and I, we'll raise swords,
       Discover our strength
       Soon. Don't slip away."

173   "I'm Patiali
       From Java. They say
       I'm brave and courageous.

174   I subdued the Javanese, my fame spreads.
       I returned to Thailand
       To show my skill and agility.

175   If you boast and brag
       You're the brave one,
       We'll battle one another."

176   Then the two took the field,
       Fighting, thrusting,
       Swinging spears aloft.

177   Grasping spears, swinging their hands,
       The two strove to win,
       Clashing with short stabs.

178   The spears' edges scraped.
       Two fighting in the field,
       How many tricks were used?

179   Two strove, two stabbed, two shielded.
       Each evaded swiftly.
       Neither overtook, both looked good.

180   Neither hit, neither touched at all:
                Swish, swish, sounds of spears
                With circling, swinging stabs.

181   Patiali, the victorious,
                Grabbed the spear and stabbed.
                And Patimanoro's strength sapped.

182   After these two thrust,
                The rhinos gathered
                To try their fighting on foot.

The Rhinoceroses Fight

183   A ferocious rhino, Ay Rangroeng,[67]
                Equal to Phra Phloeng's,
                Good enough to instill shame,

184   Chased elephants, fleeing and scattering,
                Tigers, lions, bears, buffaloes
                Scrambling, dodging, fleeing.

185   This furious rhino, Tuu Torn,[68]
                Small with a curved horn,
                Sharp and pointed,

186   Was pulled and lassoed in the forest,[69]
                Offered to the chief,
                To tend and raise.

187   Mahouts raised it, ten men
                Cut thick thorn trees
                Caring for it, duty-bound.

188   If this rhino's bold and brave,
                Bring it here quickly,
                For now they'll battle.

189   Then the two shrieked.
                Provoked, the two bit
                And clamorous sounds swept the earth.

190   Rushing in, clashing, horns aslant:
        Striking like spears,
        The two sharp horns met.

191   Circling head to head they crashed.
        Lowering shaking heads
        Phloeng shouldered it and snapped.

192   Torn body, torn head, broken legs,
        Ay Rangroeng the rhino
        Fell flat in the field.

The Cattle Compete

193   The rhino shrieked, and out came strong cattle[70]
        Which were bought expensive,
        Both for 1,100,000 coweries.

194   Jumping all around
        Like a celestial steed,
        One's called Ay Luenam.[71]

195   This one's neither low nor mean.
        Raised to be skilled in the arena,
        It's called Ay Kachaengboeng:[72]

196   Both animals young and solid,
        Vigorously strong
        Dreadful, awful, indeed.

197   If they're young and wild,
        Harness the wagon.
        In a flash, they'll compete.

198   With wagons hooked up,
        Farmers quick on the move
        Scurried back and forth.

199   One wore elephant regiment uniforms
        That reached mid leg
        With a wide palm leaf hat.

200   One covered his head down to his chin,
Went to the cow's side
With a goad to push and prod.

201   They put their carts mid field.
Farmers cheered and cheered
As they lined up in a row.

202   Rope bells jingled together,
The cattle's feet a whirlwind
As they rushed and chased about.

203   Cart creaks echoed, carts swayed,
Dust swirled overhead
Spreading through the air.

204   Ay Luenam swiftly moved,
Like the blowing wind,
And defeated Ay Kachaengboeng.

205   Victory cries echoed in the field
From glad farmers
Boisterous and babbling.

The Crocodiles Fight

206   Then two crocodiles appeared, long before[73]
Called Ay Nakleng
And Thaw Phanwang.

207   Ay Nakleng floated around looking,
Thaw Phanwang rose
From below, and the two met.

208   The two snapped and looked back
Scratching, scraping, agitating,
Struggling, swirling about.

209   Airborn tails smacked together
As they chased midstream,
Muddy water churning.

210   Pursuing, rising, sinking,
       Like wind chasing wind
       Fanning foamy waves, their fame spread.

211   The goby fish died as if poisoned
       In water dark, dark blue,[74]
       As smoke circled above.

212   Blood splattered and bubbled
       Like stirred insect-dark water
       In overflowing quantities.

213   Ay Nakleng, bold and audacious,
       Shamefully played dead
       And then swiftly fled.

The Boat Races

214   Then in the rainy month of Asvina[75]
       For ceremonies of great import
       They readied the barges:

215   On the left, mighty Kraysaramuk.
       On the right,
       Ever powerful Samatchay.

216   Filled with oarsmen,
       Bells and drums struck,
       The royal orchestra played.

217   "Hail, hail, the queen's Saramuk!
       Hail, hail, the discus bearer's
       Royal Samatchay."

218   Oarsmen bent to and fro,
       Like garlands linked left and right,
       Cramped, crowded, eyes yoked.

219   In bow and stern, flags, umbrellas stood.
       The standard bearer
       Lowered the flag halfway.

The Forester Searches for Elephants

220 They approached the starting line,
     A rope crossed the course,
     The bows sat head to head.

221 From both banks, soldiers exhorted,
     The air made dim
     And dark with troops.

222 The victory bell clanged aloud,
     Set adrift the barges,
     Both admired by one and all.

223 Golden paddles paddled in unison.
     The orchestra heated up.
     And conches echoed noisily.[76]

224 Like the sky striking the earth,
     The water splashed, resounding
     Like the crashing ocean long ago.

225 Slowness curbed, ample hands competing,
     Saramuk
     And Samatchay strove to win.

226 One in front, the other behind.
     Cheers rang at the line.
     Near land, oarsmen hoisted oars.

227 So the king's barge triumphed,
     His fame spread,
     Samatchay, the victor.[77]

228 And so showed the three worlds
     That he, the King,
     Could destroy his enemies.

The Forester Searches for Elephants

229 When the rainy season ends,[78]
     In the eleventh month.
     The moon shines in the heavens.

230   The rains retreat from the sky.
        The sun, rains, heat stop.
        Neither heat nor cold holds sway.

231   In joy, animals roam the forest.
        Water flows in streams,
        Pure and clean as though strained.

232   In joy, golden lotuses bloom.
        Bees suck pollen.
        Lotuses bloom in spreading chains.

233   In joy, deer, birds, lions;
        In joy, handsome elephants
        Nibble tender bamboo shoots.

234   In joy, golden deer
        Boldly eat kliang grass[79]
        Frolicking midst the forest.

235   Then the stouthearted woodsman
        Searched the forest
        For fun and pleasures.

236   Urgent news he revealed
        Of the forest joy,
        Animals tranquil on earth.

237   He told news of elephants there,
        Filling the forest,
        All together, in every spot:

238   Male and female, great beasts,
        Short-tusked ones near streams
        Nibbling nascent leaves;

239   Endless numbers of mountain-high beasts,
        Countless pairs of tusks
        Able to smash mountains.

Samuttakote Bids His Family Farewell

240   Then Prince Samut heard
       The woodsman's news
       And his heart rejoiced.

241   He desired the pleasure-filled forest,[80]
       To admire the woods, the mountains,
       To be content and tranquil.

242   Thinking thus, he departed
       For the king, the Follower of Dhamma,[81]
       Phintutat, Ruler of the Realm.

243   Bowing his head before the flower-like feet,[82]
       Paying obeisance, he told
       Of his departure to His Majesty, Lord of Men.

244   Raising both hands to his glorious mother,
       He told of leaving the royal capital,
       Of his intent to journey.

245   The two nobles, hearing this,
       Filled with sorrow and dismay,
       But did not forbid this Ruler of the Land.

246   He followed his heart, this precious one,
       Raised up myriad warriors
       To set forth as planned.

247   He feared for her, she who favored him,
       Surasuda, the beautiful,
       For it was inappropriate to separate.[83]

248   For their favored royal son,
       A blessing the two nobles gave,
       For their youthful son.

249   Having bid farewell, he sent his orders,
       And then, the Ruler of the Realm,
       Returned to his precious lady.

30

250   He embraced and consoled her bidding farewell.
        And splendid Surasuda
        Lamenting replied,

251   "Oh, my noble lord with a face[84]   wasantadilok
        Like the full-shining moon,
        You, O elegant one, and I, your servant, are perfect,
        Our love delicate and pure.

252   Your royal feet are lotus-like,
        And all rulers raise their hands
        Half-way to the crown
        With love, respect, and fidelity.

253   If you go off
        To the great wooded forest,
        I pay homage to you.
        I beg to be your companion.

254   Let good things be with you,
        For you'll leave, Lord of the Land.
        I pay obeisance at your feet.
        I offer love and affection.

255   I beg you to humor me, your servant,
        Who's never been separated.
        O great noble ruler,
        I'm no more than dust."

256   "O dear one, with a face
        Like a bejeweled shining lotus,
        My great beloved,
        My shining beauty,

257   The dense forest holds many things:
        Thick trees throughout,
        Tigers, elephants, of every kind,[85]
        Great lions roaring, elephants shrieking,

258   Rhinos, buffaloes, all kinds,
        Wild pigs, deer, dogs.
        Cries vibrate through the woods
        Stirring up great fear,

31

259   Should you hear those sounds,
Fierce animal cries in the forest,
For this reason, my little one,
You'd leave, no longer stay.

260   I sigh and moan for you, you know,
When we're separated, my precious.
Truly in love, my heart doesn't wander.
I do not lie.

261   Since it's a royal duty to hunt elephants,[86]
As all nobelmen do,
I do not go off to wander,
I take soldiers into the forest.

262   Don't be impatient! Grieve not!
Endure the pain,
Seek out joy and pleasure
In the jeweled palace. Grieve no more!"

263   Having consoled his beloved,   chabang
The prince prepared
To seek elephants in secret.

264   Retainers reviewed the troops,
Ordering every rank,
Every group, every duty.

265   Left, right, front, back, noise spread.
Every soldier standing forth
Covered the face of the earth.

266   Every kind of weapon abounded.
Thousands of troops
Appeared arrayed in gold decorations.

267   Flags and parasols pierced the sun.
Square and round shields, lances,
Still more shields sparkled with gold.

268   Some bore bows of beauty,
Accurate long bows.
And others gripped golden clubs.

269   Some bore breastplates, thousands.
        Some shouldered shields
        With colors glinting in the air.

270   Horses, chariots, elephants, a hundred-thousand troops,[87]
        Elephants with tusks curved
        Like the shining crescent moon.

271   Thousands of celestial and Sindhu steeds[88]
        Harnessed to gleaming jeweled carts
        With troops gloriously arrayed.

272   Horse masters mounted horses like swarms of bees,[89]
        Lances held in hand,
        Straps of arrow bags glittering gold.

273   Chariot masters raced to mount golden chariots.
        They stood to the front
        Circling war bows above.

274   Elephant masters mounted elephants,
        Right and left grasping gold hooks,
        Reflecting radiating rays.

275   Every kind of weapon sparkled,
        Glittering jeweled breastplates,
        Bright on backs of elephants.

276   Elephant trappings, wondrous finery,
        Bold, daring elephants
        Bedecked, attired, and arrayed.

277   Elephant escorts, warrior escorts of ten,
        Royal chariot escorts
        Harnessed with steeds.

278   Jeweled chariots colorfully shining;
        Gold banners, victory flags,
        Royal umbrellas, royal insignia.

279   Governors, headmen, counsellors,
        Every rank appeared
        Serving, waiting upon the prince.

280   Skilled woodsmen showed the road[90]
       Along with seers
       And then their retinue.

281   Mahouts mounted the elephant's lowered foot.
       Pikemen protected the elephants[91]
       Quickly leading them out.

282   The prince mounted his adorned chariot,[92]
       Elegant as Indra,
       King of the Thirty-three Deities.

283   The stringed orchestra strummed[93]
       The victory bell clanged
       With the conches and drums.

284   The charioteers drove the horses,
       The lightning steeds
       That sped like spinning machines.

285   Chariot sounds and elephant cries combined,
       Horses neighed whirling round
       With sounds of soldiers cheering.

286   Scrapes of eight weapons twisted together[94]
       Sent up smoke,
       Blown aloft, swirling in the air.

287   Sounds of heavenly beings blessing,
       The air vibrated,
       Sounds spread, hurrah, hurrah.

288   Sounds of Sindhu horses, echoes of swaying carts,
       Sounds of elephants trumpeting
       Resounded over the earth.

289   Flanks of soldiers sounded out
       As in victory.
       Fearful sounds filled the land,

290   Like the sky striking the jeweled mountain,[95]
       Like the sound of sea
       Waves smashing against mountains.

291   Covering the ground, covering the sky, covering the rays
          Of powerful shining Suriya,[96]
          Dust blotted them all out.

292   It hid the earth and heavens,
          Drifting to the moon,
          The sun, and the stars.

293   Prince Samut moved his company onward
          Like waves in the sea[97]
          Rolling and foaming forward,

294   Soldiers spreading out
          In glittering, gleaming, gold helmets
          Radiant with light rays;

295   Spreading out over the area, proud elephants
          With curved trunks turned to the sky,
          With swinging tails slapping side to side.

296   Countless elephants moved into the forest;
          Coughs carried over
          And soldiers conversed together.

297   Swirling, swirling, peacock tails:
          Tramp, tramp in the forest
          And tails fanned out in colors.

298   They crept along lakes, rivers, gorges,
          Crossed creeks, streams, waterways,
          Waters, crags, and mountains.

299   Deer afright,
          Lions fearing thousands of troops
          Sought caves, sought shelter.

300   Buffaloes', rhinos' screams echoed far,
          As they fled into the forest
          To wait, and to hide.

301   Forest elephants fled far to the center
          In the forest to avoid them,
          Fled far to the streams.

302   Prince Samut entered the forest,
    Crossed dense thickets
    With his thousands of soldiers.

303   They found a great river
    With crystal clear water
    Gurgling next to the path.

304   He stopped all the company's units
    And spread out in the center
    Dividing into many divisions.

305   He halted elephants, horses, chariots,
    Removed the sparkling breastplates,
    Stopped with the soldiers happy.

The Seer Opens the Forest

306   Then the prince ordered the seer[98]   yaanii/*intharawichian*
    Skilled in rites and rituals
    To enter the forest site,
    To open wide the forest.

307   The seer led the soldiers
    And the many followers
    Into the deep forest
    Skirting about for a tree.

308   They found a perfect tree,
    And their happiness spread,
    Seeing many good omens
    And auspicious signs.

309   He took out the cloth,[99]
    Wound it around this perfect tree,
    Chanted mantras, dissolved
    Perfumes and scented ointments.

310   Flags, umbrellas, ornaments,
    Were offered with rites and obeisance.
    Planks placed on posts
    Made a path for circumambulation.

311   Praising the power of the tree spirit,
        Performing every duty,
        Everything was done as desired
        To open the forest.

312   When finished, the seer   chabang
        Entered the forest and mountains
        Searching for traces of elephants.

313   And the woodsman led him
        To the forest's heart
        Where elephants thronged.

314   Traces of bamboo clumps split and rent
        He found with water in the fields
        And trees aslant, marked by teeth.

315   As before they were drawn[100]
        By the meaning of the budding tree—
        A suitable place for the rite.

316   Returning, he took the troops,
        Left and right, massed together,
        Back along the old path.

317   The seer stood before the troops
        At the budding tree,
        The special one, and offered praise,

318   Candles, incense, flags, umbrellas, scents, betel,[101]
        Liquor, rice, meat, fish,
        Wrapped in gilded cloth.

319   The area was fenced with posts and planks,
        All around as ordered,
        And the protecting spirit was set up.[102]

320   Tightly the seer embraced the tree's girth
        Chanting prayers and mantras
        In praise of the tree.

321   "This is the tree of Phra Uma[103]
        And I, in rich attire,
        Am Phra Isuan."

37

322   And thus he spoke before the soldiers,
        Who heard it all
        And then went about in every direction.

323   They put hawk's eye markers all around,[104]
        Cut many trees
        And pounded them into the ground, a protecting wall.

324   Bamboo hawk's eyes made a protected circle.
        Soldiers moved about,
        Scattered to every side, every part.

325   Numerous fires circled the fence,
        Soldiers cried out circling
        And beating on drums.

326   The weapons, the soldiers, every spot,
        The duties, all completed,
        All necessary to capture elephants.

327   Then they sent a brave woodsman
        To observe the signs
        And to guess the number of elephants.

328   Endless numbers of elephants,
        All with distinctive marks,
        And none scattered about.

329   Because of the powerful praises,[105]
        Elephants moved about,
        Moved into the kraal securely.

330   The woodsman went to the kraal
        And the seer prepared
        To report the matter.

331   He told of countless elephants,
        Captured in every spot,
        Nibbling new leaves.

332   But there were inauspicious ones[106]
        Mixed together
        Not belonging with the good:

333   Thuy, Tham, Phamla, Phahon,[107]
       Salingkhankhon,
       Chonkanloon, Ralomsangkay,

334   Plubaek, Bangkin, none good;[108]
       Thompluk, Thipasay,
       Kampotkamboon, Yongyat,

335   Prapluk, Sukrip, Kat-[109]
       Torani, Bangbat,
       Nakphan, Phinay,

336   Landat, Yurayak, Banlay,[110]
       Secretly hiding, separated out;
       Bidaw, Kanawpluk fleeing,

337   Rattan, Thorahun, all elephants,[111]
       Tradokkanthuy,
       Chipsing, Swamipote.

338   Chonchalay, Kanaekkumkot,[112]
       Common ugly elephants,
       Terrible herds moving about.

339   Tradungnak, Nakhornkat,[113]
       Khaduansuk. The treatise
       Forbids their capture.

340   These thirty-three, all thirty-three,[114]
       Followed in one group,
       Led out together

341   Because the prince's abbot
       Issued an order
       To take them elsewhere.

342   And so the seer sent the woodsman
       To take news of the elephants
       And to invite the prince to come.

343   Adroitly he passed through the trees,
       Then bowed before the prince
       And related every detail,

344   "The elephant kraal's finished.
        With soldiers surrounding
        Nothing can slip out or slip away.

345   Everything's readied,
        Every type of elephant,
        All fine animals eating together.

346   Large, lofty, and auspicious,[115]
        Similar to Ayraphot,
        Indra's elephant.

347   Eight different groups,[116]
        Beautiful beasts for riding,
        For the Lord of Men truly.

348   Some as skilled as lions
        Cross creeks, streams, and lakes,
        Nibbling bamboo sprouts.

349   Some force the females
        To move forward,
        To the forest to eat bamboo.

350   Some fear the soldiers,
        The kraal fence constraining,
        Pikemen poling them back and forth.

351   Some enraged race around.
        Reaching the stream, they wait
        To follow a clever female.

352   Some enter the stream,
        Bathe and blow water,
        Mingling with their calves.

353   Some madden with lust
        Before beautiful females
        And shake their heads side to side.

354   Endless numbers of elephants,
        Fine males and females,
        Large, lofty, and lively.

355   Choice, bright albinos;
       Dark ones sparkling
       Like black sapphires.

356   They've cleared the tall grass and trees,
       Leveled the land
       Smooth like a mirror."

357   Informed, the prince set forth
       With soldiers by the thousands
       Marching along the path.

358   Having heard the news
       The prince jubilantly left,
       Left with his thousands of troops.

359   Echoes crossed the sky, flattened the earth;
       Elephants and horses cried
       Sounds echoed, whirled about,

360   Echoing sounds of great, golden chariots
       With golden nagas
       On their tapering ends.[117]

361   Cheerful horns, cheerful conches;
       Soldiers sounded out on foot
       Squeezed together in line.

362   Fear seized the forest beasts;
       Peacocks spread their tails,
       Timid before soldiers from afar.

363   Prattling parrots took flight in fear,
       Strayed from their loves,
       Fearing the companies of soldiers.

364   Nearing the spot, the prince
       Forbid the forces
       To speak or make noise,

365   "Be still! Keep silent!
       Say not a word
       Or anger will inflame my heart."

366   The Lord of the Land with jeweled elephants
Went with his retinue
Of foot soldiers, officials, counsellors

367   And reached the golden budding tree
With retainers and Brahmins
To sprinkle holy water.[118]

368   The Lord of the Land reached the altar
For the fire ceremony[119]
To guarantee shining success.

369   The learned hatsajan offered the ashes of Siva,[120]
The prince annointed the tree for auspiciousness
With daubs shaped into mountains.

370   Ten fingers held wafting fragrances.
Candles, excellent incense
Set about, he cleansed his hands.

371   Carrying fragrant flowers at the highest point,
He offered three leaves with blossoms[121]
In the ritual of the fire ceremony.

372   And he paid respect to the three teachers[122]
With hands raised to his head
In praise of all heavenly beings,

373   With offerings for the noble lasso spirit,[123]
The prince bowed reverentially,
Acting as a preceptor.

374   The sages along with the prince,
The Lord of the Land,
And the followers radiated joy.

375   Then the prince sought the soldiers and seers
And ended the ceremony.
As the mahouts assembled.

376   They bid the tree farewell, and mounted their beasts
As did the pikemen
In front and in back of the prince.

377   With the cloth that girded the tree,
        The elephant sages
        Mixed together with the soldiers.

378   They reached the kraal gate[124]
        And offered praise to joyful Siva,
        Each of the different groups.

379   Elephants chased into the field,
        Mighty elephants
        Running, fleeing together.

380   Bamboo clumps fell broken,
        With birds and forest animals
        Startled and frightened.

381   Male giants fled.
        Calves taught to walk,
        Their mother sadly grasped.

382   The prince moved his elephant forward;
        Mahouts appeared before him,
        Swarming like bees.

383   He chased a tusked beast,
        A beauty with curved tusks,
        Dreadfully strong and frightening.

384   He carried the lasso[125]
        Ready to snare the male;
        And his sharp eyes did not move.

385   The elephant sage secured the lasso;[126]
        Troops pulled left and right,
        And the elephant turned around.

386   The elephant master drove it near, ready to fight,[127]
        Its tusks turned up,
        Drove it to the middle of the field.

387   The wild beast saw the leader follow,
        Trumpeted with no fear;
        And they intertwined tusks.

43

388   The wild one chased behind,
                But the tame one did not move,
                And the two battled to win.

389   Chat, chat, tusks scraped,
                Sparks sprang forth,
                Smoke swirled through the trees.

390   Blood flowed, twin tusks gleamed;
                The two beasts battled,
                And noise swept the earth.

391   Bamboo branches askew, mountains crushed,
                The earth swayed
                Smashed to bits and pieces

392   The wild one saw the battle elephants
                Lined up close by
                And he stopped dead in fear.

393   Soldiers called the tame one,
                The sages lay a lasso
                To clasp the bull securely.

394   Then the seers entered the thicket,[128]
                Snared the struggling elephant
                And tied it in the kraal.

395   Securely held, the wild beast
                Was driven from the pen
                And staked with cords.

396   Not even one way to escape,
                The wild beast looked about
                And the tame one pulled.

397   Leaving the forest, the prince proceeded
                To the forest tree,
                The special budding beauty.

398   The elephants' sages followed
                With elephants, male and female
                And small ones close by.

399   As before, they reached the site,
         Prince Samut gazed
         And admired the elephants:

400   Medium beasts with good signs,[129]
         Not common ones,
         But eight auspicious lines.

401   Some were albino,
         Shining like the pure Kaylat,[130]
         Sparkling like the moon.

402   Some were the lovely Chomlop[131]
         Ears flapping to and fro,
         Revolving, turning around.

403   Some were the sparkling Kobut.[132]
         Some had great significance,
         Such as the noble Sihachongkat.

404   Some had graceful creamy right tusks;
         Some had perfect nails,
         Fit for a king to ride.

405   Some walked ready for a king;
         Some were lofty and solitary
         Emitting fragrant musk.

406   There were eight lines in all:[133]
         The heavenly Ayraphot,
         Buntharuek, Komut,

407   Anchan, Phamani,[134]
         The pure Butsapatan,
         The mighty Sarawapom,

408   And Supradit. His Highness[135]
         Admired and watched over them
         In the dense forest.

409   The seer skilled in all rites
         Reported all the details
         Of the wish to leave the forest.

410   He readied all the groups,[136]
           The candles and many flags
           And gifts for offerings.

411   Leaving the forest, the prince went forth,
           Marched with the troops
           Seeking a place to camp.

Samuttakote Sets Up Camp

412   He mounted the noble jeweled chariot,
           And the myriad troops
           Set off with His Highness.

413   Midst the forest they found a Bho tree
           With unspoiled branches
           Spreading out long and thick.

414   Bamboo clumps surrounded as a retinue,[137]
           Leaves sprouting and opening,
           Golden flowers blooming.

415   Some buds grouped in graceful clusters,
           Golden gold in color,
           Fell in orderly bunches.

416   Clusters of sprouts and sprigs
           Topped the trees
           With dazzling greenness.

417   Here were countless animals, birds,
           Ponds and mountains,
           Gorges, caves, creeks, streams.

418   With Suriya at day's end,
           Contented animals throughout
           Drifted close together.

419   Stealthily the prince admired   yaanii/*intharawichian*
           The golden deer in pairs.
           Closely grouped pairs,
           The eyes of the deer sparkled.

420   The lovely eyes of the deer
       Pleased the eyes of the others,
       Captivating those looking,
       Excited by seeing these.

421   Clusters and herds of elephants,
       Together with females;
       Lions mixed with forest boars,
       The boars bowing before the lions.

422   On the mountian top
       Sat the comely jamri,[138]
       Its tail like a maiden's
       Hair swishing back and forth.

423   Golden deer wandered here and there
       In well-matched pairs.
       Secretly scanning the site,
       His Majesty moved forward.

424   The lovely eyes of the deer
       Looked about secretly.
       The prince's eyes sparkled
       Even more than the shy deers'.

425   Herds of deer hearing
       Sounds of soldiers marching
       Flew to meet their mates,
       As soldiers looked and assembled.

426   Water buffalo stomped through the forest,
       Boasting with sharp horns,
       Then frolicked in clumps of khaem grass,[139]
       Rubbing till it broke into sections.

427   The prince saw the swans,
       Elegant and beautiful,
       With slow steps like rabam dancers,[140]
       Bodies swaying to and fro.

428   The leader swan flew off
       To bathe in pleasant pools.
       Females alighted,
       Resting in orderly rows.

429   The prince thought of his lady
        Delicate with a full-moon face,
        Waited upon by handmaidens,
        Everyday at rest in the palace.

430   The prince observed the birds,[141]
        Scattered in great numbers,
        Sitting in regular rows
        Throughout the trees in the forest.

431   They circled and cried out. Sounds filled the air,
        Glorious cries blended together,
        A joyful combination
        Like a heavenly orchestra.

432   The sun ready to set,
        The winged creatures midst the wide forest
        Flew to their nests. Some in nests
        And some in pairs flew here and there.

433   Each parrot with a nest
        In loneliness flew about
        Seeking a mate, calling out
        To come live together.

434   He saw all these different kinds,
        Saw their tender care,
        Listened to sounds of songs,
        Sounds of all different kinds.

435   The husband and wife made
        A fitting couple in love.
        They chatted in their language
        As animals played all around.

436   From each nest the husband
        Flew out to compete,
        To seek food for his wife
        Swiftly diving and whirling about.

437   The prince saw these birds,
        Felt alone, strove to endure,
        But missed his heavenly wife
        As loneliness pervaded.

438   Every kind of tree
            Filled the vast forest.
            Pollen spread, unlocking
            Heavenly, delightful perfumes.

439   Flowers budded in chains,
            In clusters and bunches;
            Branches grouped together
            Like hands stretching out.

440   He gazed at the trees as the wind blew,
            As though it came to admire,
            To invite His Majesty to wander about
            To delight in the delicate plants:[142]

441   Du, pru, prayong, yom,[143]
            Sarapi, phikun, kanjana—
            Muang and monthan,
            Flowers mixed with the kamyan.

442   Budding flowers ordered,[144]
            Pleasant sandalwood perfumes,
            Wondrous jambok,
            Kannika mixed with kaew,

443   Karakate, ket, kaew,[145]
            Mali and maludi mixed,
            Bunnak beside
            Maliwan and wannawan.

444   The girth of the tree seemed[146]
            Like the waist of his beauty,
            An encircling golden vine,
            Like his Lady's arms embracing him.

445   Nangyaem, khatueng,[147]
            Dancing and pulling lamduan,
            Jik, jaeng, maeng, mong-
            Khut, khuy, khu, khlay.

446   Trees stood high and low
            As though dancing and turning.
            Branches, when breezes blew,
            Swayed as dragons lifted high.

447   Fragrant scents and aromas hung,
        Gentle breezes blew,
        Ready ripe mangoes exuded their aroma,
        And the monnak tree flitted uneasily.[148]

448   He finished admiring every tree
        As evening drew near,
        Suriya late in the day
        Hiding behind Mount Meru.

449   And now with Suriya hidden,[149]
        "Surasuda, my beauty,
        Now, looking before me
        You're not there, only loneliness!

450   Now these pictures
        Show my beauty's heart burns alone.
        No one comes to soothe,
        To cherish, to care for you, my love.

451   Oh, I pity your heart,
        You who begged to follow,
        Oh, I pity your heart,
        It was wrong to forbid you to come.

452   I was wrong, fell into error
        By some sin, or some trick,
        Not to bring my elegant beauty
        As my forest companion.

453   In pain, trembling alone,
        I journey through the forest,
        Separated from my beauty,
        Forever thinking of her.

454   No, I won't stay here;
        I'll hurry on to the city
        To remove this vexation, this irritation,
        This sorrow we two bear."

455   The prince stopped his chariot and soldiers,   chabang
        Confused sounds reverberated
        As they set up the carts.

456   Weapons and shields were placed as posts;
       Soldiers whirled about,
       Front, back, the right flank.

457   The head counsellors
       Advised the prince,
       Invited him to the royal bath.[150]

458   And he descended from the chariot,
       Went forth
       Next to the splendid pool.

459   The pool of beauty brimmed with jewels:
       White night blooming lotuses
       And other spotless species.

460   Red lotuses and other blooms
       Bloomed and spread their perfumes
       Drifting into the air.

461   Pearls and gems lay scattered in the sand,
       Radiant golden ground,
       A smooth dais of cat's eye.

462   Bees swarmed around in pairs;
       Pairs replete with pollen
       Circled the fragrances buzzing.

463   Melodious buzzing honey gatherers
       In pairs hovered over flowers,
       Never leaving their pleasing blooms.

464   They moved over the fragrant lotus
       And aromatic scents spread,
       Diffused, sprinkling the water.

465   The water was an emerald
       With blooming lotuses
       Shaped like rubies.

466   Every shape and size of bird
       Flocked about the pool
       Alighting on the lotuses.

51

467 Intimate pairs mouthed the pollen
   And the pollen spread about
   Saturating their bodies.

468 Whirling sounds combined
   Like an orchestra striking up
   In praise of the splendid pool.

469 The golden Bho drooped its branches,
   Shade and vines fell
   Over the splendid pool's edge.

470 Flocks of feathered creatures[151]
   Flew down alighting
   And singing soft lulling sounds.

471 Kungok, kungan, kungon:[152]
   Jip and jap birds hid
   Sheltered in the screening lotus.

472 Klingklong kept close to the nest,[153]
   The jaw sat quietly listening,
   The happy krasa sang out.

473 The rangnan abandoned its nest moaning,[154]
   The nangnuan's like a woman
   Beautiful with creamy white skin.

474 The kanam dived, a fisherman.[155]
   Petnam floated by
   Diving down into the water.

475 The ngua bird crowded with the khaw,[156]
   The ten bird followed
   And the kranay grasped a blooming flower.

476 The red-eyed stork seemed brave[157]
   Chasing after the huakhwan
   And shrimp leaped about.

477 The plaw played in pairs[158]
   The cuckoo cooed
   Together with the sarika.

478   The prik billed water weeds like a beard,[159]
The iang and aen plucked it out,
And appeared abashed and ashamed.

479   The sangsaew strew down straw[160]
Up and down secretly,
Startled over each flower.

480   The phay pursued the lang,[161]
The pling clung above
The lovely fragrant lotus.

481   The bawkhun and kangkhen whirled about,[162]
The khwaek kept a stick in its mouth
And the ilum and khum laughed.

482   The say sat sad and solitary,[163]
The pairs waited together,
Saw their mates and then flew off.

483   Flapping, flapping, the huahang sought the yung,[164]
Landed on a bamboo clump
And the branch danced swaying.

484   The saek, khwaek, and khaw guarded[165]
The mango tree,
Bothering and annoying the crow.

485   The bird's mouth was open, laughing loudly,[166]
The khapkhae sat close together,
Both pairs with sad eyes.

486   The yang sat in noisy rows[167]
Looking at the strange plaw
Mingling in the peanut bushes.

487   The kwak bird gazed at its friends,[168]
Shook its wings, shook its tail,
Called out 'kwakkwak' introducing itself.

488   The pharahit and crow laughed out,[169]
The jak cried out
Separated from its love.

489   The topyung and thungthong looked about[170]
        Searching for swimming fish
        And quickly the fishermen dropped.

490   The nokkajok told its friends to come fast,[171]
        Together the khonhooy looked
        And then ate the fish.

491   The phuradok and kokma sat red faced,[172]
        The kot phloeng with great strength
        Circled and cried from above.

492   The thin birds passed through the thatch grass,[173]
        The changlek made 'lek' sounds,
        The krawan and krawaen sat scared.

493   The lang from midst the flock[174]
        Landed on a tree seeking husbands,
        And the khamin squirmed after.

494   The crane cried echoing[175]
        As geese and swans swept by,
        And sorrow gripped the Lord of the Realm.

495   Wondrous parrot and cuckoo sounds,[176]
        Melodious sweet talk,
        Combined creating pleasure.

496   Every kind of gold fish
        In the crystal bright pool
        Excitedly jumped and leaped.

497   There were red-tailed kraho and krahae;[177]
        The wua fish hid in fear
        By the bank along the edge.

498   The krim and kray circled while the saway swayed,[178]
        Stirred up the trees
        That shook in the water.

499   The khangbuean turned, the angry khaw spun,[179]
        And many submitted,
        The salit, pho, and phruan.

500   The khemakroy swam with the namlang fish,[180]
        Never ending numbers of eels
        Flew along looking for the hualuang.

501   The phram, salumphon, pluang,[181]
        The phrom in great numbers,
        And the pliaplen,

502   The thong, kanthong, henglen,[182]
        The kabork and kaben,
        The khemakroy and kray.

503   The thepo and chado swam about,[183]
        The kaemcham turned red
        And let the maw see.

504   The maew, linma, mu,[184]
        Kotchara, rahu,
        Janthamet and thoramang.

505   The wan chased behind moaning,[185]
        The tatum was in sorrow,
        And the chon splish-splashed around.

506   The kathing swam up in the water,[186]
        And the aw, the royal one, saw
        All these varieties in the water.

507   The ma rose up like a pony,[187]
        And the khlang in fear
        Swam back and forth into the water holes.

508   The ka jumped after the hera,[188]
        Mixing with the fish
        As the soy and saway swam overhead.

509   The fakphra, sa, suea,[189]
        Sup and khuea
        Mingled with schools of fish.

510   The rakkluay, hangkiw, and kuraw,[190]
        Kanaek and khaw
        And kot dipped up and down.

511   Many mukam dove into the water[191]
        And siw swam side to side,
        Numerous sets of bodies.

512   The kradi and kratrap followed[192]
        With big, beautiful bodies,
        Leaping in paddies, leaping above the water.

513   The chorn, chawat, and chawaeng,[193]
        Hangkiw and thukang
        Jumped and swayed in the pool.

514   The phuang leaped to eat,[194]
        Swam next to the chawaeng
        And turned the taphian shy.

515   The paen and paep kept to the sand[195]
        Snatching the abundant bait
        Bubbling through the pond.

516   The juat went without food waiting,[196]
        And the lot coiled in the mud,
        Quickly they startle.

517   The maew chased the morm,[197]
        The chalamnu seemed strange
        Wanting to come up close.

518   The kralumphuk, duk, daeng, khayaeng,[198]
        The uk and amphan
        Swam through the streams.

519   The fish swam back and forth
        And somersaulted
        And played, swimming upside down.

520   Turtle shells and the khuea all around[199]
        Swam to every place,
        Swarming like bees.

521   The wind blew captivating fragrances
        To the Lord of Men
        As a flower messenger at the pool

522   Invited the Lord of Men
       To enter the pool
       And admire the beautiful blossoms.

523   Then His Highness, Lord of the Earth,   *yaanii*/intharawichian
       Went forth into the water,
       Frolicked in the pleasing pool,
       Delighting in his royal bath.

524   His high officials, ministers,
       Valiant soldiers, each descended
       To bathe in the pool
       Of blooming jewel-like lotuses.

525   Wandering about, admiring
       The pool, the budding blooms,
       They picked the fabulous flowers
       And offered them up.

526   Crystal clear water brimmed
       Pure and shining.
       Like the form of Naray[200]
       Bathing in the milk sea,

527   The prince peered at the buds,
       Peered a long time at the buds
       So like his beloved's breasts,
       And his sorrow swept through him.

528   He finished bathing in the pool
       Of pleasing, pure, cool water,
       His outside a cool exterior,
       But inside he heated thinking of her.

529   The prince peered at lilies and lotuses,
       Reflected and dreamed
       Of his spotless lady
       So like the lovely lotus.

530   Suriya hid behind the mountain,
       Shining rays hid behind Mount Meru,
       Suriya now obscured and darkened
       As the prince lingered and waited.

531   With the prince's ablutions performed,   *chabang*
The ministers reported
And supplicated the Lord of Men.

532   As he left the pleasing pool,
Soldiers and ministers
Surrounded and ministered to the Great One.

533   The prince donned his raiments,[201]
Arm ornaments,
Jeweled rings and bracelets.

534   He drove his gem-encrusted chariot
As Suriya set
And hid behind Meru.

535   Evening drew near
With thousands of soldiers
And a flood of retainers.

536   Lamps and lanterns flickered in every spot.
With golden tapers, flags, and garlands,
The prince began his homage and praise

537   To the Bho spirit who guarded[202]
The noble Bho tree,
Where the prince would sleep.

538   In the east, the Lord of Light beamed,
Rays illuminated the spot
Sparkling over the forest land.

539   Fragrant scents drifted from the lotus,
From blooming flower buds
Shaped like women's hands offering.

540   The prince reclined on his pillows
In the sparkling jeweled chariot,
Desire agitating his heart.

541   The moon moved with beams shining
And it was as though he had seen
The face of Surasuda.

542   The prince reflected upon his precious,
       Indulged in his sorrow,
       His heart desiring his queen.

543   The trumpets and conches joined the drum;
       Orchestra sounds combined
       With echoes from the great drum.

The Spirit Transports Samuttakote to Phintumadi

544   The prince worshipped and praised[203]
       The beautiful tree
       And then began intently:

545   "O spirit that protects the animal world,   wasantadilok
       That governs the world,
       O spirit that protects and assures
       Compassion for the animals of the world,

546   O spirit that protects, guard us!
       Do not curtail your help.
       Ward off all wickedness,
       Prevent the dangers from the forest.

547   Respectfully, I ask, protect all soldiers
       Who come to sleep in the forest,
       Ward off all wickedness and misfortune,
       Have no anger, worry not."

548   Prayers to the immortal protector over,
       The noble prince slept,
       Content upon the jeweled pillows
       In the golden chariot.

549   And then the Great Noble Spirit   chabang
       Who inhabits and protects
       The great Bho, which spreads in all directions,

550   Heard the blessings from the Lord of the Realm,
       And smiled happily
       As when eating immortal ambrosia.[204]

551   The cries of the swan
        And the heavenly karawik blended[205]
        As the spirit listened smiling.

552   Leaving his arboreal celestial palace,
        He set forth
        And saw the soldiers like a stream of water,

553   Countless warriors, thousands of troops
        In the dense woods
        That surrounded, circled the groups.

554   He saw the elephants, horses, golden chariots, flags
        Colorfully blowing in the air,
        Shining bright all around.

555   The Bho spirit gazed with amazement
        And thought intently,
        "Who's this? some noble?

556   Or a god from the giants?[206]
        Or the God of Love?
        Or the Lord of the Discus,

557   The one with the discus and mace?
        Or the Trident Bearer[207]
        With the noble beauty Uma?

558   Or Kuvera, the Lord of Wealth,[208]
        On his royal swan,
        The golden, celestial bearer?

559   Or the noble king Garuda?[209]
        Or the naga changing form
        In the milk sea?

560   Or a hermit? a phittayathorn?[210]
        A khonthan? a leader
        With mighty power

561   Changed to a spotless form
        With powerful soldiers
        Arrayed all around?

562   Or groups of demons with a giant?
        Or Lord Indra
        Changed to a comely-shaped figure?"

563   Looking from his royal head
        To his splendid feet,
        This figure had no comparison.

564   He reflected, then smiled, confusion gone.
        "Ah, it's the prince,
        The noble Samuttakote.

565   For what reason does he sleep here
        On the chariot's cushions,
        Handsome, vexed, and alone?

566   Countless consorts should gather close,
        Cling to his lotus feet,
        Serve and attend him.

567   He usually sleeps on the celestial dais
        With jeweled curtains, gold gleaming,
        Perfumes floating and wafting about.

568   Ladies-in-waiting ply plumes,
        As his arms embrace
        Young maidens he desires.

569   Now this handsome prince is alone,
        His arms grasp golden pillows
        And desire inflames his heart.

570   Breezes blow, moonbeams shine,
        Dew drifts down,
        Cool and shady, it's late in the day.

571   It's not right to be indifferent.
        I should look after him,
        Take him to a precious lady."

572   The spirit thought of the noblest lady
        Over the face of the earth,
        No one comparable to her splendid form.

573   He thought of Lady Phintumadi,
                Daughter of the king
                There in Romyaburi.

574   "A woman like an apsara,[211]
                When she marries,
                Every king will seek her."

575   Comparing them, their families,
                The two the same,
                Two to dally in games of love.

576   Thinking thus, the spirit was pleased.
                He approached the prince
                And quickly cast him into a deep sleep.

577   The prince slept; soldiers, warriors,
                The assembled brave troops:
                No one awoke, no one stirred, all slept soundly.

578   Embracing the Lord of the Realm,
                The spirit flew through the air
                And disappeared in the distance,

579   As when Phra Phrom[212]
                Took Anirut, the same way,
                To dally with Queen Usa.

580   Alone they reached the mountains
                Of splendid Romyaburi
                Brimming with brave soldiers.

581   They crossed over the eternal seas,
                Crossed over secured doors
                In the walls and ramparts.

582   They crossed over Romyaburi
                To the golden palace, to the audience hall,
                And made their way inside.

583   He looked at the Palace of Suriya,
                So like the Palace of the Moon,
                Jewels sparkled and rays flickered.

584   Like the palace of the Great Earth King,
        The palace of the queen
        Shimmered with shining mixed jewels.

585   Closely he examined the Palace of Suriya
        Where finials tore the sky[213]
        And beams of beauty bounced about.

586   Here was the palace of the daughter,[214]
        Phintumadi,
        Who lived in joy and pleasure.

587   Secretly he peeped at the orchestra playing;
        Secretly he peeped at the consorts
        Chanting chan verses far off;[215]

588   Secretly he peeped at shouting soldiers marching;
        Secretly he peeped at groups scurrying about,
        Stationed to watch over the city.

589   He flew to the top of the jeweled palace,
        Mount Khanthamat,[216]
        And looked at the people bustling about.

590   He opened the lotus doors, returned[217]
        And took the prince
        Into the pleasure-filled prang.

591   He saw comely consorts and courtesans,
        Piles of bodies, floods of breasts,
        Breasts revealed in sleep.

592   Some slept soundly,
        Garments lowered showing stomachs,
        Bellies, tightly bunched breasts.

593   Some forget to ply their plumes,
        Eyes drowsy with sleep
        At the foot of the golden dais.

594   Some slept supinely on others,
        Hands grasping waists
        And squeezing lotus bud breasts.

595   Some had cheeks in anticipation
       Of lovers slow to go,
       Asleep, awake, murmuring.

596   Royal courtesans filled the golden hall,
       Piles of bodies, a sleeping mass,
       Courtesans and consorts covered the room.

597   He stopped, looked uncertainly,
       Then took the prince
       Quickly to the jeweled bed,

598   Placed the two side by side,
       And with pleasure
       Gazed at the splendid pair.

599   He looked at the lady, and forgot the prince;
       He looked at the Lord of Men
       And forgot the precious lady.

600   The two, different figures, counterparts,
       And the spirit gazed happily,
       Praised them and offered a blessing.

601   Then he awakened the Lord of the Realm,
       Awakened the attractive Phintumadi,
       And quickly the two rose from their sleep.

602   And then the spirit flew off
       To his celestial palace,
       There in the lovely Bho tree.

603   Excited, the two were enamored.
       Each in amazement,
       The two moved closer, shyly, puzzled.

604   "I dream, no I do not," the two smiled
       Moaning in their hearts,
       Gazing, turning aside bashfully.

605   The lady's eyes were lovely arrows.
       Both breasts heaved,
       And desire vexed their inner hearts.

606   He saw a becoming nose to smell;
       He admired crystal clear cheeks
       Emitting intense fragrances.

607   He thought, "Just last night
       I slept near the pleasant Bho tree
       Shaded by dense branches."

608   He saw the royal bed,
       "It's not the royal chariot
       Under the shining Bho tree."

609   He saw the elegant ceiling overhead,
       "It's not the stars
       Scattered in the sky's expanse."

610   He saw golden dragons
       On the royal couch
       With wondrous blossoms,

611   All kinds of trays with dragons,
       Many aromas of betel
       Already prepared;.

612   Precious stones on the bed; fragrances spread;
       Perfume from the splendid lady;
       And he was long uncertain.

613   He knew surely a god created this
       For wondrous love-making,
       Just as a heart would wish.

614   His arms encircled her waist;[218]
       His beauty, his beloved,
       Her breast beat excitedly.

615   His royal face
       Above his lady's face,
       Their two fragrances mingled.

616   His stomach covered her circular one;
       Breasts bumped together;
       On top he squeezed the glorious flower.

617   She rejoiced in her heart;
        Her hands grasped the Lord of Men
        And led, offering no resistance.

618   He fondled, cheeks glowing with lust;
        He caressed the elegant beauty
        Who embraced his neck.

619   He kissed the liquor of her lips;
        His hands stroked lines of her stomach
        And caressed the beauty's breasts.

620   Her breasts adhered to his chest;
        Her waist his hands
        Encircled trembling with desire.

621   The two dwelled in certain pleasure;
        Delighting in the great fortune
        The spirit had created.

622   The two devoured love's pleasures;
        Happiness filled the royal bed
        And fragrant scents wafted overhead.

623   In joy the two romped and merged;
        Desire mounted
        In every way wondrous.

624   Afterward they lay drowsily on the gold dais,
        Lamps and lanterns flickered
        As beams of light bathed their bodies.

625   In one more watch the night passed;[219]
        Night ended and light rays
        Flowed in, forcing his return to the heavens.

626   Parrots prattled in the trees,
        Deer awoke from sleep
        And the cock crowed.

The Spirit Transports Samuttakote Back to Camp

627   The Bho spirit from his celestial palace
        Quickly flew back
        And arrived at Romyaburi.

628   He entered the palace filled with sleep
        And saw the Lord of the Realm
        Asleep with the young maiden.

629   The two together seemed as one,
        Fair faces fit together,
        Both full like the moon.

630   His hands encircled the beauty's waist,
        Better than a golden vine strung around,
        Close together they slumbered.

631   Asleep after wondrous loving,
        Great happiness arose
        As desire returned to them both.

632   Near the dais stood the spirit;
        He stopped, saw them turning,
        And thought without moving,

633   "It's not right to take him
        From his precious lady,
        Separate him from his elegant beauty.

634   But to stay brings evil for certain;
        A friendship destroyed
        Quickly for both kings.

635   She alone is her father's great love;
        Whoever touches her
        Brings ruin and destruction for sure.

636   This is right, this is wrong, which?"
        And he disputed in his heart,
        Seeking the correct way.

637   Wrestling through the night,
The spirit pondered;
Searching, searching, till decided.

638   So he lifted the prince's hands,
Loosened them from the lady's waist,
That beloved beauty.

639   And he lifted the lady's hands
From the noble prince;
And then removed him without his knowledge.

640   The spirit peered at the pure face,
Clothed him
And supported him with his arms.

641   Clasping the prince to his breast
He flew off without delay
And placed him in the jeweled chariot.

642   With Suriya about to shine,
The animals of forest and mountain moved,
And sounds drifted to every corner.

643   Deer left their haunts,
Parrots squabbled
And birds chirped and cheeped,

644   Circled, hovered, cried in the sky,
Alighted in trees,
Joining and blending their voices

645   Like an orchestra awakening.
Sounds without stop:
Crickets and cicadas sang out;

646   Elephant trumpets reverberated;
Horses neighed at jeweled carts;
Soldiers' shouts resounded.

647   Sounds of creatures: elephants, great lions,
Vibrating sounds
Echoed over the Himaphan forest.

648   Animals from every forest corner
       Opened their eyes, awakened
       With tumultuous sounds over the land

649   That happily called Suriya.
       Melodious sounds sounded
       When the rising sun sent its rays.

650   The dawn filled with sunbeams
       As majestic Suriya rose
       Over the encircling mountain tops.[220]

651   The day-maker sent golden beams,[221]
       Radiant rays,
       Jeweled horses glittering.

652   In the east, the light-maker
       Created glimmering designs,
       Powerful Suriya, the splendid light.

Samuttakote Searches for Phintumadi

653   Then the prince awoke from his sleep,
       Opened his eyes searching,
       His hands empty, grasping the pillow.

654   He thought of the precious body,
       When he dallied in love
       With his beauty on the golden dais.

655   He remembered the two united as one,
       A precious golden wire,
       The two intertwined.

656   Her fire heated his breast,
       Brought on pain and confusion,
       "A dream or reality, I'm lost."

657   The prince smelled her fragrance
       Clinging to his body
       And felt the pain in his heart.

658 Confused, he cried "A dream or not?
    Why this agitation?"
    And he fell into sorrow.

659 Clearly the earth and sky were inverted;
    Clearly the great mountain[222]
    Now rested upon his royal chest.

660 Long he endured the grief,
    Grieving for the princess,
    Moaning and groaning.

661 He set forth on the golden war chariot
    With soldiers and warriors
    Throughout the forest and mountains.

662 They searched the deep, dense forest,
    Hills, mountains, caves, streams,
    Crevices, gorges, and woods.

663 Soldiers stumbled through forest and mountains
    Circling round and round
    Over every surface, in every cave.

664 The forest was quiet with solitary animals,[223]
    Every parrot flew alone,
    With no calls, no answers.

665 Breezes failed to move trees;
    Not one thing stirred,
    No garlands spread their perfumes.

666 Elephants forgot their bamboo and hid;
    Midst the trees, great lions,
    Disheartened, forgot to chase elephants.

667 Deer forgot to eat grass;
    They feasted on sorrow everywhere
    In sorrow with the prince.

668 In every direction, he looked and sought
    But failed to meet his love,
    And then laments came without stop,

669 "O beloved, you came with the face[224]   yaanii/*intharawichian*
Of a shining moon.
In the evening we two
Frolicked, our happy hearts content.

670 I dream of your lovely waist,
O woman so excellent.
I think of your bunched breasts,
Divine jeweled breasts.

671 I dream of your arched eyebrows,
Curved like the bow.
Eyes as round as bamboo sections
No longer there to enamor me.

672 I dream of your tight, flat stomach
With down glistening like gems.
I dream of your smooth, bright cheeks
Perfect in their fullness.

673 Some merit we two made[225]
Brought me to her,
And now some sin
Separates her from me."

674 And so he kept searching
Every part of the forest,
But failed to meet his delicate beauty,
This prince separated afar.

675 The ministers advised the prince,   chabang
Told him he should leave,
Return to the city to rule.

676 The charioteers returned the jeweled chariot
And a flood of troops
Surrounded it, coming together.

677 They went along the old roadway,
Crossed over the forest levels,
The thousands of lakes and mountains.

678   "How near, how far this great forest?
        How near the city?"
        He cried desiring to sight the ramparts.

679   Outside the city, the prince rejoiced
        Reaching the royal pleasure park,
        The garden of beautiful blossoms.

680   And then came great Brahmins,[226]
        Four men journeying
        To the land of Romyaburi.

681   Having finished studying every treatise,
        Knowledgeable in every way,
        They sought a holy ascetic life.

682   They met the Lord of Men,
        Gave him great blessings,
        Extolling the Lord of the Land.

683   He saw their wondrous forms,
        And conversed amicably,
        "Why do you Brahmins come?"

684   And the Brahmins paid respects
        To the merciful prince
        Whose power spread afar,

685   "We come from Romyaburi
        Hearing that you, Lord of Men,
        Care and support those such as teachers.

686   Over there, it's heard,
        This Lord of the Land and his honor.
        We come to admire and praise this universal ruler."

687   The prince asked of the city
        Romyaburi
        And the wondrous sights therein.

688   "O Prince with superior might   wasantadilok
        In every way and manner,
        Who shows power with arrows
        Cowering enemies everywhere,

689   The distant city rejoices
        With citizens far and wide,
        Elephants, horses, soldiers like streams,
        Great streams of water.

690   All things superior and wondrous
        Equal the royal daughter,
        The one beauty, the pinnacle
        Of the King's heart forever.

691   Her form is one to soothe[227]
        All places on earth and heaven.
        She's named Phintumadi,
        The elegant beauty.

692   A youthful beauty[228]
        Like a flower delicate and budding,
        Her skin's perfection,
        No other's the same.

693   Her fresh hair sways to and fro
        Like the tail of the golden peacock.
        Her golden hair glistens with light,
        One of the eight desires.[229]

694   Her whole face's spotless,
        A beautiful flower
        Like the full moon,
        Lovely, creamy white.

695   Her ears are like lotus petals,
        Fine and delicate
        With sparkling gold earrings,
        Glorious, glinting gems.

696   Her delicate nose is a pleasing curve
        Like the hook of love;[230]
        Cheeks please with scents;
        Whoever sees her is lost.

697   Her legs are golden bananas,
        Straight with crystal, clear hair.
        Two breasts, wonderfully tight
        On her chest, finely wrought jewels.

698   Arched eyebrows curve like a bow,
       Curved and smooth;
       Eyes sparkle clear and bright,
       More attractive than the deer.

699   Her lips, brilliant as jewels,
       Glisten and glimmer
       With wide smiles. No one
       Equals this youthful beauty.

700   Teeth like diamonds
       Form orderly rows.
       Her smooth chest's a jeweled bed
       For celestial games of love.

701   Precious arms as lovely
       As noble Ayra's trunk;
       Curved fingers with lustrous nails
       Taper to fine points.

702   A curving waist induces desire,
       A splendid flowery vine;
       To find another like this on earth,
       It's said no one's the same.

703   A curved chin of gold.
       A throat for clear laughter,
       Whoever sees, when he sees,
       His heart agitates desiring to caress.

704   When you see the paired breasts,
       You'll fail to blink, seeing their shapes;
       You'll forget the jeweled stomach down
       Set in lines and rows.

705   When you gaze at the face, you'll rejoice
       And forget the smooth cheeks.
       Gazing at the shining hair,
       Gazing at the lustrous strands,

706   Gazing at the clear, arrow-sharp eyes
       Of this ravishing royal lady
       Arouses desire in the heart.
       In confusion, you forget the ears.

707   Gazing at the slender straight legs,
        The beautiful breasts,
        All the heavenly divinities,
        All the world forgets to gaze upon her.

708   Gazing at the bejeweled body down
        Of this wondrous woman,
        You'll forget to gaze at the lotus breasts,
        Jeweled and beautiful.

709   A heavenly, marvelous woman on this earth,
        This one we've seen.
        Such a fragrant queen as this,
        None exists in the three worlds.

710   A suitable one for caring,
        This radiant royal woman,
        She's the great queen
        That all the nobles think of.

711   Comparing the noble lineages
        And the royal kingdoms,
        Comparing the merit,
        In all things you two are suitable.

712   This then is the situation:[231]
        The Ruler of Men, her father,
        Wishes to give her in marriage,
        This woman, in seven days."

713   Listening to the Brahmins   chabang
        Relate the beauties
        Of the young princess,

714   The prince became jubilant,
        His face beamed,
        His heart's agitation extinguished.

715   Two thousand leather bags of gold,
        He bestowed as reward
        Without delay to those Brahmins.

716   With the Brahmins, soldiers, and retinue,
        From the pleasure garden,
        The prince entered Phromburi.

75

717   When dusk had fallen,
The prince proceeded
To the glittering golden palace,

718   Where gems glittered brilliantly
And a flood of consorts
Waited upon, attended the prince.

719   He sat alone in sorrow.
Countless consorts offered comfort,
But indifferent, he ignored them.

720   He forgot to answer his wife entreating,
Forgot to offer obeisance
To his royal father and mother.

721   He forgot his wife beseeching,
Even the lady Surasuda
Could not comfort, put out the pain.

Phintumadi Searches for Samuttakote

722   The princess Phintumadi with a face like the   sathun
moon was agitated upon waking. She shook
and quivered.

723   She sought the Ruler of the Realm, but failed.
Spreading grief filled her. Confusion filled her bed.

724   She beat her heart in agony, sad and mournful.
Her heart felt as though a torch flamed within.

725   "A dream or reality" back and forth, over and over,
she thought of him. She knew not how often.
Instantly, she awakened.

726   "How strange," the maiden cried in grief.
Awakened Thari came to see her.

727   Then the maidservant of the maiden   chabang
With the beautiful face
Awakened instantly.

728   Comforting, caressing, she asked,
      "What's wrong? Why are you confused?
      What do you dwell on?"

729   Caring for the maiden,
      Admiring and cherishing,
      "Why did you awake so startled?

730   Your servant wants to know
      What grief you endure.
      Don't hesitate! Tell me!"

731   The noble lady weeping in pain,
      Sobbing, worn out,
      Told her tale of sorrow.

732   "I returned here drowsy,
      Ready to sleep in the royal bed
      In the shining palace of gold.

733   Not long after, a handsome man
      Came and caressed
      And cared for me here.

734   I didn't know the ways,
      I wasn't skilled in love,
      But he came and taught me to smile,

735   Induced me to indulge in love.
      With pleasure, we slept
      In the royal bed.

736   I awakened alone. My eyes sought him,
      But failed to find the prince.
      Separated my heart was forlorn.

737   My grief and anger are restrained;
      No one sees inside my heart
      Where I sorrow and grieve."

738   Thari comforted and consoled the lady,
      Embraced her waist
      And praised the one with flowered feet.

739   "You're sad and vexed,
O little one.
Lament not! Don't do it!

740   No one entered this golden room,
Secretly passing in and out,
Coming to this splendid couch.

741   Listen to me, to my advice!
Don't strike yourself, my princess,
Don't grieve and sorrow, my life.

742   Soon there's the wedding
With you alone as bride
With all the kings coming for you.

743   Because of this you dreamed.
It's not real! Sorrow not!
Let me grieve for you."

744.   The lady was dismayed, her heart broken.   *yaanii/*
With grief and desire inside,   intharawichian
She threw herself on Thari's lap,
Her skillful maidservant.

745   Her hands beat her breast,
"O precious Thari,
It wasn't a dream! Don't confuse me!
Show mercy and compassion."

746   "Your cheeks are hollow,
Come let me look.
There're teeth marks on your cheeks[232]
Shaped like a stringless bow.

747   Your lips are bruised
As from some boy."
"This sorrow kills me,
Without death, I grieve.

748   The smell of his cheeks
Mixes with sweet fragrances
And fails to leave my breast.
The taste of love remains and soothes.

749   My heart pains, I complain.
       I'm not mad!
       I know clearly in my heart
       Where there's unseen suffering.

750   You're skilled in these ways.
       I beg for help. Don't withhold it.
       One time you came
       As a refuge for me in pain.

751   I think but remain confused
       Before the power of desire.
       Desire destroys me!
       Exhausted, I cannot endure.

752   If you won't help me,
       The grief will remain within my heart.
       O my beloved and respected,
       Please don't refuse me!

753   Since I was small you reared me,
       That goodness is hard to repay.
       Now it's the second time
       For your goodness, greater than the earth.

754   Come, find a way
       That reveals the proper action
       So that I, your little one,
       May meet with the prince.

755   If you love me, don't wait for long.
       Come help draw a picture
       Of kings and gods,
       Nagas and kinnarees,

756   So we'll know who it is,
       Who dared to hug and caress,
       Fooled and played with me
       And when I was happy, sneaked away."

757   Thari listened to the maiden,   chabang
       Saw her sorrow
       And grew alarmed.

79

758   "How strange some person
       Dared enter
       These royal chambers.

759   With many levels and doors
       With impassable secret ways,
       A fearless one came through.

760   He came to soothe and caress you,
       Showing no fear
       Of your father, the king, who watches over.

761   If the king knew, he couldn't escape this earth,
       No way to escape at all."
       And thinking she laughed.

762   "She asked for a series of drawings,"
       Thari thought,
       "I'll draw kings from every corner."

763   She drew a powerful king
       In many raiments and chains,
       Draped with the naga king,[233]

764   Along with the great bull.
       The maiden grieved
       Did not look, remained puzzled.

765   She drew colorful Naray in colors[234]
       Along with Garuda
       Flying mightily in the heavens.

766   Her lady looked, never ceased moaning.
       It wasn't this king
       Who came secretly, came to caress her.

767   She drew the great Lord Phrom[235]
       On the shining swan
       Glowing lustrously.

768   None were the prince
       So elegant and handsome,
       Superior beyond all others.

769   So she drew Indra[236]
        On the elephant Ayra,
        Marvelous and handsome,

770   He carried the diamond weapon.
        It wasn't he.
        That king was not this shining form.

771   Then she drew the God of the Wind[237]
        On the Sindhu steeds
        Shining with glittering rays.

772   Phintumadi grieved becoming
        Sorrowful twice over,
        Thinking, reflecting, her heart dismayed.

773   Then she drew the protector of the world[238]
        On his lotus throne
        Gleaming, glittering, glinting.

774   Phintumadi swooned,
        Her heart heated more
        And her confusion increased

775   She drew the Lord of Fire[239]
        With his powerful beast
        Shining with a hundred-thousand rays.

776   She drew giants,
        But the maid sat listless,
        Neither looked nor changed her sorrow.

777   She drew a kinnaree, a golden naga,
        A noble khonthan.
        How sad she stayed!

778   Then she drew the royal prince,
        Samuttakote
        With his shining power,

779   A face like the unsullied moon,
        Eyebrows arched like a bow,
        And each eye an arrow.

81

780   A handsome waist aroused her heart.
        She stretched her hands,
        Saw the body and changed nothing.

781   She placed the plack against her heart,
        As her fire flamed up
        And she forgot her sorrow-filled story.

782   "Oh, this one makes me die,
        Forces my heart out,
        Far from my body."

783   She examined this honored one;
        Desire intoxicated her;
        Her eyes no longer confused.

784   She asked her maidservant,
        "Who's this elegant prince?
        A godlike noble from where?

785   Thari answered quickly,
        "This prince is famous.
        Over the three worlds, his praises spread.

786   His elegance covers the world,
        The son of the Lord of the Realm.
        Powerful Phintutat.

787   This noble prince is named,
        Called Prince
        Samuttakote, the immortal."

788   When she heard this,
        The fire advanced little by little
        And she groaned as her heart moved.

789   Her tears welled up and flooded over.
        Thari comforted and consoled,
        Soothing the princess' heart,

790   "Grieve not, your servant Thari,
        She'll go out.
        It's not difficult. Sorrow not!

791   Tell not even one person!
       Watch what I do!
       I say worry not!"

792   She listened relieved.
       Her sorrow dissipated
       And the maidservant laughed.

793   She sent Thari, the maidservant,
       To the prince,
       To invite His Highness, the Ruler of Men.

794   And then Lady Thari
       Consoled the princess
       And paid her homage.

Phintumadi's Servant Meets Samuttakote

795   In an instant she flew into the air
       With sparkling gold ornaments
       Glimmering in the moonbeams.

796   Reaching Phromburi,
       She looked all around,
       At tiers of impregnable walls.

797   The palace was arrayed in gold,
       Shining like Suriya's rays,
       Glittering gold in the heavens.

798   All the soldiers slept soundly,
       Quietly she landed
       In the eternal jeweled palace.

799   She entered the palace,
       Saw precious stones shimmering
       With glittering rays of light.

800   Nearing the splendid celestial bed,
       Heavenly Thari
       Secretly gazed upon the prince,

83

801   Saw him sleeping in the royal bed,
       Alone in deep sorrow.
       She moved closer to give her message,

802   "O noble prince, most worthy of respect,   *yaanii/*
       Your fame spans the earth,   intharawichian
       You fill maidens' hearts
       With your elegant form,

803   The Lady Phintumadi
       Equals you in rank,
       She groans with grief,
       Yet Your Highness shows no compassion.

804   Awakened, she missed you,
       O Lord of Men,
       Her heart confused,
       Confounded with eternal sorrow.

805   This lady dreams of you
       Without end. She's vexed,
       Her breast seeps tears
       From true sorrow and longing.

806   Intentionally, she sent me
       To Your Majesty, O Great One,
       To tell you of the Lotus-like feet,[240]
       To tell you of her great grief."

807   The Ruler of the Earth hearing   chabang
       Of this maid's sorrow
       Grieved for the maiden,

808   "You came here and no one
       Soothes the lady, all alone
       In her agony and her longing?

809   Little did I know that when
       As usual I went to the forest
       There, I'd encounter sorrow.

810   Take me to her quickly,
       To end her heart's torment!
       Immediately, without delay!"

811   Then the Ruler of the Realm and his retinue
Left the royal chamber
And his splendid slumber.

812   He ordered his ministers,
Those noble men,
To watch over with care,

813   "Report my journey,
Tell my royal father
Whose name spreads far and wide.

814   Then bring the royal soldiers
With the Brahmins,
All four, to Romyaburi."

815   Then he sent the ministers
And readied to set forth.
And Lord Indra knowing his desire

816   So sent his charioteer Matuli[241]
With a celestial chariot
To offer to the Royal Master.

817   He mounted the jeweled chariot;
And Matuli drove the steeds,
Beating each, the chariot swaying.

818   Thari showed the way
Before the chariot set off,
Climbing into heaven's expanse.

819   The jeweled chariot shed light
And glittering gold garments
Covered His Majesty

820   Like the Maker of Light in his gold chariot.[242]
And the celestial horses leaped boldly
Across the earth and sky.

821   So they reached Romyaburi,
Its glittering jeweled palace
Bespeckled with rays of gemstones,

822   And the golden chariot
Reached the jeweled throne room
Where the royal maiden slept.

823   Thari led the prince
To lie with the beauty
Comparable to ambrosia.

824   The two of equal rank
Told of their sorrows
Since the night he left

825   And a thousand sorrows filled their hearts.
He caressed the princess
And his arms quickly embraced her.

826   And she cried, "O Lord of the Realm,
My heart left me
And in agony I sent her for you.

827   You caressed and consoled me in the royal bed,
Enticed me into love,
Till we blended into one.

828   And you so filled with emotion
Had no time to awake me
And you, my noble, fled from me.

829   I knew not the reason,
Awakening I beat myself,
Lamenting my ruin, searching for you."

830   The prince's hands embraced his precious,
"Remove your confusion,
O my beloved lady.

831   Close we lay in the royal bed,
Delicious desire arose,
Then we slept not knowing time.

832   For long we knew no weariness.
Then the spirit took me
And instantly I cried when I awoke.

833   I searched through the forest,
        Met no one at all,
        My heart devastated thinking of you."

834   Speaking of sorrow he embraced her,
        Comforted his young maiden,
        Soothed her agitated heart.

835   With joy their confusion subsided
        In the royal bed
        With flowers opening wide.[243]

836   On the royal jeweled bed
        With the decorated cushions
        And the handsome ceiling above,

837   With golden pillars sparkling
        And pendulous pearls swaying,
        Desire lasted long.

838   Scattered begemmed pillows gleamed;
        Candle rays illuminated;
        Flames sparkled like jewels;

839   Ladies-in-waiting, courtesans
        Sat in close groups
        Paying obeisance.

840   Some plied plumes and fans;
        Some played music
        Blending sounds together.

841   Some offered trays of betel;
        Some offered blossoms,[244]
        Stringing strands together;

842   Some offered scents and fragrances,
        Alluring aromas
        Wafting through the celestial palace.

843   They tasted desire till replete;
        His arms encircled her waist
        As they luxuriated in love.

87

844   For seven days the two loved
        In the pleasure-filled bed
        Bedecked with jewels and gems.

845   Then ministers ordered the troops,
        Warriors stood all around
        Like streams to the sea.

846   They sent the prince's message
        To Phintutat,
        The Ruler of the Earth.

847   The chariots, elephants, soldiers, and horses
        Parted Phromburi
        Along with the four Brahmins.

848   The soldiers led the way
        With the warriors who arrived
        At Romyaburi.

849   The news of these troops spread,
        And Thari bowing
        Before the king told her news

850   She'd bring the Lord of the Realm
        That evening
        To order up the soldiers.

851   And the news spread to all corners,
        All over the land,
        To citizens of every city,

852   That dawn commenced the engagement.[245]
        From every direction, every continent,
        All the noble rulers came:

853   Deities, giants, kings,
        Heavenly musicians,
        And soldiers everywhere.

854   They brought troops, set up lines
        In glorious Romyaburi,
        All over the city plain.

Samuttakote Bids Farewell to His Wife

The Seer Opens the Forest

Elephant Groupings

Samuttakote Snares an Elephant

Samuttakote Bids Farewell to His Parents

Samuttakote and Phintumadi Adrift in the Sea

The Wedding Contest

855   Then the king of Romyaburi,   *yaanii*/intharawichian
                    The great, royal kingdom
                    With the power of might
                    To defeat all enemies,

856   Arranged the contest
                    For the royal daughter.
                    Kings from every continent
                    Came with their leaders.

857   The king readied
                    The iron bow heavy[246]
                    With such great weight
                    That fear spread far and wide.

858   And so he told every king
                    From every direction with power great,
                    And with the ability
                    To battle in every corner,

859   "Whoever can lift the bow,
                    Hold it way overhead,
                    Show his skill with arrows
                    In ways devised,

860   To that Lord of Men I'll give
                    This royal princess
                    And the wealth and treasure,
                    Allow them to rule Romyaburi."

861   Pleased, the kings from all the lands   chabang
                    Readied to contest for victory
                    On the face of the field.

862   Groups of kings, powers in war,
                    Mounted their chariots
                    And one after another rode out:

863   First Maturarat,[247]
                    Chariot harnessed with horses,
                    In his hand a long lance;

864   Then Kawsoek
His chariot with dragons,
And he with a bow standing forth;

865   Then Thepanikorn,
A crossbow in hand,
His chariot harnessed with tigers;

866   Then mighty Mattarat
Riding in a glittering chariot
With the swish of a sword;

867   Then Thepphitchay
In a chariot with his hands
Swinging a mace of gold;

868   Then splendid Phitthayut
Rode in a chariot with a tusked lion
With countless capable soldiers;

869   Then Makottarat
In an adorned chariot
With a ferocious lion;

870   Then Jittarat in a gold chariot
With two lions
Skilled and powerful;

871   Then Jitasen, lion-strong,
His chariot swaying
Harnessed with a jamri;

872   Then Chumpasun set forth
In the zodiac chariot
With giants by the thousands;

873   Then the giant Nikum[248]
Like Kumphakan, the leader
Of all the giant soldiers.

874   They mixed extolling their might,
But became discouraged,
Ashamed and abashed.

875   Each thinking to snatch the lady
In vain attacked many times
Without wavering even once.

876   None succeeded;
Indifferent they looked on,
Not entering the field.

Samuttakote Shows His Skill

877   Then Samuttakote appeared
Showing his warrior skills,
His might and his intent.

878   With the power of a naga
Able to battle with special powers
He took to the field.

879   He seized the iron bow,
Swung the powerful weapon,
And proved his power to all.

880   Drawing the bow with mighty arrows
The lotus-foot prince drew back,
Showing the bow in the field.

881   His magic might instilled fear;
As he showed his superior force
In battle on the field.

882   Like Rama of the Solar Race[249]
He lifted the iron bow
With might and magnificence.

883   He plucked the string and clear thunder
Echoed across the earth
Shaking every corner.

884   He grasped a glinting arrow,
Curved and bent
The handsome bow in a flash.

885 To all directions, he was polite, courteous,
But his power was feared
By enemies across the earth.

886 He showed his skill
Like Saraphang[250]
Who proved his power long ago.

887 Quickly he showed his skill with arrows
As the King of the Realm,
Sri Narakup, decreed.

888 Shooting one arrow he demonstrated:
The shot became a flood
Covering the earth:

889 Hundreds of graceful arrows,
More than imagined,
Innumerable and countless.

890 Then he shot an arrow with full strength,
A high powerful shot
That hung in the heavens,

891 And then spread like falling rain
In the rainy season
And noise reverberated over the land.

892 To cover the earth and sky,
He shot an arrow
Showing his intent.

893 He shot one full strength
Into the air as a naga
And then another killing it.

894 One became a palace room
All across the sky
Shining with arrows.

895 One became a jeweled orb,
And the soldiers admired
And praised the Lord of the Land.

896   Then he shot another with full strength
               And it became a golden flower
               Sparkling over the ceiling.

897   Flowers hung at the top,
               A many-hued jeweled place,
               A city of many things.

898   Every king, soldier, warrior
               Praised the prince's power,
               His perfect skill and ability.

899   Then the king ordered hung a hair
               From a jamri,
               Twisted into knots in a circle,

900   Far, far out, a full yoot.[251]
               To those looking it was unclear,
               Farther than the eye could see.

901   He had the prince shoot one arrow
               Into the heavens high
               To make it evening.

902   He had the prince quickly shoot an arrow,
               Shoot the jamri hair,
               Split it in half.

903   The prince listened, with no hesitation
               Shot it flying
               To the heavens with skillful tricks,

904   Created darkness over earth and sky
               As though it were midnight,
               A day with no moon.

905   The kings, soldiers, warriors
               Milled about in every spot
               Confused, startled, frightened.

906   The prince strung one arrow, a barrier,
               Shot it into the sky
               Shading all from sight.

907   It struck one strand of the hair,
Cut it from sight,
Felled it quickly before all.

908   Deities and ascetics sang praises,
"Victory, victory, fight on fiercely,"
Cries of approval rang out.

909   They cast heavenly flowers in praise,
And all the enemy
Trembled in hair-raising fear.

910   News of the majestic power spread,
And the populace and troops,
One after another honored the prince.

911   Orchestras, trumpets, conches, drums
Sounded gloriously,
Combining in celebration.

912   King Narakup was jubilant
Every wish completed
To win His daughter.

913   His heart was satisfied,
All done perfectly
With no desire undone to disappoint.

914   At once he announced
He'd join his dear child
In union with the splendid youth.

915   He'd offer her in marriage,
Soon to become queen
For the Lord of the Land.

The Suitors Ready Their Forces

916   This the kings from all the lands heard,
They gathered, lined up duties,
Hoping to begin battle.

917   In great indignation,
        Desiring the comely woman,
        Each argued his point,

918   "Each of us has thousands,
        Hundreds of thousands of soldiers
        That surpass all others.

919   To win that lady we'll bring the army,
        So many it'll be a mass;
        It's wrong to back down!

920   We must prevent ignominy,
        Preserve honor,
        Allow no one to belittle us.

921   Though we die on the battlefield,
        Honor replaces life,
        It's greater than life.

922   We're with our soldiers,
        Skilled in all arts.
        It's improper to allow such shame.

923   We'll gather soldiers from all over,
        A single thread, one mind,
        One person unstoppable,

924   A like-minded force we'll battle him
        And take the precious princess
        In revenge for the shame."

925   Having shown their intent,
        They ordered up their troops,
        Spread them over the earth.

926   They readied chariots, readied elephants;
        And sent skilled soldiers
        To every spot on the battlefield.

927   The mighty Mathurarat
        First provoked battle
        Before all other kings.

Samuttakote Readies His Forces

928   Samuttakote heard this news
        That kings from all corners
        Had readied all their troops.

929   Fires of fury encroached upon his heart,
        His whole body
        Appeared to be ablaze.

930   He desired to destroy all
        And his soldiers assured of victory
        Readied for great destruction.

931   He reviewed the brave battalions,
        Ordered every rank,
        Their numbers unknown.

932   He chose the warriors,
        A fearless group to harass
        The enemy on the battlefield.

933   He chose the warriors
        With ability and skill
        To suppress in the fight.

934   He sought them with art and no fear,[252]
        For it was an auspicious time,
        An astrologer's prediction.

935   He sought brave ones, the best of all,
        Asked them to volunteer,
        To follow without question.

936   He sought a group of keen minds,
        That knew all strengths,
        All ways the enemy fought.

937   He sought brave ones with stamina,
        Experienced in battle
        With strength and fighting skill.

938   He sought those who knew all
In war, skilled in ways
To defeat the enemy.

939   He sought a group firm in fidelity,
Who loved the Ruler of the Land
With no treason, no deception.

940   Before the prince they volunteered
To support him,
Never to be remiss in their duties.

941   He sought those with stout hearts
Who'd incite each other
With echoing cheers and cries.

942   He sought those to unite,
Nobles who would not waver,
An advantage to him in his goal.

943   He sought those who knew ways,
The many ways of war,
Skilled in the battles on earth.

944   He sought those bolder than lions
With great power and strength,
Capable of killing elephants.

945   He sought those skilled with arrows,
Bold enough to kill enemies
With tactics and strategies.

946   He sought those with brave hearts
To destroy the enemy
With hearts forever strong.

947   Finished inspecting thousands,
He chose ten warriors,
Surpassing all others in all ways.

948   He sent them right and left,
Front, back, all around
With their companies of soldiers.

949   Hundreds of soldiers
        Covered the ground and the sky
        Going in all directions:

950   Sparkling weapons and ornaments,
        Shiny breastplates
        Of every different kind.

951   He readied elephants, horses, chariots;
        Skilled soldiers did their work
        With their fearful weapons.

952   The prince offered blessings
        To all of the warriors
        Along with a glorious victory,

953   "Success, success to you brave, bold soldiers;
        Victory, victory, battle boldly;
        Fulfill, fulfill your powers;

954   Victory, victory, all around;
        Victory, victory, defeat,
        Destroy enemies by the thousands;

955   Victory, victory to skilled Satsatrachit;
        Victory in destroying
        Those giants in the thousands.

956   Victory, victory to Rutaratit,
        Cruel, pitiless,
        With power supreme.

957   Victory, victory to Sonjak
        Splashing swords in a killing rain,
        Completely filling the air.

958   Victory, victory to famous Ronamuk;
        Victory, victory to the renowned,
        Phimsin, his name.

959   Victory, victory to feared Thotsaron,
        Victory to Phanthasongkhram,
        Phinpanpiri, one after another.

960   Victory, victory to brave Phirenthorn,
       Ronnasing who shows
       Power and determination."

961   The blessing of the soldiers over,
       He arranged them all
       Into a mass that filled the earth.

962   These ten readied
       Filled the area
       All over every surface.

963   Having chosen the brave ten,
       The leaders of the soldiers,
       Special in their everlasting power,

964   He readied chariots, horses, elephants
       That echoed the prince's fame
       Over the three worlds.

965   He inspected the skilled warriors
       With their swinging swords,
       Shiny shields, and lances in the lead.

966   Flags, umbrellas filled the sky
       Hiding the Maker of Light
       With sparkling flags, umbrellas.

967   Some nobles rode elephants oozing musk,
       Trunks and tusks waving,
       Rolling and rippling back and forth.

968   Some nobles rode horses, drilled donkeys;
       Troops whirled and swirled
       With hands swinging lances.

969   Some nobles drove golden vehicles,
       Bows and arrows in hand,
       Skilled on the battlefield.

970   Some nobles rode elegant camels
       Brandishing swords,
       Showing special skills.

971   Some nobles rode rearing antelopes,
Rode fearful lions,
Experienced in flourishing swords.

972   Some nobles rode arrogant nagas
With shiny white fangs,
Instilling hair-raising fear.

973   Some rode ferocious tigers,
Rode lions brandishing
Swords in great numbers.

974   Some nobles skillfully rode buffaloes,
Fierce musking buffaloes
With magnificent power.

975   Some nobles rode jamri
With marching soldiers all around,
Arrayed with knives and long swords.

976   Legions of companies, legions of vehicles,
Many knew animal languages,
Unending lordly companies.

The Minister Attempts to Stop the Battle

977   When the king of Romyaburi   *yaanii*/intharawichian
Learned these kings
From every land were enemies,
Angry and ready to fight,

978   He sent a high-ranking soldier,
Valiant and able,
Named Susangkan
And with great intelligence.

979   He was ordered to stop, oppose
Those kings from every land,
Elephants, horses, warriors,
The companies of brave soldiers.

980   The minister Susangkan
        Received his royal order
        And went without delay
        Before the ten warriors,[253]

981   Arriving, he claimed
        "King Narakup, general,
        Has sent me here in haste
        To you ten majesties.

982   He's sent me to stop you.
        Quell your angry!
        I didn't come on my own!
        Restrain your anger!

983   Now, His Highness
        Samuttakote
        Alone raised the bow,
        Displayed his skill with the arrows.

984   And with great dexterity
        This prince showed his strength.
        And thus the king ordered
        The wedding ceremony.

985   So you, noble lords,
        Ready to start any destruction.
        You know his arrow has power,
        Stop boasting about yourselves!"

986   As these nobles listened   chabang
        Their illusion and folly rose;
        They missed the proper action.

987   The comely figure of the woman
        Produced a rising lust
        Which they could neither restrain nor stop.

988   None feared death, each proud.
        They readied their troops
        To fight, no change in their intent.

101

989 The minister Susangkan   *yaanii*/intharawichian
    Returned to the king.
    Hearing this report,
    He sent Susangkan

990 To Samuttakote
    To reveal the enemies' ways.
    Susangkan returned
    And told the news,

991 "With my life I beg you,
    O noble one, to look quickly,
    Gaze upon the valiant soldiers
    Spread across the earth.

992 The air's clouded over
    In all directions, dust blots out,
    Covers over the rays
    So the Maker of Light cannot shine.

993 There are complete companies
    Bold and brave soldiers,
    Elephants, horses, closed tight,
    Companies ready to fight."

994 The prince gazed at the forces,
    Soldiers equal in strength,
    And asked Susangkan,
    That noble minister,

995 "Which noble rides the chariot of gold,   wasantadilok
    Harnessed with horses,
    With the long lance
    Of majestic power?

996 Jamri, horses, umbrellas,
    Tight together, cloud the air,
    Cover the Maker of Light
    So no rays reach the air.

997 Leaders of the companies
    Left and right swing swords,
    Each yells out
    All around, on all sides."

998   "That noble's Maturarat
        With power greater than all celestial cities.
        The earth shakes all around;
        None can fight him."

999   "Which noble's with the dragon
        Harnessed to the chariot?
        With a shining crossbow,
        He boldly grasps arrows.

1000   Skillful soldier companies
        Enter fearlessly,
        Jeer at the arrows
        With no fear of death from this power."

1001   "That noble's Kawsoek
        And his fame spreads.
        Capable of fighting celestial armies,
        He's filled with dreadful plans."

1002   "Who's the noble in the camel chariot
        The brave and bold one,
        Raising high the mace
        Like the famed Lord of Maces?"[254]

1003   "That noble's Phitchaychan
        With superior skill and vehemence,
        Able to kill great giants.
        His might never weakens."

1004   "Which noble rides the victory chariot
        Harnessed with elephants
        Displaying power, skill, great magic,
        A bold power with a two-edged sword?"

1005   "That noble's named Phitthayut,
        A mighty king who quickly
        Slays nobles all over the earth,
        Within the boundaries of the universe."

1006   "Who's that superior noble
        Carrying the excellent discus
        Standing center chariot
        With the great naga?"

103

1007   "That noble grasps Phutchakaro,[255]
        Powerful and majestic,
        A strong and mighty soldier,
        A hero with a king's regalia."

1008   "Which noble rides the golden chariot
        Harnessed with a great lion,
        Carrying a superior bow and arrow,
        Boasting of boldness midst battle?"

1009   "That noble's Makottarat
        With a daring power
        Who arrogantly kills his enemies,
        Destroying enemies all over the land."

1010   "Which noble carries that diamond weapon
        On the broad lion chariot,
        The sky brilliantly glittering
        As he stands midst the battlefield?"

1011   "That noble's Jittarat,
        Bold and vicious,
        Subduing the demons
        Proving his power and skill."

1012   "Which noble wears the gold crown,
        Grasping the club and yelling out,
        Flying straight up in the chariot
        Harnessed with the jamri?"

1013   "That noble's named His Majesty
        Jitasen, a khonthan,
        With a magic verse
        To change into different shapes."

1014   "Which noble rides the gold chariot
        Harnessed with the daring donkey
        With the radiant weapon
        Glittering in his hand?"

1015   "That noble's the great one
        Named Chumphasun.
        Able to destroy Indra's soldiers,
        He's evil, bold, and arrogant."

1016   "Which noble rides the handsome chariot
        Harnessed with two lions that fly,
        Who raises the hammer, swings it back
        Leaving giants shaking in fear?"

1017   "That noble's named Nikum,
        Fearful and dreadful,
        His mighty magic, famed magic,
        Greater than others, crosses the earth."

1018   The enemy already admired,
        The enemy soldiers and forces
        Ordered and arrayed their forces,
        Countless elephants, and horses.

1019   The first was Maturarat,
        Fearless with magic power,
        Who led the great force,
        Creating a fearful fire.

1020   They came out to battle the prince's troops,
        Ferocious groups of soldiers,
        Fighting on the battlefield,
        Showing power and skill.

1021   The elephant leaders of the forces
        Moved out in a stream
        Covering all the groups
        With soldiers meeting face to face.

1022   On all sides soldiers shouted,
        Great cries called out,
        Echoing and reverberating
        For victory one after another.

1023   Curved horns resounded,
        Conches together with drums
        Crossing the three worlds,
        Sounding out destruction.

Samuttakote Battles the Suitors

1024   Mathurarat quickly called the brave noble,   chabang
        Skilled in all aspects,
        And Ekkajak answered fearlessly.

1025   He mounted a horse with a lance
        Boldly laughing,
        Skilled in brandishing the sword.

1026   He stood in the victory chariot,
        Darkness covered the three worlds
        From a myriad of numbers.

1027   So the prince sent his splendid warrior
        Satsatrachit
        With power exceeding the rest.

1028   They stabbed, struggling mightily,
        Countless troops
        That evaded, avoided, then cut.

1029   They rushed, pushed, and clashed;
        And enemy companies
        Piled up, strewn across the field.

1030   The prince's soldiers pounced,
        Scattered the enemy
        As Ekkajak fumed and flamed.

1031   Next they flew their horses
        Shouting victory.
        They threatened and groaned fighting.

1032   So with golden spears flying
        Satsatrachit
        Appeared midst the battle.

1033   Satsatrachit skilled in victory,
        With an iron hammer clanging
        Fought Ekkajak on and on.

1034   But he fell from his horse rolling,
The earth shaking
And trembling across the land.

1035   Mathurarat with fiery fury
Readied his others
And returned to the conflict.

1036   He stood in the gold chariot
With a handsome lance
Flourishing in bravery.

1037   Fighting furiously, battling,
Elephants, chariots thick in line,
He ordered the warriors to charge.

1038   The prince's soldiers pressed;
The prince proceeded ahead
In the glittering, gold chariot.

1039   With arrows, bows, and breastplates
Charioteers like bees
Sent up their magnificent chariots.

1040   With joyful cries of battle
The soldiers instilled great confusion
Turning over the earth.

1041   The leaders pressed forward
With loud noises issuing forth
And chariot horses hurrying on.

1042   Mathurarat cried out his command,
"You, Lord of the Realm,
Noble Samuttakote,

1043   You'll fight with me,
On this field. Whose might
Will you battle with?

1044   You're still a child! Which way,
Against me,
Will you try on the battlefield?"

1045   And the prince answered back,
"You, Mathurarat,
Quell your arrogance!

1046   In no time you'll see.
It's either you or me.
We'll know who the winner is.

1047   Don't boast and brag too much.
I'm the one that'll destroy you
With all my tricks and ways."

1048   The two entered the field,
Pushed their forces forward
And met face to face.

1049   Elephants and horses screamed out;
The infantry fought head to head;
And the dead piled up all around.

1050   The prince shot arrows forward,
Smashed the chariot retreating
With banners bending and breaking.

1051   In a fury Mathurarat grabbed
His handsome diamond club,
Thrusting and jabbing at the prince.

1052   The prince sent an arrow aloft
And struck the diamond club,
Smashing it with a powerful arrow.

1053   The prince sent another arrow aloft,
A great naga hovering
That hit Mathurarat's chest.

1054   And Mathurarat dropped down;
His defeated soldiers scattered,
Tilting and turning the earth.

1055   So Kawsoek the giant
Moved his troops up
Without stopping in the field.

1056   He sent Jakjon with his troops
        Readied in a great mass
        With superior soldiers following.

1057   Elephants, horses, jeweled chariots advanced;
        Earth and sky trembled in fear
        As dark clouds covered all points.

1058   The prince sent Rutaratit;
        Fearless, intrepid with shiny magic,
        He led his warriors,

1059   Thwarting the brave Jakjon,
        Scattering soldiers.
        Both braves boldly battled.

1060   The brave two shot quickly;
        Striking sounds sang
        With the mighty diamond.

1061   Victory cheers: chaw, chaw;
        Smash, slash: sword sounds;
        Striking, cutting with many dying.

1062   Jakjon grabbed the arrow whisking by,
        And sent to every point
        Hundreds of arrows shining.

1063   Rutaratit skilled in war
        Carried the diamond club behind
        And in a flash struck Jakjon.

1064   Jakjon fell. And arrows from the prince
        Smashed Jakjon to pieces,
        Flattened him on the field.

1065   King Kawsoek alone looked on,
        His anger grew
        And he pointed boldly.

1066   In haste chariots and soldiers lined up
        With bows and arrows ready
        And he called out,

1067   "Quick, strike the Lord of the Land,
        Splash arrows
        Like sparkling rain over the earth."

1068   But the prince shot a single arrow aloft,
        Covered the earth and sky,
        Covered them in great darkness.

1069   Great sounds rang from the great arrow.
        Soldiers cheered,
        Spread the sounds of victory.

1070   Kawsoek sent an arrow as fire;
        The prince sent an arrow
        As water flooding the sky.

1071   Kawsoek shot an arrow hanging,
        Changed it to a naga
        Twisting slowly above.

1072   The prince fired off an arrow
        As Garuda, King of Birds,
        Seizing and destroying the snake.

1073   Kawsoek shot an arrow
        As a charging elephant
        There replacing the naga.

1074   The prince sent an arrow
        As a lion that grabbed
        The elephant falling dead in a heap.

1075   Kawsoek shot an arrow
        As smoke obscuring earth and sky,
        Clouds shading the eyes.

1076   The prince shot a blowing wind
        To clear the clouds,
        Revealing all directions.

1077   Kawsoek shot a mountain,
        Closing the way in darkness,
        Hiding the thousands of soldiers.

1078   The prince shot with great skill
        A diamond that split the rock,
        Pulverizing the peaks.

1079   The troops were crushed;
        Kawsoek confused
        Cried out in surprise at his ways.

1080   An arrow split Kawsoek in pieces;
        Quickly he fell
        And the enemy shook in fright.

1081   Deities and ascetics sang praises,
        Offered flowers and sounds
        Of accord reverberating.

1082   So the skilled Thepphitchay,
        Filled with fire of rage
        Arising midst his heart,

1083   Ordered his soldiers to follow,
        Royal soldiers
        In hundreds and thousands.

1084   He assigned fearless Ukarasena
        As commander
        To lead the troops.

1085   Thousands spread over the land,
        Assembled on the field
        Like streams in the sea.

1086   The prince sent ever faithful Sonjak
        To lead his soldiers,
        To destroy the enemy.

1087   The earth and sky inverted;
        Dust billowed out, hiding
        Suriya's rays without end.

1088   Ukarasena led Kartikeya's troops[256]
        Into the battle,
        Clashing with the enemy.

1089   The prince's soldiers slew the enemy;
        Dying in disorderly heaps,
        They piled up over the earth.

1090   Ukarasena called out,
        "Sonjak, I pity you,
        You arrogant child.

1091   Let's fight on the field,
        You're not worthy
        Fighting and fleeing death."

1092   Sonjak called back,
        "Ukarasena, you've no shame
        Bragging and boasting of your bravery.

1093   Fight me real soon
        And I'll destroy you
        So you can fight no more."

1094   Ukarasena angered fast
        And with a mace
        He grasped at victory.

1095   Sonjak brandished bow and arrow,
        Swung them in the field
        Ready to destroy every foe.

1096   The two fought on the field
        Smashing clumps of trees
        And shattering mountains.

1097   Ukarasena struck Sonjak,
        But Sonjak revealed his power
        Midst the field without moving.

1098   Then Sonjak shot an arrow
        At Ukarasena
        Striking him dead.

1099   Phitchaychan saw
        His soldiers dead
        And indignation filled his heart.

1100   Charging chariots, elephants, soldiers,
The leaders looked on
As the noble chief became enraged.

1101   He drove his royal chariot forward,
Seized the iron mace
And dared the prince to fight.

1102   And the prince with the bow and arrow
Shot and destroyed
The chariot, smashed it to pieces.

1103   Umbrellas broke and flew off;
Phitchaychan with the mace
Ferociously screamed out.

1104   The prince shot the mighty arrow
Zigzagging like lightning,
Spinning through the vault of heaven,

1105   Till it struck Phitchaychan,
Who fell stunned,
Shaking the whole earth.

1106   Phitthayut led out his thousands,
Stood in his place
On the field of battle

1107   And struck the fleeing foe,
Chariots, elephants, one after another
By the hundreds of thousands.

1108   So the warrior Petcharom was sent
To lead the troops
To fight the soldiers of the prince.

1109   Both battalions with battle skill
Cried out shooting,
Striking, killing, piling on one another.

1110   And so the prince sent Ronamuk
As the leader
With special power of victory.

113

1111   Ronamuk pressed forward;
        And the enemy on the ground
        Piled up higher and higher.

1112   Phetcharom did not rest, but carried on;
        Each fought on the field,
        Neither crying out in defeat.

1113   Ronamuk thrust his diamond spear;
        Phetcharom returned harassing
        But quickly fell in the field.

1114   Phitthayut flamed like fire,
        Showing no fear in his fury,
        Drove his chariot forward.

1115   He carried a gleaming sword
        To the middle of the field
        Roaring like a lion.

1116   The prince skillfully shot an arrow
        Shaking the earth,
        Turning the world around.

1117   He struck Phitthayut and his soldiers
        Scattered the dead,
        No one living on the battlefield.

1118   Phitthayut fell there,
        His pain doubling
        No longer causing fear.

1119   Jitasen saw the warriors
        And quickly came out,
        His anger burning like fire.

1120   He drove his chariot, called the soldiers;
        And they pounded over the earth
        As the noble leader drove forth.

1121   They returned to fight, unsure with fear,
        Victory cries echoing,
        Resounding in every corner.

1122   They fought the prince fearlessly,
        Ordered infantry to follow
        Darkening the heavens overhead.

1123   The front lines of steeds swung swords;
        Clamoring cries spread:
        With strength they pressed on.

1124   Prince fought prince, both equally brave;
        Charioteer against charioteer,
        Both sides striving for victory.

1125   Foot soldiers fought and died.
        Assured in their strength,
        None unsure of victory.

1126   Staggering and falling, wading in blood,
        Waist high in blood,
        Thousands fell defeated.

1127   Bodies heaped high in piles;
        The prince's forces slashed forward,
        Beheading and scattering the soldiers.

1128   Some hit in the stomach, their innards protruded,
        Entrails dangled out,
        And the dead piled up one after another.

1129   Some hit in arms and legs
        Ground their teeth in pain,
        Then jumped to fight the enemy again.

1130   Swords knocked down, spears snatched,
        Grabbing and running, none fled;
        With power, they knew no fear.

1131   Some fell, some ran to their station;
        Clamoring soldiers cried
        And shouted out stridently.

1132   They snatched spears to thrust;
        They snapped all around;
        In confusion, back and forth, they fought.

1133   Striking, slashing, fearless soldiers
Chopped and yelled,
Rays from their swords gleaming.

1134   Slipping, falling, blood overflowing,
Warriors waded back and forth
With no sounds of complaint.

1135   The prince shot a smashing arrow;
Jitasen showed no fear,
With no retreat before the arrogant enemy.

1136   He lifted a jeweled thunderbolt, and club,
Brandished it
And struck Prince Samut in the field.

1137   And the prince smashed the chariot;
It broke and fell
And the mace flew into the heavens.

1138   The arrow hit Jitasen
Devastating him, his blood
Covering the earth in a river.

1139   Heavenly flower garlands fell
From heavenly hosts
That hailed and sang the prince's praises.

1140   The splendid Chumpasun
Drove his chariot,
Pressing hurriedly his thousands of enemies.

1141   Chumpasun's side had demons;
Thousands with him
Lined up in the field,

1142   One after another, elephants, chariots, horses,
A mass military movement
With great giants following.

1143   They were fearless on the field
With one warrior
Called Thoramuk.

1144   With might he led the troops,
Pressed the valiant forces
Against the Lord of the Realm.

1145   The prince sent Phirenthorn, the brave,
Powerful and skillful
To lead the warrior units.

1146   Out he came to fight Chumpasun,
Both bold and brave
Striving for victory.

1147   More giants than could be numbered,
As great as mountains,
Threatened and gestured.

1148   Phirenthorn ordered the soldiers to follow,
To fight in the field's middle,
With no hesitation before magic and arrogance.

1149   Battle cries with horses and donkeys
Mingled back and forth,
And foot soldiers slashed with swords.

1150   Dust swirled about the sky;
Brave soldiers bellowed with cries,
Exuberant brave sounds.

1151   With cheers of victory,
The prince's side destroyed
The great, giant soldiers.

1152   Endless numbers died
With corpses mountain-high
That sent fear and terror.

1153   Some fell, some ran to their place;
Battle cries climbed
As they ran about.

1154   Some were struck down
While running around
Brandishing swords and spears.

117

1155 Some rolled around, stretched on the ground,
     Fell and rose again,
     Startled they fell destroyed.

1156 And then Phirenthorn destroyed
     Brave Thoramuk,
     Who crashed down like a mountain.

1157 Chumpasun angered and arrogant
     With his magic power,
     Quickly moved forth in his chariot.

1158 Myriad forces of giants
     And skilled fighting soldiers
     Met with striking swords.

1159 They speared and fought and yelled,
     The giants boasted
     Not standing his anger.

1160 He drove the chariot to the prince,
     And they fought back and forth,
     Neither able to destroy the other.

1161 The prince shot elephants, chariots, soldiers.
     Flooding the earth,
     They fell scattered in every corner.

1162 The prince shot the arrow in many ways;
     With its great power,
     It reached Indra's celestial city.

1163 He hit the leader Chumpasun
     Who fell dying
     While heavenly hosts hailed the victory.

1164 So the superior demon Nikum
     Raced into battle
     In haste setting up the field.

1165 He sent out a leader,
     Fearless Thuraput,
     Who led the thousands.

1166   And the prince sent Ronnasing,
        Brave and happy in battle,
        Skilled and ready for the field.

1167   Ronnasing, a proud lion,
        Shot arrows destroying
        Thousands of gigantic giants.

1168   Thuraput, the arrogant, fought on;
        Threatened Thuraput
        Growled about his bravery,

1169   "Hey you, Ronnasing, I guess
        You should meet
        With me alone. Right?

1170   You alone have no power;
        You're no soldier,
        Bold and brave in the world.

1171   Look you, all your leaders,
        All your groups
        I'll fight and ruin you."

1172   "You, Thuraput, low and cruel.
        With false bravery, you boast.
        You don't know right from wrong.

1173   With no shame you came bragging,
        With no thought for your life,
        You came to meet Ronnasing.

1174   I'll destroy you!
        Forget your companies;
        They'll be eliminated soon."

1175   The two fought pressing near.
        All over earth and sky,
        In every corner, echoes resounded.

1176   Boldly they rushed in
        Crying loud with a cheer.
        With no stopping they pushed on.

119

1177   Ronnasing, a rampaging lion,
Thuraput, an elephant,
Shook the earth through and through.

1178   Nikum ordered the march   *yaanii*/intharawichian
Of great companies of soldiers,
Quick the chariots, quick
Repeated intimidation.

1179   Still standing midst the field,   wasantadilok
A dreaded leader,
Ready to fight the Lord of the Land,
Nikum, a valiant instilling fear.

1180   Prince against prince,
Soldier against soldier,
They fought back and forth,
Powerfully, bravely in war.

1181   Elephants, horses, chariots, soldiers
Skilled and able in battle;
Weapons, swords, lances
Sparkled with scattered rays.

1182   The prince's soldiers killed,
The enemy piled up,
Numerous to the eye
Lined up like mountain ranges.

1183   In fury, Nikum swung about
Carrying a hammer,
Fought Samuttakote
No longer tolerant.

1184   He carried his bow and arrow,
Shot Nikum, the leader,
Scattered the horses
And destroyed the chariots.

1185   Nikum ran mid field   chabang
Strutting fearlessly
And met the Lord of the Land.

1186   The prince shot his powerful arrow
        Striking the weapon,
        Smashing it to bits.

1187   He destroyed the famous Nikum,
        Dispersed his soldiers,
        Piled the dead on the battlefield.

1188   All over the sky, battalions of soldiers   sathun
        wandered about,
        Crying out in pain and sorrow.

1189   Elephants, horses, soldiers, ruined corpses,
        Blood like a lake covered the earth.

1190   The dead became food for vultures, crows, garudas
        hovering,
        Flying around, crying out.

1191   Bending over, they tore at the corpses, pleased and
        content, Not meeting anyone or anything.

1192   The ten nobles, each brave,[257].   chabang
        Thought wrongly
        To win with unrestrained revolt.

1193   Hoping for the precious lady,
        They assembled troops,
        Became mortal enemies.

1194   They fought the Lord of Men,
        Not knowing his strength,
        This prince, powerful victor.

1195   Like grasshoppers entering a fire,
        They fell dead
        Midst consuming flames.

Samuttakote Weds Phintumadi

1196   Romyaburi, nobles of the city,   yaanii/*intharawichian*
            The Lord of the Realm
            Arrayed and readied all
            For the splendid ceremony.

1197   Kings gathered from afar
            With coteries of ministers
            And Brahmins learned
            In rites and rituals.

1198   They readied the royal regalia
            Marvelous and abundant,
            They decorated the city,
            That royal earthly site.

1199   Quickly they bedecked
            The celestial palace
            With nine shimmering gems,
            And pure shining sapphires.

1200   Ladies-in-waiting were adorned
            More elegantly than city ladies.
            Whoever beheld them changed not his mind,
            Seeing their shiny radiance.

1201   They compared and divided these handmaidens,
            Personal attendants paying respect,
            Enough to adorn
            The prince and his precious lady.

1202   Glittering gold necklaces,
            Jeweled crowns and diadems,
            Equal in beauty to the one wearing them,
            An excellent figure of beauty,

1203   Elegant crowns, necklace chains
            Fell around the neck,
            Royal regal raiments,
            Adornments and ornaments.

1204   At the time of ceremony,
        That auspicious hour,
        All duties were set
        For the great event.

1205   Their dressing and adorning set
        With regalia appropriate for the Lord,
        The prince and lady held
        A special happiness.

1206   A messenger was sent,
        One with great knowledge,
        To take the glorious news
        With all its details,

1207   To go and pay obeisance
        To his Royal Majesty,
        His Highness Phintutat,
        The King of Kings.

1208   "I'm the messenger
        From Romyaburi's king,
        Who's all powerful
        With great auspicious signs.

1209   I was sent, I, the servant,
        To bring the royal news,
        For you to come to this land,
        Powerful and prosperous.

1210   His Majesty King Narakup,   wasantadilok
        Ruler and Master of Men,
        Gathered all kings together
        To give his daughter in marriage.

1211   Numerous nobles beyond count,
        Soldiers by the thousands
        Were readied in their units
        In every part, every place.

1212   He readied the iron bow
        Named Sahatsaphan
        And gave it to the judge
        To be admired midst the field.

1213   He announced to all the kings
Whichever person, whoever,
Could lift the victory bow
And show it to the battlefield,

1214   Any king who could raise it up
And shoot an arrow powerfully
With both skill and art
And show His Majesty, the King of Kings,

1215   Would receive in marriage
The noble virgin, the precious one,
And rule the kingdom, greatest in the universe,
In bliss and happiness.

1216   The noble son of the king,
Prince Samuttakote,
Equal to the great Rama,[258]
The great and fearless warrior,

1217   Raised up the great bow;
And warriors praised him in the field.
He showed his weapon and power
And his fame spread over the earth.

1218   Kings from every corner
Gathered to wrestle away victory.
But he scattered these enemies,
Destroying them in the field.

1219   And then, His Majesty, Lord of Men,
As planned, readied
To perform the ceremony,
Complete in all rites and rituals.

1220   He directs me to welcome you,
Two nobles so loving,
To offer blessings and joy
In the wedding ceremony."

1221   Hearing from the messenger
This royal decree
Was like bathing in ambrosia,
And the queen's heart rejoiced.

1222   Quickly they made ready
        The massive elephants and horses
        With warriors and soldiers
        Like the immortal sun god Athit.[259]

1223   His Majesty and the Queen
        Adorned in ornaments
        With thousands of ladies-in-waiting
        Like stars around the moon

1224   Reached the great land,
        The heavenly kingdom,
        The city of Romyaburi,
        Eternally noble and regal.

1225   They entered the royal city
        And His Majesty Narakup set forth
        To welcome the Lord of Men,
        Phintutat, to join them.

1226   In the royal throne hall,
        Proclaimed to thousands,
        The two sat together
        And talked of the great love.

1227   The queen and the great queen
        Both happy and content
        Went to their eminent thrones
        To speak as old friends.

1228   They gathered together
        For the royal son and daughter,
        For the one skilled in all ways,
        Whose fame spread far.

1229   Spreading over the three worlds,
        Orchestra sounds echoed,
        All over the vast world
        And the magnificent festivities.

1230   All kinds of music played,
        Every kind and type
        And variety readied
        For special entertainments.

1231 With the ceremony completed
The royal princess
And the noble son,
Their fame and honor spread afar.

1232 With the ceremony finished,   chabang
The Lord of the Land,
Phintutat, bid farewell.

1233 And His Majesty Sri Narakup
Invited the King of Kings
To return to his city.

1234 He returned with nothing impeding
And the people rejoiced
As they ruled with joy and happiness.

1235 The Protector of the Land and Phintumadi,
The queen content,
Remained happy in body and spirit.

1236 They entered the palace
With glorious ladies
Ready to serve them.

1237 They reveled in joy and affection.
Induced into love play,
They found their hearts' content.

1238 Their fame reached the three worlds;
In every direction, every king
Pronounced their love and perfection.

1239 All the nobles came to offer   *yaanii*/intharawichian
A flood of jewels and gems.
From every corner,
They came to pay respects.

1240 Happiness and content filled Romyaburi
And midst the people too.
Peace and happiness heaped together
As the populace praised them.

1241   And then Lady Phintumadi
        Honored the King of Kings,
        "May I explain
        What I thought so long?

1242   O famed Lord of the Land,
        I grieved long,
        Hoped for a life together,
        Thought this with a pure heart.

1243   I paid homage and made offerings[260]
        To the guardian spirit
        Who holds the power
        To grant success in all things.

1244   This I've already gained;
        My heart's desire fulfilled,
        Together with you.
        I bow before your splendid feet.

1245   I delight in pleasure with you
        In overwhelming happiness,
        This I know well,
        The spirit has great power and might.

1246   I beg you, your majesty,
        To make an offering to the spirit.
        Do not dismiss this,
        Lest unrest and confusion follow."

1247   The prince listened to his jewel   chabang
        Tell of her offering
        To the heavenly spirit that spreads good.

1248   And with an exultant heart,
        He embraced his beauty,
        Urging her to go forth.

1249   They readied the food offerings,
        All the various things
        Along with the flowers.

1250   And the two rode their chariot in regalia
        With their great retinue
        Arrayed in great splendor.

1251   Going forth, the prince and his lady
        Reached the hermitage
        Of the spirit they were to honor.

Samuttakote and Phintumadi Visit the Kudi

1252   They gazed at the kudi,[261]   yaanii/*intharawichian*
        That wondrous hermitage
        Studded with innumerable gems
        Set close to one another.

1253   The extended portico was lower[262]
        And the upper room, a place for pleasantries.
        The verandah was arranged
        In the customary way.

1254   Golden poles glittered with jewels
        In circular arrays,
        Like Brahma's golden palace,
        Equal to Brahma's world.

1255   Various carved designs
        Created a close-knitted cover.
        Precious stones blinked brilliantly
        Along with the pure gold.

1256   Embellishments of gems
        Intertwined in vine-like designs
        Equal to Visanukam's work,[263]
        Skilled and detailed workmanship.

1257   Carved kinnorns sparkled,
        Their arms embracing kinnarees,
        Their forms as lovely as
        Kinnarees in the heavens.

1258   Delicately polished purlins
        Shone with decorations,
        Glorious gems that shimmered
        As though they were stars.

1259   The superior, lofty beams linked,
        Precious jewels spread light,
        And blazing gold shifted back and forth
        On delicately carved mouldings.

1260   The golden floor with pieces of cat's eye
        Closely inlaid seemed smooth.
        Crystal streams of gems shimmered
        Like ambrosial vines.

1261   Doors with sapphire settings[264]
        And other jewels,
        Their golden surfaces glittered
        With the royal lotuses.

1262   Groups of small sconces,
        Naga shaped, lined the walls,
        Golden walls that glinted
        With glittering jewels.

1263   Leonine designs
        Covered the splendid windows,
        Pearls and gems
        Radiantly beautiful.

1264   The forward pillars were carved as lotuses,
        Lotus blooms inverted,
        Lotuses blooming everywhere,
        Flowers blooming everywhere.

1265   Suriya's rays shined through,
        With beaming rays of beauty
        That glimmered and gleamed in the air,
        Tongues of fire pleasing the eye.

1266   Serrated eaves in cat's eye
        Caught the eye glinting
        With unobstructed views of jewels,
        Sheets of cat's eye and gold.

1267   Jeweled beams and joists crossed
                With carefully constructed surfaces;
                Beams and purlins in gold
                Lay linked close together.

1268   Like flowers ready to bud,[265]
                Budding flower designs,
                Buds of phuttan,
                Appeared in skillfully carved designs.

1269   Jewels studded the inner walls;
                Ruby lotuses shimmered
                And when Suriya shined,
                Fiery flames flared up.

1270   A spire lofty and soaring
                With glittering rays,
                A finial magically made[266]
                Sat in the heavens.

1271   Ordered tips at the top,
                Sitting side by side,
                With reflecting mirrors
                Decorated the celestial palace.

1272   Ramparts and walls
                Encircled the shining kudi
                With pure golden projections
                Built to catch the eye.

1273   Before the temple was a jeweled mirror,
                Spotless and pure.
                The rays of the gems, like the rays of the sea
                Glistened and glimmered.

1274   The pedestal for the fire ceremony[267]
                Was heated and steamy smoke
                Covered all directions
                Blowing into the forest.

1275   Sounds from the Fire Brahmins
                Rose in praises and chants
                And the sounds mounted
                With a mantra of magic.

1276   They gazed at the gold and jeweled bench
        Required by ceremony,
        That pre-eminent seat
        For worshipping and praising the fire.

1277   The bathing pool overflowed
        With pure white lotuses;
        Delicious smelling pollen
        Diffused fragrant perfumes.

1278   Gurgling and bubbling water in streams
        Crashed noisily between mountains,
        Splashing against the crags,
        Spraying the mountain projections.

1279   Vishnu rode upon a lion[268]
        Golden and strutting.
        He embraced a naga
        Great and and all powerful.

1280   Finely outlined heavenly beings,
        Divine forms from past eons
        Paid respect and obeisance
        As a giant naga crawled back and forth.

1281   A royal lion attacked,
        Biting an elephant.
        It displayed its power and might,
        Sufficient to destroy the earth.

1282   The white deer retreated to hide,
        Reflecting the light's rays
        Near the wall's edge
        All studded with jewels.

1283   In the trees the breeze swayed
        Flowers and branches.
        Blossoms and betel
        Emitted enticing scents.

1284   The breeze blew the branches,
        Dancing, swaying to and fro,
        The tree tops tilted
        Bending back and forth.

1285   The tree tips shaded
The kudi along with fragrant flowers,
And fantastic ambrosia-like fruit
With their captivating tastes.

1286   Jik, jaeng, maeng, strong[269]
Sandalwood, kannika,
And karakate spread memories
With heavenly maludi.

1287   Phikun, bunnak,[270]
Asok, surapi
And ramduan diffused scents
With marvelous maliwan.

1288   Krisana, krawan,[271]
Karabun, kun, kraniat,
Kanbun, kamkhun
And scents of sandalwood spread.

1289   Suphanka clusters clung[272]
With bees and also pheka.
All kinds and varieties
Grew through the forest.

1290   Rang, rak, and sakraw,[273]
Jaraling and kok.
The nangyaem no longer smiled,
Too little joy in the ramyai and phai.

1291   Pho, theptharu,[274]
Lampu in three-pointed spears,
The tongtaek bent back,
Plentiful pradu, prayong, yom,

1292   Tatum, rakam,[275]
Jambok, fantastic flowers,
Ratchaphrik like silk
In Brahma's palace.

1293   Wild figs with no flowers,
But with wondrous fruit;
The khanang was like women dancing,[276]
Moaning in grief, swaying back and forth.

132

1294   The raksorn remained[277]
        Like love that's true.
        Laepnang, the lady's nails,
        Circled swirling about.

1295   Flowers and blooms of all kinds.
        Pure flowers, when the breeze blows,
        Gently spread their scents
        In the luxuriant forest.

1296   The points of lamjiak,[278]
        Jan, marvelous malika,
        Ket, kaew, kumari,
        Floated all about.

1297   Fragrant scented garlands
        Diffused their heavenly perfumes;
        And the woman's heart rejoiced
        Overflowing in happiness.

1298   Alternating delicate flowers
        Draped and drooped in a line
        Like golden necklaces
        Arrayed on beautiful trees.

1299   Coconuts, sugar, wondrous tastes,
        Pure liquids,
        Delicious captivating tastes:
        How could any compare?

1300   Phlap sprouted and budded,[279]
        Mixed with trakop, khanun,
        Khanang and chamchun:
        Ready ripeness hung about.

1301   Quantities of khwit and khwat[280]
        Hid the trees;
        Mangosteens, lamut, all sweet,
        With boundless durian covered the land.

1302   Mayhiang, charahan, mahat[281]
        Along with sweet mangoes,
        Ripe fruits in clusters
        Hung dangling together.

1303   Clumps of bamboo, one after another,[282]
        Covered the land with bong
        And changyang
        Closely intermingled.

1304   The breeze briefly blew;
        Sensuous sounds spread;
        Sounds of the saw swirled above:
        A stringed orchestra strummed.

1305   Sounds of swans resounded,[283]
        Crossed with the karawik,
        Light-hearted nanwika,
        Kronca and kokin.

1306   Crows cried listening to sounds
        Sweetly issuing forth,
        Melodiously filling the heart:
        What pleasure equaled this?

1307   Moved by these sounds,
        Startled, the hermit
        Forgot his duties, his contemplation,
        Lost his concentration.

1308   The jip and jap whispered,[284]
        "Why do jip and jok fight?"
        Kangkhen played with its tail spread out;
        The ilum, khum, and khaw flew skyborne.

1309   The iang and aen mixed together[285]
        Laughing and awakened the karian.
        The phuradok cried out
        Midst the mixed forest voices

1310   The yangthon, krasa,[286]
        The sarika sad and silent;
        The sun almost setting
        Sympathized with the woman.

1311   The say grew fearful[287]
        With evening closing in;
        Husbands and wives separated;
        The tranay circled, returned, and laughed.

1312   The khapkhae, two tight together,[288]
        Two together, an appropriate pair,
        Bemoaned and lamented,
        Playing and fearing.

1313   The plaw bird didn't change its heart,[289]
        But called for its mate.
        The khaektaw came and looked,
        Saw it gone and thought it strange.

1314   Each parrot in each nest
        Flew looking for its mate.
        Missing and thinking of them,
        They called to come and stay.

1315   The prince and his bride looked at all of life,
        Each animal closely paired;
        They listened to sounds together,
        Every different kind.

1316   Monkeys joined joyously sporting in the trees,
        Running and jumping together,
        Playing in groups,
        Running and hiding in the forest.

1317   Skittish squirrels scampered away;
        Rabbits regrouped in bunches;
        Lizards gazed at mongooses;
        Anteaters glanced back and forth.

1318   Male elephants stalked about
        All the corners of the forest
        In royal and elegant order
        With females running behind.

1319   Elephants reached to grasp
        Clumps and sprays of flowers,
        And sniffing the scented blooms
        They grew elated.

1320   All around the bamboo clumps
        Searching for love,
        The elephants trumpeted in streams
        In all protecting groups.

Samuttakote and Phintumadi Visit the Kudi

1321   Cicadas sang melodious songs
For dancing peacocks,
Living in the high trees
Dancing and swaying in the tops.

1322   Little monkeys from monkey packs
Ate little langling fruit;[290]
Some monkeys leaped and snatched
And then quickly fled in fear.

1323   Lemurs, squirrels, golden deer:
Animal paired together
In close loving pairs
Happily nibbled leaves.

1324   Herds of golden deer,
Animals grouped close together,
Stared at the reindeer,
Stared at the dark eyes.

1325   In the forest bison romped.
In the forest mountains,
Antelopes, forest buffaloes
Walked fiercely about.

1326   Thengthut called out[291]
"See the gibbons!"
Their calls echoed in the forest,
Their cries fanned fear.

1327   Trees and flowers
Bud and bloom:
Every kind of flower
With the golden lotus.

1328   Bees with sounds like plucking strings
Played together to and fro.
Near the lotus they looked
And moved over the fragrant scents.

1329   The different fragrances
Brought happiness to the forest;
As breezes from the south
Gently wafted over the area.

1330   Fragrances spread their perfumes
Around the forest kudi
And the committed ascetic
Sat enamored.

1331   The two nobles gazed and admired
The forest and splendid kudi
In happiness and pleasure
And with great fun.

1332   The fire ceremony finished   chabang
The spirit propitiated,
Their hearts satisfied,

1333   The two nobles left the spirit
Setting forth in the jeweled chariot
Like the sun and moon.

1334   With retinues of attendants
In uncountable numbers
They entered the gold palace.

1335   The two excellent nobles exulted
As desires of all types
Filled their hearts.

1336   In one year to Phromburi
They would return,
And the prince's fame spread.

Samuttakote and Phintumadi Visit the Royal Gardens

1337   One day the Lord of the Land
With his queen
Left for the royal garden

1338   On the bejeweled chariot
With thousands of attendants
And royal counsellors.

1339   Like Indra on splendid Phaychayon[292]
With royal heavenly deities
They made their way.

Samuttakote and Phintumadi Visit the Royal Gardens

1340   In the royal garden precinct
        Stood a forest
        With wondrous sights.

1341   And when they reached the trees,
        Flower garlands bloomed
        Spreading their scents.

1342   Countless colored lotuses
        Sent their perfumes
        Wafting about the royal garden

1343   With cliffs, mountains, creeks, streams,
        And a wondrous wood
        Filled with fragrant scents.

1344   Ten thousand princesses, four thousand ladies-
        in-waiting
        Attended the two nobles
        With hearts united in joy.

1345   Contented, they strolled about gazing while the   sathun
        trees swayed overhead bursting in blooms.

1346   They enticed each other to gather lotuses, then tucked
        them behind their ears and scattered them in the stream.

1347   In every corner they found delicious scents in the
        pool, and fragrances spread to the forest.

1348   Walking they saw flocks of birds, swans flying
        and alighting in the pool.

1349   The swans called their mates as the sounds of the deer
        mixed together.

1350   Countless golden deer ran about, leaping and running
        midst the wondrous scents.

1351   The royal counsellors, the retinue, the queen, and the
        Lord of the Realm went forth

1352   Picking the fragrant lotuses and flowers that covered
        the area by the thousands

1353   Like Indra and the joyful apsaras in Nanthip, the
celestial garden of joy.[293]

1354   Indulging in pleasure the prince found contentment in
the royal garden with the spreading scents.

The Battle of the Phitthayathorns

1355   Then a phitthayathorn   chabang
Flew over
On his way to majestic Meru.

1356   Called Ronapimuk,
His power and authority
Manifest throughout,

1357   He carried his bride,
Eminent and elegant,
To Kaylat, the silver-pure.[294]

1358   There bathing, he plucked lotuses
And offered them
To his bride to admire.

1359   Gathering golden garlands,
He arrayed himself
And his chief consort.

1360   In bliss they frolicked
With tender thoughts,
Two happy hearts together.

1361   A breastplate donned, a sword
And gold shield grasped,
He embraced and carried her away.

1362   Then came a phitthayathorn,
Ronabut, his great power
Beyond all others in battle.

1363   Sprightly he sported in the pools
On the gold mountain,
The divine jewel, proclaimed everywhere.

1364   One hand held a shield of gold,
        The other a sword
        Capable of destroying the world.

1365   Each flew through the heavens
        When suddenly
        The two valiants met.

1366   When Ronabut saw
        Ronapimuk's wife,
        All beauty, light, elegance,

1367   Lustful desires arose.
        He groaned with love
        While lust vexed his inner heart.

1368   Crudely, he yelled, "Who are you
        To bring your wife here?
        I speak and you fail to stop.

1369   Don't you know that I—
        I, Ronabut, rank highest
        Over these many lands.

1370   If you value life, fear death,
        Give her to me! Leave!
        Go elsewhere! Depart! Shame remains!

1371   If you fail to give her to me,
        You cannot leave.
        I'll rip her away with my might."

1372   The phitthayathorn listening
        To Ronabut's boast
        Replied with no words of fear:

1373   "You, phitthayathorn, I too am a deity
        Wielding power,
        A splendid great power.

1374   You're called Ronabut, the great,
        I, myself,
        Ronapimuk, the battlewise.

140

1375   All your weapons are lustrous gold.
        But I, myself,
        Have great and mighty power.

1376   If you wish to fight,
        Do not hold back,
        Soldiers should do thus."

1377   The two showed their might,
        Duelling, maneuvering,
        Jousting in heaven's heights.

1378   Then two armies,
        They made with magic,
        With mighty mantras, two powerful sides.[295]

1379   All the sky filled full
        Like Indra's warriors
        Arrayed on the battlefield.

1380   Each held a full array of weapons
        Glittering gold
        To destroy the world flying through the air.

1381   In flight, they fought. Swords swung up
        Whirling, sparkling
        In the lustrous heavens.

1382   Each stabbed, each raised up, each equal.
        Each stuck with bright knives,
        Rings of rays appeared in the heavens.

1383   Each side fighting, flying
        With airborne colors gleaming
        Mixed special strategems.

1384   Earth and sky lay confused
        As Mount Meru's peak
        Fell to the earth.

1385   They were like Sumpa and Nisumpa,[296]
        Two valiants
        Battling long ago with terrible power

141

1386   Who tore away a woman,
        The noble Tilottama,
        A beauty famed over the earth.

1387   If not these, then Phali,[297]
        And Sukri, the monkeys,
        Warring in ancient ages,

1388   Till the earth lay ruined,
        Till the seven seas[298]
        Splashed the mountains.

1389   Bright blades, their light spreading,
        One against the other,
        Neither side relented.

1390   Swish, swish, slash, slash: slicing sounds;
        And their soldiers expired
        In fighting and thrusting.

1391   Blades dulled, the mantra's power gone,
        Only two bodies remained,
        And mightily they collided.

1392   Sword against sword, forward, backward,
        In heaven's middle,
        Crash, crack, clang, they battled.

1393   Ronabut pounced and slashed
        Ronapimuk swerved,
        His heart weakened, his strength gone,

1394   And fighting he carried off his wife.
        Weakening, distrusting,
        He reached the center of the battlefield,

1395   Defeated by the power.
        Ronabut ripped the beauty away,
        Raised his sword and threatened.

1396   His desire gained, Ronabut,
        Swan-like flew away,
        Rapidly growing smaller and smaller.

1397   Then Ronapimuk,   wasantadilok
        Injured, his heart destroyed,
        Rapidly fell from the heavens
        To lay upon the earth

1398   In that place of flowers
        And great trees, the royal garden
        Of His Majesty,
        Samuttakote the great.

1399   He fell filled with tears,
        A shrunken heart[299]
        Sorrowing, grieving, still angered,
        Moaning and groaning in sorrow.

1400   Distressed, he sought to change the mantra,
        The details of the past.
        But in sorrow he realized
        His power was useless.

1401   Great sorrow and mourning
        Shook the ruined heart.
        Anxiety arose from the thoughts of his beauty,
        But the thinking never stopped.

1402   "O god, now I must endure great sorrow[300]
        Separated from my bride.
        My heart's always lost
        In suffering, sorrow, and longing.

1403   O dear one, you beautiful lotus,
        Bees swarm admiring you;
        My life's come to know
        Your delicacy and innocence.

1404   Oh, I went out and met
        That enemy attacking with evil intent,
        Ripping away my beloved beauty,
        My bride, and flying away.

1405   When I embraced you, my beauty,
        Hugged you, we went off
        To frolic in the forest,
        To find joy in every corner.

143

1406   I embraced you tightly, noble one,
        And took you to the garden
        At majestic Meru
        And Himaphan, the mountain of pleasure.

1407   And then we entered the forest
        To admire the precious blooming blossoms,
        The golden lotuses, the red lotuses.
        And there we picked them.

1408   And then I caressed you,
        Embraced you, my precious,
        Arrayed your perfect body,
        O my lovely one.

1409   And then we went to play in the forest.
        We saw a pool and went to bathe
        At that jeweled bathing place,
        O precious jewel.

1410   We two were content and filled with joy.
        We didn't dare leave.
        What evil could come
        And separate you, my glory?"

1411   Then Ronapimuk's face
        Filled with great despair,
        Pain and sorrow,
        Great despair from the separation.

1412   "O my young love, my youthful loved one,   sathun
        you with the face of the young moon,

1413   No heavenly nymph can match your alluring, your
        captivating form.

1414   We two found happiness and pleasure journeying through
        the flower-filled forest.

1415   Filling us with desire, fragrant flower garlands spread
        their perfumes about you, O enraptured beauty.

1416   We marveled at the trees, the waters, the forested mountains;
        we delighted in the lotus blossom pools.

144

1417   Flowers and bright-petaled lotuses diffused their pollen
        and their luscious perfumes.

1418   Bees swarmed like flawless black sapphires; ruby red blossoms
        resembling lotuses grew scattered about.

1419   Tiered green leaves sparkled like emeralds; limpid water
        shone with rays of the cat's eye.

1420   Turtles teeming in the water swam with fantastic fish, crabs,
        tortoises—complete contentment in the pool.

1421   Enraptured prattling parrots flew overhead; peacocks danced
        and strutted by the brimming pools.

1422   Cicadas sang out like melodious instruments; waters mingled
        their powerful sounds, lulling us to sleep with song.

1423   Elephants, tigers, lions and other animals in pairs wandered
        side by side filled with joy.

1424   Embracing you, O noble one, we flew through the air in fun,
        in happiness, in everlasting delight. What evil could come
        and force us to separate?

1425   Then—the pitthayathorn, wicked and wanton, savage and
        fierce, ripped you away from me, my beauty.

1426   Anguish mounted upon anguish because of our separation, our
        calamity. My heart's scorched, parched, withered, shriveled
        from the heat.[301]

1427   Ruin mounted upon ruin because of defeat by this enemy.
        Boldly he came firing anger, generating shame:

1428   Shame before all the deities, shame before all the demons.
        If my life ends, I am happy.

1429   So the battle would be unfair, without form, without propriety,
        that evil enemy boldly attacked.

1430   Because I was carrying you, my beloved, he had power and
        strength. So out he came fighting and attacking.

1431   Superior he was, but who flatters a felon? No one! In
        ignominy and disgrace I shrink.

1432   I think only of you, my beloved—the purest on the earth,
        O fragrant one.

1433   My heart, my bride with everlasting beauty, how will you
        endure the torment?

1434   I moan, I groan, I search for you, my lost bride, my auspicious
        beauty. My heart will break, my mind's overwhelmed.

1435   I long to meet you, but I do not. I only meet sorrow like
        fire. Better death than separation from my beloved.

1436   I die, but I do not. Sorrow and memories are the same. My
        strength gone, what'll I think of next, reflections nearly gone.

1437   Cease heart, heart without joy, heart with its everlasting
        memories of her beauty—memories that remain with me.

1438   I remember her face, an unsullied spotless moon. I remember
        her night-dark hair.

1439   I remember her dark sapphire eyes, blooming lotuses, purple
        dark. Her ears golden lotus petals.

1440   I remember that flower's skin, delicate as the blossoms of
        the blue climber. Each side with gracefully arched eyebrows
        —she with the eight desires.[302]

1441   I remember the fragrance of her cheeks, the perfumed essence
        of blossoms in full bloom. None to compare with that beauty.

1442   I remember her nose, an incomparable curve. I remembers its
        full splendid tapering.[303]

1443   I remember her luscious lips. My appreciation never stops.
        Her sweeping smile's now gone, no longer here to admire.

1444   Like the God of Love with a joyful woman, all through night
        and day glorious scents arise.

1445   O my heart, my jewel shining through the night, must you
bear this burden?

1446   I remember her angelic voice, the melodious cooing bird—
now distant from my ears.

1447   Her throat, the throat of a deer. Her chin, the chin of a
lion. Her breasts, round like the moon.

1448   Her swaying arms, elegantly curved elephant trunks. I
remember her shape, a beautiful woman, delicate and smooth.

1449   I remember her waist and stomach. Her beauty excites love.
Pure and innocent she is.

1450   I remember her legs, her lotus-like feet, like those of
the apsaras, spotless and pure.

1451   O god, I've reached my end, helpless and forlorn. My aching
heart almost shatters.

1452   Sleeping, I used to cling to my beloved's body. Now I sleep
alone in the forest.

1453   O god, my heart's in torment. I don't think of my life. I
think only of my beloved. I can't forget her beauty. O god,
I lament.

1454   Bathed in blood, bathed in tears, my heart's bathed in utter
sorrow that seeps through my whole body.

1455   Now, my beloved, I'm maimed and wounded. It's difficult to
see you, my bride.

1456   I'll die, die alone. Who'll see me? My jewel and I, we do
not see each other."

1457   The phitthayathorn in pain and agony[304]   chabang
Cried and groaned
Not knowing how long he suffered.

1458   Stuck and slashed by weapons,
His body covered with wounds,
His blood flowed like a stream.

147

1459   Wounds covered him completely.
        From a weapon his body lame.
        Maimed, crippled, he bowed his head in grief.

1460   As if water covered him,
        Covered his whole body,
        He struggled for breath from sorrow.

1461   "With pain and shame my torment increases.
        Whose pain compares with mine?
        My pained heart cries!

1462   There's pain from separation;
        There's pain from defeat and fear;
        There's loss and forlorness.

1463   I can't find a friend. No one comes;
        The pain's almost death.
        Little by little I'll die alone.

1464   I grieve to have lost her;
        Who can get her back?
        This lady once so close to me.

1465   When I die, pain and agony disappear,
        Confusion's eliminated,
        Longing's diminished."

1466   Groaning in sorrow, he sighed
        And his two hands
        Beat his chest over and over.

1467   With pitiful moans
        For his great adversity
        He grieved in the royal garden.

Samuttakote Receives the Magic Sword

1468   Now the one to be born a Buddha,[305]   *yaanii*/intharawichian
        The incomparable one of the world,
        Rested in the royal residence
        In the royal pleasure garden

1469   With his unequalled lady,
       The heavenly Phintumadi.
       And it was midday
       Filled up with the sun's rays.

1470   In the evening's waning light
       The breeze gently blew diffusing
       The scents of sumali and surapi,[306]
       Spreading their delightful perfumes.

1471   And the prince summoned two close advisors,
       One a son of a Brahmin,
       And one a counsellor
       By the name of Susangkan

1472   To follow him out
       Into the forested garden
       With the countless graceful trees,
       Marvelous fruit, and majestic flowers.

1473   Then they saw the phitthayathorn
       In a death-like sleep,
       Blood flowing over his body,
       Mutilated and lame.

1474   And they asked the reason,
       "Why this condition?
       Did you meet danger?
       Fight with an enemy?"

1475   And then the phitthayathorn
       Bowed to the Protector of Men,
       Relating and explaining
       In spurts the story from the first.

1476   "I'm called Ronapimuk.
       Ronabut persecuted me,
       Stole my beauty with no fear
       Of sin or kamma damning him.[307]

1477   I fought him closely
       In the sky, fighting long.
       But I was defeated, no further trying
       For my power weakened.

149

1478   I was defeated by Ronabut;
                 My beauty snatched by him;
                 And I fell here,
                 In this royal garden, utterly alone.

1479   I beg your Majesty for help;
                 I have no one;
                 Who'll help cure me
                 Of all these wounds and troubles?"

1480   Listening to all, the Master of Men replied,
                 "Look no farther for help.
                 Your fever's great, it confuses.
                 My duty is to cure you."

1481   And then the three carried him
                 Along to the royal palace,
                 To the skilled physician,
                 Adept in healing medicines.

1482   In five days passing,
                 In no time, the afflictions
                 Abated, disappeared completely,
                 His body returning to normal.

1483   Overjoyed, the phitthayathorn,
                 Without delay, paid his respects,
                 Gave a thousand blessings
                 To the great and noble prince.

1484   He offered him a magic sword,
                 Guaranteed success to the splendid leader,
                 Demonstrated its power to raise him
                 Over the many worlds.

1485   "This magnificent sword   todokka
                 With its dreadful power,
                 If in a battle,
                 It'll sustain you.

1486   With it you'll raise up,
                 Over the earth
                 Standing or as you wish,
                 Going in any direction.

1487   So make a wish
From your heart
Of places to go
For success is yours.

1488   To the king, great and mighty,
I repay with this favor.
Your highness will rule
All the world joyfully."

1489   With a reverential bow,
He returned to his home,
The Himaphan forest
On the pleasure-filled mountain.

Samuttakote and Phintumadi Visit the Himaphan Forest

1490   And then the great prince   wasantadilok
Of power and virtue
Gained the powerful fortune
Found in the incomparable sword.

1491   Pleased with his gift
Bright and happy
He wished to see and admire
The Himawet forest.

1492   So he invited his perfect mate,[308]
That graceful lady.
"O dear one, together in joy
Let us visit the great wide forest.

1493   To admire the mountains, the area,
To adventure in the streams,
To see wondrous animals and birds,
Each different in design.

1494   The caves, rivers, streams,
Crystal clear water, lucid,
We'll find joy in the forest,
Pleasure in every spot."

1495   The royal lady listened
To the prince's plan.
Delighted she raised her hands
Ready to follow her lord.

1496   The prince embraced his chief consort,
His pre-eminent beauty,
Grasped his magic sword
And flew into the heavens.

1497   When they reached the northern sky,
Like birds flying through the air,
They hid in the clouds, concealed,
Floating high in the sky.

1498   Reaching that delightful area,
Himawet, the joyful,
It soothed in every way,
Opening up their hearts.

1499   He pointed out for his beauty
The great golden mountains
Covered over with silver, gold,
And precious stones in countless numbers.

1500   84,000 they counted,[309]
High peaks scattered around;
Five hundred princely mountains
With medium-sized peaks.

1501   There were great crags,[310]
Five mammoth peaks created there,
Stretching up, touching the heavens,
Illuminated with rays of jewels.

1502   These towering mountains
Lie in the Himaphan forest;
These five reached high,
Hundreds of yoot, it was said.

1503   The peak named Sutat[311]
Glinted with gold;
And Kaylat, multi-hued,
Was made from sumptuous silver.

1504 One peak, Kan, gleamed as lovely[312]
 As a black, sparkling jewel;
 One peak, Jit, radiated colors
 With seven kinds of gems;

1505 One called Khanthamat mountain[313]
 With beaming, brilliant light;
 Countless jeweled veins shimmered
 As though inlaid there.

1506 Five great mountains surrounded,[314]
 Encircled the pool,
 Anodat, the great water
 Seemingly filled with crystal rays.

1507 There atop midst the great Himawan
 Mountains, it reached
 One hundred yoot in width,
 A crystal pure lake.

1508 A myriad of trees bore fruit
 Along with eternal flowers.
 Scattered here and there lay lotuses
 And black parasol-trees hid the sun.

1509 Long living trees, giant trees,
 Forest treasures complete and full;
 Any and every desire was satisfied
 With everything to eat and taste.

1510 Countless different flocks
 Of most excellent birds
 With noisy love calls,
 Warbled sounds calling and answering.

1511 The hongsa, suwa, kukkut, konca,[315]
 And the sari, kungan,
 Karawik circled around;
 And the kunan called clear melodious songs.

1512 Kinnarees and kinnorns, heavenly beings,
 Danced with swaying arms,
 Chanting, their melodious voices
 Blending in unending delight.

1513   The prince led his lady
To the mountains and hills,
Inviting the beauty to admire
All the four-footed beasts.

1514   Tigers, lions, elephants, bulls, buffaloes
Scattered through the forest;
Horned beasts and horses joined voices
In joyful unison.

1515   Deer, antlered deer, and bison
Ran about the woods
With rhino herds, wild boars,
Lizards, skunks, and bears.

1516   Foxes and dogs, fierce and furious,
Whole nations of beasts, jamri,
Goats, monkeys and antelopes
Leaped and walked atop the hills.

1517   They encountered countless beasts,
Unlimited numbers in the forest;
The number they knew not,
But their hearts rejoiced seeing their beauty.

1518   At the same time, he embraced his beloved   sathun
and descended into the waters of the lake.

1519   In pure Anodat, the ambrosia-like water, they
bathed in pleasure and delight.

1520   The cool, moist water filled their heart and body with
happiness and content.[316]

1521   They picked flowers, fragrant lotuses blooming, and he adorned
his comely youthful bride.

1522   At the same time, they gazed at the schools of swimming
fish, jumping, diving, mixing, seeming the same.

1523   Kung, kang, kumapin, makorn shook the water swimming
with the kot, ka, krim, kray, and kratrap.[317]

1524   The kralumphuk and duk swarmed; the salat and salit swam
one after another; and the lot lay hiding in the mud.[318]

1525   The ma, maw, and mu with the bu and ba mingled together as
did the paen and paep.[319]

1526   Families of khaw and khuea swam by the chorn after
the sangkhawat and saway.[320]

1527   Malaengphu, chanak, chalam churned in the water with the
thepo and thepa and trapak.[321]

1528   The krapaep and krabork mixed with the chado and kraho.
Countless krahae and khangbuean gazed at the bank.[322]

1529   The soy, say, suea and beautiful kradi and kradong massed
together floating high on their backs and tails.[323]

1530   The turtles, karakot and katchaba, mixed with the jariew and
jaraw; the aw and uk, fresh bait, swam down the river.[324]

1531   The nuanjan, the hangkiw, bait which the kukkura eat,
filled up the waters.[325]

1532   Thousands of schools, thousands of kinds scattered about in
the wondrous Anodat.

1533   The two from the Solar dynasty   chabang
Finished bathing
With happy and contented hearts.

1534   And then he invited his cream-colored queen
To leave the glorious pond
To journey through the forests and mountains,

1535   Picture-beautiful mountains,
Smooth and shiny with gaps and edges
As though artists had carved them.

1536   Tortuous and overhanging cliffs, rocks and hills,
Valleys, caves, waterfall pools,
Creeks, chasms, abysses, streams,

1537   Water sprays in rocky fissures and ravines
                  Flowed and shook, sending drops
                  Like rain all over the earth.

1538   Rocks jutted out, ready to fall,
                  Splendid radiances
                  Interspersed with mountain passages.

1539   Colors alternated,
                  Yellows and golds and whites,
                  All shimmering lotus gems.

1540   Green and blue jewels,
                  And red ones like the sun's rays:
                  Royal lotuses reflecting the light.

1541   Dark blue ones like the heavens overhead;
                  Blue ones like dark sapphires
                  And purple-red ones like dark red garnets.

1542   Pink ones like zircons
                  With sparkling colors:
                  Every color gleaming brightly.

1543   The rays from splendid Suriya
                  Mixed them together
                  Like seven jewels set close.

1544   And along with those, countless trees
                  Of all different types,
                  Spread across the mountain.

1545   They picked the jasmine;
                  Surapi's perfumes diffused,[326]
                  Pleasing fragrances wafted about.

1546   Some bore abundant fruit
                  With the honey-sweet taste
                  Of celestial food.

1547   The prince picked this wondrous fruit
                  And invited his beloved
                  To eat the many fruits of the forest.

1548   With joy and content in their hearts
        They wandered about
        Into the caves and other forest places.

1549   With pleasure they slept in the forest,
        Staying in the cave,
        Sleeping and passing away the time.

The Royal Couple is Missed

1550   And then the ladies-in-waiting, the attendants,[327]   wasan-
        And the royal retinue,   tadilok
        All the retainers and soldiers
        Who watch over Samuttakote

1551   Missed the ways of the prince,
        The Lord of the People.
        Each trembled in fear, in anxiety,
        Their breasts racked with pain:

1552   "O noble two,
        Why did you go beyond
        This quiet place of content,
        This garden, Nantawan?[328]

1553   What enraged your heart,
        Caused irritation in your heart?
        What thing caused sorrow?
        What in the past? What was wrong?

1554   There's no reason, no fault
        To make you problems.
        All of us are devoted followers.
        But no one's met or seen you.

1555   Or did you wish to sojourn
        Through the Himawat forest?
        What's the reason?
        What induced you to go?"

1556   Each looked in every garden corner
Neither met nor saw anyone.
In every forest place they went,
But in every place found no one.

1557   Each sorrowed for the prince
With tears gushing out in a stream
And returned to the jeweled city
Safely and ready to report.

1558   And to the great King Phintutat,
"Your two noble children are gone.
We sought them throughout the forest,
We went, but met no one."

1559   Hearing thus the two nobles
In sorrow and despair
Grieved and agonized in their hearts
As though life were gone.

1560   They lamented and grieved for the two youths;
Their sorrow neither left nor lessened;
A hundred sorrows beat their bodies
As hands beat their chests in sorrow.

1561   Consoled, the king sent retainers
To ride forth quickly on horseback,
"Proceed to Romyaburi in haste
To find out, to discover

1562   If our precious ones
Have wandered off, as I suspect.
Ask the Lord of all the World
To explain all, where they are."

1563   Receiving the royal order
From the greatest of crowns,
The two left by horse
And reached the city of Romyaburi.

1564   With respect they gave the message
Of the great sorrow and unhappiness,
Of the king's wish to see his son's face
And his royal daughter-in-law.

1565   And the king, Sri Narakup,
Father of the beloved,
The royal pair, understood, and afire
Were their breasts as over a spit.

1566   A thousand sorrows and griefs
Tortured them endlessly.
Sorrow heated their breasts
As though life were over.

1567   And then he sent thousands
Of soldier battalions
To search the forest area
And every cave, hill and mountain.

1568   "Oh to meet the Solar dynasty two,
Our distant royal son."
The two moaned and groaned oppressed,
Constantly bewailing their absence:

1569   "O son with the sustaining power
Like the descendant of Rama;[329]
O daughter with delicate beauty,
Modest and polite as Sida;

1570   O son, you with power like the sun,
Bright colors in the sky;
O daughter like the lovely moon,
Full and bright in the sky;

1571   O son, you with the power
Of Indra, Thunderbolt Carrier, One-Thousand Eyed;[330]
O daughter, you with the lovely face
Shining like a heavenly nymph;

1572   O son, you like the four-armed Phra Naray[331]
Who rides the Garuda through the air;
O daughter, you heavenly nymph, an apsara
Like the lovely Laksami.

1573   O son, you the great king[332]
Of the noble trident;
O daughter, you, a celestial woman,
The beautiful Uma;

1574   Your fame and power
                 Spread over the earth and heavens;
                 Your famed form soothes the world
                 And all the people praise;

1575   Why did you go? Why do you fail to appear?
                 Tell us your place, your way.
                 We, everyone, sorrow,
                 Our breasts heat in great pain."

1576   Their grief lessened and the two soldiers
                 Left Romyaburi,
                 Left for Phromburi
                 To report before the king

1577   The reason the royal couple,
                 The royal pair, have disappeared;
                 "They're not in Romyaburi;
                 No one saw them go."

1578   The two listened and moaned;
                 Their sorrow repeating;
                 Their hearts writhing in pain,
                 They cried and moaned piteously.

1579   A hundred thousand officials and ladies-in-waiting
                 And all the retinue
                 Bowed their heads moaning,
                 Their sorrow and grief doubled.

1580   In the two countries, Phromburi
                 And radiant Romyaburi,
                 No heart was content, happy;
                 Hearts only filled with sorrow.

Samuttakote and Phintumadi Visit the Kinnarees

1581   At that time the Lord of the People,   *yaanii*/intharawichian
                 The two royal personages
                 Ventured into the forest
                 Into every cave, hill, and mountain.

1582   They admired the four-footed creatures
        And the winged creatures in the forest;
        And their hearts filled full
        With joy, content, and delight.

1583   For nearly two months,
        Every evening and day,
        They remained in the Himawan
        With no sorrow or danger.

1584   And then the prince embraced her,
        His beloved, and flew off,
        Leaped into the heavens
        Reaching every corner.

1585   They saw the shiny mountain peak,
        A brilliant sparkling crown,
        The peak Kaylat,
        This is its name;

1586   There lay a city of glimmering gold
        With a celestial palace
        With bright golden designs
        Of radiant lotuses.

1587   A site on the golden mountain,
        The pre-eminent mountain;
        Tiaras arched the doors
        With gems and gold mingled.

1588   Turrets and porch posts
        All gilded in gold;
        Superior excellence
        Equal to Indra's celestial city.[333]

1589   Many groups of male
        And female kinnarees
        Filled this city,
        Supreme and numerous.

1590   The King of the Kinnarees,
        Thumarat, gave his name.
        "I rule with joy and delight,
        Complete peace and content.

161

1591   My family and lineage
Possess great power and magic,
Wings and tails appear
Through the power of magic,

1592   I'm able to fly
Through the air into the heavens
As do the kinnarees
And other winged creatures.

1593   You should go to the city
To admire that royal place
To reside in happiness
Complete in every way."

1594   Having considered thus, the two entered
That golden city of beauty
And proceeded to the palace
Of the King of Kinnarees.

1595   And the King of Kinnarees
Looked into his eyes
And asked why men
Come to his palace.

1596   Waving his hands, he called
The youthful handsome couple,
Invited the two to enter
The gold embellished throne room.

1597   Together on the throne they spoke
With happiness and joy.
The king asked his name and city,
His place and country.

1598   Greeting and answering
The prince revealed his name,
"I'm the son of the King
Of Kammalasontani.[334]

1599   His name is King
Phintutat
And my name's
Samuttakote, famed throughout the world.

1600   I take my beloved
        To the forests and mountains,
        Through the vast forest
        Himawat, the great.

1601   Reaching this city
        Of the magnificent king
        I come to visit the palace
        Wishing to see the celestial city."

1602   Hearing their tale
        The king rejoiced in his heart
        And touching them on their backs
        His arms embraced them.

1603   With satisfaction, on their topknot
        The two royal youths wore
        Decorations and crowns
        Of great beauty and elegance.

1604   He ordered they be given the treasure,
        The entire kingdom,
        "O honored one, it's not fitting
        That you return to your city.

1605   Please remain and rule here
        This kingdom complete
        With every possible thing
        Like the celestial world of Meru.

1606   Your merit brought you here[335]
        To this glittering gold palace
        Shimmering with nine jewels,
        Lustrous glowing gems.

1607   Become the King of the Kinnarees,
        Rule this heavenly place in joy,
        Assume the royal duties
        On this joyous golden mountain."

1608   The prince listened to the king's greeting
        And then spoke, "It's impossible;
        This I cannot do,
        Accept your offer.

163

1609   I cannot rule this city
        Following your royal order.
        I'm not an evil person,
        One that's greedy and envious.

1610   I hope to see and admire
        All these heavenly treasures;
        And I wish to stay
        About one month and go around."

1611   The king listened to this speech
        And became happy;
        So he gave his approval
        And consent to the prince.

1612   He invited the two to stay
        In that glorious, gold palace
        And to dine on celestial food
        In content and happiness.

1613   The two nobles sojourned happily
        Midst the hills and golden mountains,
        Visiting all the reaches
        Midst the mountains in the heavens.

1614   For one month they stayed
        In that golden city,
        And then they bid farewell
        To the king and left.

1615   They left the summit of Kaylat
        In the land of the sky
        And moved swiftly to the edge
        Of Anodat pond.

1616   Four sides brimmed with water,
        All four sides for bathing
        With the seven wondrous jewels
        Heaped in piles upon the shore.

Samuttakote and Phintumadi Visit Anodat and Chattan Ponds

1617   At one landing all the giants and celestial
        musicians bathed in the pure waters.[336]   sathun

1618   At one landing heavenly apsaras, nymphs, and
        heavenly deities bathed in the waters, rinsing away impurities.[337]

1619   At one landing phitthayathorns and kinnarees and Brahmins
        rested on the bank.[338]

1620   At one landing numerous arhats, their anger and dishonesty
        gone, walked out to bathe.[339]

1621   A cool and moist spray made their body mild and moist
        outside. And they absorbed the coolness into their bodies.

1622   And so the prince invited his beloved to bathe in the waters
        heedless of time.

1623   They remained in Anodat contented as children until one
        month passed.

1624   And then they flew off, went on the wind, to visit the lucid
        waters of Chattan pond.[340]

1625   Seven levels of mountains called Sattaphan surrounded that
        area shedding a special light.[341]

1626   One was called Suphanbat, towering, wide mountains, seven
        yoot in dimension and all shining gold.[342]

1627   They gave the name Manibat to the jeweled mountains, and
        Suriyabat to the ones brilliant like the shining sun.[343]

1628   One was called Janthabat, the mountains of gleaming silver,
        and another Uthokbat, the mountains of crystal.[344]

1629   One was called Mahakanbat, those of excellent sapphire, and
        Julakan like ink-dark stone.[345]

1630   Arranged in tiers a yoot high, each stood out like an umbrella,
        large and beautiful.

1631   And so he carried off his beloved bride and descended into the pond about fifty yoot in size.

1632   All around, its circumference reached fifty yoot in total.

1633   And in the middle of that lotus pool were pure, clear waters.[346]

1634   Shade from trees reflected in the water, jewel-like, with all the water lettuce gone.

1635   Twelve yoot of pure water surrounded with a forest of jongkonni lotus scattered around.[347]

1636   And there forests of creamy ubon lotuses stood separate from the blue-black nin and the red lohito.[348]

1637   And still another forest of white lotuses, patthama, sawet, and kamut: seven types of lotus scattered about.[349]

1638   And then they reached Indra's Mitsakawan, where every kind of bloom grew together in mixed profusion.[350]

1639   And then they reached the shallow water, shallow enough for elephants to stand and eat the wild rice.[351]

1640   These nine flower forests stood alone and separate, each useful and great.[352]

1641   Around the edges in many places other marvelous flowers grew here and there.

1642   Yellow and green blooms were interspersed with red ones, along with scattered pink ones in great numbers.

1643   Four flower colors with their fragrant scents. Fragrances wafted about the bunches, each a forest.

1644   Clouds of bees, honey-makers, swarmed over the lotuses drawn by the flower fragrance.

1645   Hovering over the flowers, the bees gathered the pollen from the blooms and then drifted through the air.

1646   And then the two reached a forest with countless trees, trees in every corner of the area.

1647   Cardamom, pumpkins, green squashes, vines and creepers covered the area.[353]

1648   And another pumpkin with its special flowers; and the sugar cane stood as tall as the betel tree.

1649   Banana forests of every type and kind produced fruit curved like the fangs and teeth of the naga.

1650   And then they reached an area of trees lined up next to each other one after another.

1651   Overflowing fruit in each tree, fruit as big as water pots in unending numbers:

1652   Mongoes, tamarind, wood apples, marvelous kinds, all sweet and delicious.

1653   And then they reached Mitsaka, Indra's great forest, a bamboo forest at the foot of the mountain,[354]

1654   A forest of trees in every way for a yoot, spread out over the great land.

1655   The prince admired the great pond
        and royal forest   chabang
        And invited his heart-like love
        To gaze upon them also.

1656   In the clearing behind the mountain
        Lay a rounded area,
        Chattan, its name.

1657   And there many elephants,
        Many different kinds,
        Male and female filled the pond,

1658   Descending to bathe their bodies
        With trunks drinking water
        And trumpeting loudly.

1659   Jumping and diving, the groups there
Numbered hundreds and thousands,
Their thousands unknown.

1660   Some elephants, heads and trunks scooped up,
Sucked up and shot forth the water,
Making great foam and froth.

1661   Some elephants played up and down,
Crowded all together
Full of vigor and desire.

1662   Some small calves followed behind
Sucking milk,
Both big and small mixed together.

1663   Some ready to run amuk;
Some skilled in fighting
Began knocking tusks together.

1664   Some trunks reached and grabbed branches
From various trees
Searching for their food.

1665   Some pruned the bamboo; some broke
And destroyed the bamboo;
And some moved carefully nibbling grass.

1666   All elephants had auspicious signs,
A group of ten elephants[355]
In the lineage exceeding all others.

1667   Some elephants were the Chattan[356]
With skin shining
Like auspicious silver rays.

1668   Some elephants were the noble Ubosot,[357]
Their bodies gold,
Different from the other groups.

1669   Some were yellow all over, pleasing to see,
The Hemahatthi group[358]
With beautiful skin.

168

1670 Some were the Mongkonayra;[359]
 Some purple like the anchan flower,
 Covered with auspicious signs.

1671 Some elephants, the great Khanthakhot,[360]
 Had feces wondrous and fragrant
 With the fragrance wafting about.

1672 Some were light orange: the Bingkhon,[361]
 Marvelous skin
 With eyes like a cat.

1673 Some were red, the Damop,[362]
 These elephant bodies
 Shining like copper.

1674 Some were the great Banthon group,[363]
 Albino white bodies,
 Their whole bodies beautiful.

1675 Some were in the Khangkhay group,[364]
 Their color like water,
 Crystal gems lustrous and glimmering.

1676 Some were the wondrous Kalawaka,[365]
 Dark bodies mixed together,
 Glimmering dark jewels.

1677 Ten groups, male and female,
 Delighting in desire, living happily
 Around the seven mountains,

1678 Around the jeweled forest pond,
 In the great Himawan,
 These were content with delight.

1679 The prince invited his precious
 To delight in the forest
 With a heart filled with joy and content.

1680 And so the prince told his beloved
 Through supernatural knowledge
 An ancient story from eons ago:[366]

1681   "This pond I remember from long before,
       A place I stayed
       For an endless time.

1682   There I was Chattan, the elephant,
       Leader of all the groups,
       Eight different ones."

1683   And his beloved explained to him,
       "In that former life
       Before, I was the same.

1684   When you were Chattan,
       I was born,
       I was your wife, your servant,

1685   With the name Lady Supattra.
       And I cared for you,
       The royal king,

1686   An honest and loyal husband
       Like the one now
       In the life today."

1687   The two talked to one another,
       Explaining the former life,
       Speaking of the time long gone.

1688   And so he invited his beauty
       To gather the lovely blossoms,
       The prince with his beloved.

1689   Embracing he cared for his wife,
       Flew into the sky,
       Leaving behind the glorious pond.

The Magic Sword is Stolen

1690   They floated about the heavens[367]   sattharaa
       And sighted a great land,
       A golden land,
       A great and vast place.

170

1691   And a sparkling jeweled dais
        Like an emerald
        Lay midst the wondrous place,
        Lovely and beautiful:

1692   As high as fifteen sawk,[368]
        Measured thirty sawk
        The width and length
        Both equal in dimensions.

1693   Two similar gold pools
        Adorned and decorated,
        Sparkling with heavenly colors
        Shining and glimmering bright:

1694   One was deep with water
        Like a crystal jewel;
        One with fragrance
        Wafting about the air.

1695   The phitthayathorns together
        Bathed in this delightful place
        And dabbed their bodies
        With aromatic scents.

1696   A place for contentment
        For the two royal heirs:
        With joy and happiness
        They descended to the spot.

1697   On this sparkling dais,
        Created by the deities,
        Their hearts found content
        And their bodies delight.

1698   The two nobles finished bathing,
        Water dissolved
        With fragrant scents
        All over their bodies.

1699   Then the two drifted into sleep
        Midst light green gems,
        Shimmering precious stones,
        Jewels set in the throne.

171

1700   Rested, their weariness abated,
They set off on heavenly paths
With thoughts and desires
Of the things they wished to do.

1701   And the wind touched the two
And they drifted into sleep
Relaxed and relieved,
A time of resting again.

1702   Evening neared and Suriya's rays slackened
As he began to hide
And dusk fell all around
At this time of evening.

1703   The jewel's hand embraced the Lord of the Land
And the Lord of Men
Embraced his beauty,
Perfect in every respect.

1704   Like vines clasped close
The two lost consciousness
And through the second watch
They slept on and on.

1705   With the hot rays of the sun rising,
When they rose and spread
Into heaven's realm,
Then the prince twisted in the heat.

1706   And at that very time   todokka
The arrogant phitthayathorn
With the wicked heart
And with the wanton power

1707   Descended to earth
And instantly saw the two nobles,
The prince and his lady,
The two deep in sleep

1708   On that jeweled dais,
Unconscious in sleep,
And so he flew down
To admire their noble bodies.

1709   He wasn't clear or sure
If both were royalty,
Or human beings,
Or heavenly deities:

1710   "Why do they sleep
In this forest deep
On this jeweled bed
Here in the Himawet?

1711   Is it noble Siva
With the heavenly queen Uma,
The two playing in joy
In this forest area?

1712   Is it the god Vishnu
In the fun-filled forest,
Close to the unsullied one,
The auspicious Laksami?

1713   Is it the King of Thunderbolts[369]
On Mount Meru
Journeying through the forest
Happy with his wife Sucha?

1714   Is it Brahma
Who refused happiness in love?
For what reason do they sleep?
He never had a consort.

1715   Is it a man taking
His love to the forest
Himawan
To delight in their sleep?

1716   His fine personal sword,
His hands always grasp.
Perhaps it holds
Great magical power.

1717   If I snatch it and run,
That noble sword
With its great power,
How'll he get out?

173

1718   If it's a god, he'll awake,
        And awaken quickly.
        If it's a man who sleeps,
        He won't awaken fast."

1719   Thinking thus,
        He seized the sword in a flash
        And fled, flying far
        From the Lord of Men.

1720   He fled into the heavens,
        That road into the sky,
        With the prince and his consort
        Knowing nothing at all.

1721   And passing down the road,
        The dawn arrived
        With Suriya's shining rays,
        Glimmering beauty in the skies.

1722   And then the Leader of Men   wasantadilok
        And his young consort,
        Their sleep of pleasure slackened
        In the sun's golden rays.

1723   Searching but not finding the sword,
        He bowed his head in grief,
        And as if life itself had ceased
        He moaned with oppression:

1724   "Who? Which one came down
        With wicked intent,
        Sneaked in and stole from my body
        My mainstay, my magic sword?

1725   How'll we return to the city?
        I know not how.
        Turning to every direction, every place
        It's unclear which way to go.

1726   To leave from this forest,
        This great Himawan forest,
        Not in one hundred years will we find a way
        That leads to our city.

1727   We'll leave our lives
In the Himaphan.
We'll sleep deep, forever helpless
Like pieces of wood piled up.

1728   Who'll go and tell
The two noble kings
Of this destruction,
Their tears springing forth?

1729   And so too our royal mothers,
The two great queens,
Will be in sorrow and pain,
Their hearts in endless agony.

1730   In great sorrow from the separation,
They'll lament mournfully,
Beat their breasts, shake with grief,
Sighs and sadness will increase two-fold.

1731   If these four nobles, the world's leaders,
Our fathers and mothers,
Burn with flames of sorrow,
Their lives'll come to an end.

1732   The two cities freed from rule
Will fill with vexation;
The citizens will turn cold,
The place solitary like a cemetery.

1733   Enemies will boldly make war,
Arrogantly rush in
And begin to destroy
This capital so bereft of joy.

1734   In fear and horror, the people,
They'll scatter and flee in disorder
Because there's no king
To destroy and eliminate the enemy.

1735   Both cities and world will be abandoned;
Happiness will disappear
For all the people;
It'll wither, be ruined, become a forest.

1736   O evil enemy, take pity,
        Make merit. Do not persecute us.[370]
        Return my weapon in haste
        So that we may return.

1737   If you desire any thing,
        We'll give what you wish.
        Show us mercy, end this grief,
        Or our lives will end here

1738   Like a pair of birds
        That a wicked man comes to kill.
        Their feathers destroyed, they fall deformed,
        No longer able to fly."

1739   Burdens and sorrows overwhelmed the two,
        And from all over the earth,
        All the heavenly deities heard
        And sat in fear,

1740   Pitying the King of Men
        And his beautiful queen.
        Sadness and grief
        Filled the hearts of the gods.

1741   And all the heavenly deities
        In the Himawan forest
        Lacked the bravery to force the cruel foe
        To return the sword of victory.

1742   And then the pair from the Solar dynasty,   *yaanii/*
        The two noble children,   intharawichian
        Filled with thousands of sorrows and longings,
        Thinking of the powerful sword.

1743   And the prince embraced his love,
        That youthful beauty,
        And she the major queen
        Embraced her king.

1744   Each spoke, infused with pain
        And weeping at the same time,
        Hearts filled with sorrow
        As though their lives would end:

1745   "O my beloved, where will we go?[371]
        In which direction? I'm lost and confused.
        I see trees standing all around,
        A forest surrounding and I don't know the way."

1746   "O my husband, if we go
        Into the forest, I'm unsure.
        Lofty mountains and hills surround
        And obstruct. How'll we go on?"

1747   "O my beloved who's tortured,
        It's necessary that we go;
        This isn't our place to stay;
        It's not fitting."

1748   "O my husband, we must walk
        Along the hills and forests,
        And in the forests undergo hardships
        And troubles as we walk."

1749   "O my beloved, last night was hard,
        Difficult to walk about;
        Our hearts must persevere;
        Don't be discouraged, disheartened, dismayed."

1750   "O my prince, on this difficult path
        We must tolerate no sleep, no food,
        Taste sorrow forever
        With no decrease in afflictions."

1751   "O my sweet one, cease your suffering.
        Griefs only increase meeting danger
        With oppressed hearts.
        Let us press on little by little."

1752   "O my prince, we must leave
        The Himawat forest
        For we will die for sure,
        Our life will not last long."

1753   "O my sweet, don't be disheartened,
        Discouraged with an embittered heart.
        With our merit we won't die;
        We'll escape and return."

177

1754   "O my prince, if sins oppress,
Something that returns cannot be avoided.
Should our life extend,
And we continue to live on, this we don't know yet."

1755   "O my beloved, if merit supports,
Nourishes, helps, we will not die.
Our lives will go on and on
In our cities and homes."

1756   On and on they talked
As they slowly walked;
Leading her by the hand,
He gently urged her on.

1757   And from the jeweled dais, the throne,
They went down the path
Crossing hills and mountains,
The limits of the Himaphan

1758   The path obscured
In the distant mountains
Unsure they walked through the forest
Moving carefully through the trees.

1759   Densely packed trees surrounded
With bright green bushes,
A thick undergrowth
With some bearing flowers and fruit.

1760   Many special kinds
They could see
With enticing scents
And tastes spread on the breezes.

1761   Some places in the mountains fell
Into many different levels
With valleys and streams,
Caves, lakes, gorges, and stream trickles.

1762   Streams gushed up,
Streams swiftly flowed
With spray splashing endlessly
Like a never-ending rain.

1763   Some places were like rows of flags,
A wide flat place
With many kinds of grasses,
Covering the earth all over.

1764   Some places were dark and dense,
Great dark forests,
With roads and paths made
Onerous with barbs and thorns.

1765   Some places were tall and stately forests,
The land blanketed with trees,
Regularly spaced trees,
Not too close or too far apart.

1766   Various birds and animals
Filled up the forest in great numbers;
Some flew, some walked,
Some went back and forth in the forest.

1767   Countless birds in the tree branches
Blended their voices in pity
As the two from the Solar dynasty
Forced their way midst the forest.

1768   The two nobles groaned in grief
Wandering through the forest
With no joy and delight in their hearts
To admire and enjoy the forest.

1769   Sorrows as heavy as golden Meru
Forced happiness and content to disappear
As they gathered the fruit from trees
To stave off cruel hunger.

1770   Passing through the forest
On that wooded path,
They walked slowly
As many days passed by.

1771   They slept on thick forest leaves,
Like a covering over a bed
And the shade from the trees
Like a sheltering roof overhead.

1772   The sounds of the animals
        Echoed like an orchestra,
        A forest orchestra
        That soothed the two to sleep.

1773   The two nobles wandered
        Through the Himawan forest
        Until passing through the forest
        They reached the banks of a great sea.

1774   Like the region
        Of the five great rivers,[372]
        Its very great width
        Stretched as far as the eye could see.

1775   Human power was insufficient
        For swimming to the other side,
        For many swift currents entwined
        And echoed rushing with noisy sounds.

1776   The prince and his beauty stopped,
        Disorientated from sorrow.
        And he spoke soothing words
        Talking endlessly of different things:

1777   "O my darling beauty, my life's mate." We meet   sathun
        increasing dangers so we must persevere.

1778   We search for a boat or raft, but there's none for sure,
        None to be seen here on this bank.

1779   Our lives will be destroyed crossing this water; there's
        no chance.

1780   To stay or cross the deep water's the same. Either way we lose
        our lives.

1781   We'll live or die swimming in this great water according
        to the merit of all our deeds before.[373]

1782   If merit helps, we won't die; we'll escape and live; if
        sins remain, we'll be destroyed and we'll die.

1783   Any mistakes I made were careless and unintentional toward
you. I beg of you, my sweet, to forgive my faults."[374]

1784   The noble beauty listened to the words of the prince and
answered, revealing her thoughts,

1785   "My sins too were unintentional, my prince, from actions,
words, and thoughts.[375]

1786   I beg you to forgive the sins which were in my heart;
quickly, so there's no punishment, rid my heart of those sins."[376]

1787   Their talking done, each embraced the other and lamented
their fate.

1788   Tears flowed from their eyes, flowed down and soaked their
breasts.

1789   They pined in their sorrow, begging forgiveness; but
their immeasurable grief did not cease.

1790   They turned their faces toward the sea and gazed at the great
waves and water.

1791   They looked at a kapok tree floating midst the currents and
suddenly

1792   The two nobles saw the sea splash it up on the beach nearby.

1793   And so the prince entered the fast-flowing current
with his young bride.

1794   They grasped the log floating and bobbing in the water
and neither sank nor were destroyed.

1795   Down they floated with their great trouble and sorrow,
their lives nearly spent.

1796   The prince on the log grasped first his young bride.

1797   Floating in the flowing water, water splashing them, they
reached the middle of the great water.

Samuttakote is Separated from Phintumadi

1798   And then at midnight   maalinii
        There occurred
        A dire event.

1799   The sky darkened
        Hiding all ten directions,
        And this took place.

1800   A great wind blew,
        And waves rose
        With tossing foam.

1801   The log with the royal two
        Rolled midst the waves,
        Then split down the middle.

1802   The two nobles in fear and dread,
        Each of them
        Was separated from the other,

1803   An evil accident
        That scattered those two
        From the Solar dynasty.

1804   Hands grasped each piece,
        The two filled
        With endless sorrow.

1805   The beloved lady thought of the prince
        And the prince thought
        Of his beloved lady.

1806   Sorrow and longing remained,
        Their hearts like meat
        Midst tongues of fire.

1807   The King of Men saw her no more;
        His beloved saw no more
        The King of Men.

1808   Waves and water fumed,
        A destroying wind
        Blew and blustered.

1809   And for the noble lady,
        Her sorrow and grief
        Increased two-fold.

1810   Gazing, their eyes separated,
        Abandoned and pitiful,
        They drew away.

1811   Agony, near death,
        There at sea
        In the night.

1812   No time of fortune,
        They endured grief
        With cries and laments.

1813   With dawn near
        Each thought of the other,
        No lessening of sorrow.

Phintumadi Mourns for Samuttakote

1814   Suriya's rays glimmered at dawn,   chabang
        And the young shining moon,
        The crest of the palace,

1815   Reached the bank
        And sought the prince,
        Her husband,

1816   But failed to meet the lord
        Midst the hills of water,
        Great, wide, and powerful.

1817   And more grief bent her
        Pitying the Lord of the Land,
        Mighty over the earth:

Phintumadi Mourns for Samuttakote

1818   "O my husband, noble one,
        Are you safe?
        Do you still live?

1819   Or have you reached heaven
        In the watery currents
        So great and deep?

1820   You left me, your slave,
        Alone, in grief;
        To die is my wish.

1821   To live my life alone,
        So long without you,
        No escape from grief comes.

1822   Should I follow and die,
        Stop the increasing sorrow
        That burns within my heart?

1823   To follow him and be two,
        This is better
        Than apart from him.

1824   Why live? Who'll care for me,
        Support me—no one.
        They'll belittle me.[377]

1825   Even a widow with great fortune
        No one respects;
        They despise her. No one to love.

1826   There's no one to care for me,
        Protecting, his duty;
        There's no place to stay.

1827   Waning joy disappears
        Like a fire
        Separated from its smoke.

1828   If not that, a river empty
        Of brimming currents,
        Dry as a bone.

184

1829   If not that, think of a city
Abandoned by its king,
No longer there ruling.

1830   If not that, a royal chariot
Without a noble flag
Elegantly curved, but missing.

1831   All gone, the security;
No throngs of people
To call out praises.

1832   My life with no content
Equals a life
Of burdens and confusion.

1833   Think and watch over myself;
Wait for the message,
News of the king,

1834   That he lives or not
Or destroyed
His life is.

1835   Still I don't know
About the Lord of the Land,
Uncertain, still desperate.

1836   If he's dead and gone
Then I'll follow.
If saved, then I'll stay.

1837   And then he'll return,
Rule the land,
Increase the peace and content,

1838   Reign in peace and happiness
In the golden residence,
The palace of pure gold.

1839   It's right to find a city,
A place to stay,
A residence

1840   And listen for news,
              Good or evil, whichever,
              Until all is certain."

1841   Thinking thus, she removed her adornments
              And wrapped them up,
              Then took the difficult path.

1842   Rows of trees shaded the road
              Bearing fruit and flowers
              In all their varied profusion.

1843   She looked at the forest groves,
              Her heart longing with sorrow,
              Unable to stop thinking of him.

1844   No relief from the sorrow,
              Her breast grief-laden;
              Her heated heart beat rapidly,

1845   And she looked at the trees and mumbled,
              Making moaning sounds,
              Lamenting the king.

1846   "The sawat tree is like the pleasure[378]   wasantadilok
              With my royal mate;
              The rak tree is like my love for the Lord of Men,
              Now abandoned for a long time;

1847   The sala clump reminds me of relinquishing[379]
              The noble feet of the prince;
              The clumps of rakam tell the cause
              Of the bruised heart, the love-sorrows.

1848   The kratum tree reminds me of hands beating[380]
              The chest with a weak and shaky heart;
              For the heated heart there's no loss of grief,
              Pitiful, sad, heated grief.

1849   The tum tree reminds me of sounds of hands striking[381]
              The chest about to break;
              The sok reminds me of endless sorrow,
              Impossible to escape from.

1850   The phanlawk blooms are called akhani[382]
Just like the fire akhani;
Sorrow and sadness gather;
Neither dying nor fading.

1851   The sayyut stops its streams of scents,[383]
The pleasing tastes stop at evening;
Shaking sorrow and grief never depart,
With no stop at any time;

1852   The sukkrom is melancholy, bereft of joy;[384]
There's weariness from moans;
With grief and sadness my heart hurts
For my husband, the prince.

1853   The sathorn is like agony and grief pounding.[385]
The breast recoils, the sobbing heart sighs.
I yearn for him, my heart breaks;
I die unable to endure life.

1854   The thingthorn is a piece of firewood[386]
Thrown away upon the bank;
The pieces tossed away are those they
Grasped and held in the currents.

1855   The rok tree is like a diseased chest[387]
Separated from the Lord of Men;
More pain, more sorrow covers the body;
No disease of the body equals it.

1856   The kanphay will prevent danger,[388]
But fails to protect against even one;
Danger of separation it didn't stop;
Separation comes to us face to face.

1857   The marum tree is like the breast gathering[389]
Grief and irritation in the heart;
How long before sorrow's gone?
There's no one to sleep with.

1858   The kamjat are scattered trees[390]
But they can't limit the gathering sorrow;
The tortured breast is like a fire offering;
Without limit, how does it disappear?

1859   The makawk is like sucking[391]
     Blood out causing great pain;
     Why not suck out the sorrow,
     Soothe the bruise, make me happy?

1860   The jak is like the prince separated,[392]
     Separated when the log split;
     Not seeing the lord's face,
     Separated from him, a two-fold sorrow;

1861   The teng tree is like weight scales,[393]
     Those for weighing,
     Knowing, not knowing the weight of grief,
     Which is the greatest?

1862   The mafaw tree is like a withered heart in agony,[394]
     Depressed and exhausted from grief;
     How much time, how many years
     For the withered heart to recover?

1863   The saba is like endless crazy talk,[395]
     Pitiful speech for the one gone;
     Not seeing the great prince changes
     The heart with crazy, delirious talk.

1864   The ramngap tree does not curb[396]
     Regret, speaking with no meaning;
     Speaking and not meeting him
     Difficult and impossible to see.

1865   The nat is like being destitute,[397]
     Separated from the prince how difficult;
     The breast hot like fire, when will it cool
     And put out the caused grief?

1866   The suramarit is like heavenly ambrosia[398]
     That puts out the burning heart;
     Sorrow's flames extinguished as a stream
     Of heavenly water poured in a bath.

1867   To think of these trees is like a raging river,
     Neither stopping nor disappearing;
     Thinking of my mate brings grief
     With unchanging heat in the heart;

1868   The wannam is like the day[399]
      We entered the water splashing and then separated;
      Grief came from the water, how many tears,
      As the name wannam shows.

1869   The dapphit tells the ways[400]
      To stop the poison with no worry,
      But it didn't stop the breast's sorrow,
      For a virulent poison remains.

1870   See all the different trees,
      Stately and scattered about;
      Compare them with the grief
      Showing everything lamented for.

1871   But they fail to stop my agitation for him;
      The sun already moves overhead,
      And the sorrows from separation
      Doubly increase the struggle."

1872   When she looked at the birds
      Throughout the forest trees,
      She met all the different kinds,
      Thousands upon thousands.

1873   She admired the birds
      And thought of the prince,
      Moaned and sighed considering,
      The sorrows from separation:

1874   "The jak phrak is like separation[401]
      From the prince, separated far;
      How many years, how many months
      Before we two meet?

1875   The phirap laments while[402]
      Thinking of her tears;
      With groans the tears fall,
      How many thousands of basins?

1876   The thengthut sends out messages,[403]
      But doesn't put clear news in the ear,
      News of the noble one's troubled path;
      The area he travels, it doesn't reveal.

Phintumadi Mourns for Samuttakote

1877   The khokma is a messenger on horse[404]
Looking for the king's traces everywhere,
But it doesn't tell the place to see,
The place the prince rests.

1878   The krawaen watches the sky,[405]
Sees his majesty somewhere;
Please reveal it, clear the heart
So that I may follow.

1879   The khawmong thinks about time,[406]
Counts in order the watches;
But there in the forest
Time passes so very slowly.

1880   Khawkun help me look and call out[407]
For that great noble of the land;
Where did he go; he's not near;
I cannot meet him face to face.

1881   The saek calls out urging,[408]
Makes clear my sorrow;
Pity me walking in the forest
Lonely and alone.

1882   The khwaekkhwan is an ax cutting wide,[409]
Splitting the breast and destroying;
A life lost and sought for;
Without the king I'm in sorrow.

1883   The ragnan long abandoned[410]
Separated from the walled palace.
How long before he returns
To rule the abandoned palace?

1884   The lang is one sign[411]
Clearly showing the prince's story,
When and how he died,
This for sure is still in doubt,

1885   The sarika fails to speak of love;[412]
Please help and tell Indra
Who knows my husband
And which way he went.

1886   Beasts, don't keep the secret.
Truly tell the story, reveal
The news that he's far
Or near. Tell me the news.

1887   Nori if you know the place,[413]
This noble's place, I ask;
Favor me and speak it clearly;
Speak honestly without confusion.

1888   Khaektaw take the guest[414]
To the place the prince rests;
Please reveal, don't lie;
Let me follow you.

1889   Benjawan tell the reason[415]
The prince stays in the forest;
Tell me straight
Where the noble one resides.

1890   Kayfa swim into the heavens,[416]
Seek the Lord of the Land;
Swarms of bees fly about
Seeking to help, but see him not.

1891   None of the birds speaks,
Neither alleviating my sorrow;
Nor pitying me,
One without friends in the forest,

1892   Moaning while walking
Along this path, troubled
With a heart barren of joy
Or happiness at any time."

Phintumadi Builds an Alms Hall

1893   She gazed at the four-footed beasts,   chabang
Filling the forest,
But did not know how many kinds.

191

1894   Tigers, lions, bears, boars, herds of deer,
        Great lions, cows, buffaloes,
        Reindeer, rhinos, all moved swiftly.

1895   Wild bison ran noisily through the trees,
        Elephants, male and female,
        With groups of forest animals.

1896   Iguanas and lizards went in and out
        Hiding in shaded groves to sleep
        While some ran to hide.

1897   Short- and long-tailed monkeys, squirrels, shrews
        Grabbed the branches together,
        Climbed with their hands, jumping and leaping.

1898   Antelopes took short steps and attacked,
        Jumping and colliding,
        Neither contused nor bruised.

1899   "All these forest animals," she thought,
        "Form a picture, a feeling
        With no pleasure, with no sorrow abating.

1900   Oh that former sin, from which life,[417]
        Separated me from my husband?
        My heart squirms in sorrow.

1901   But the prince has more sorrow
        Which does not abate."
        And tears welled up and flowed.

1902   And then she reached the road,
        The cart path,
        And her heart rejoiced.

1903   A small path went along
        From the city,
        The outskirts of the city.

1904   To protect herself she changed her appearance
        To ward off men desiring her,
        Wanting to console and soothe her.

1905   Men think of desire
        Planning to speak and chat
        But prefer to sleep with them.

1906   At the same time she scooped up dust
        Spread it over her body,
        Dust mixed with dirt,

1907   All over the body,
        Her face soiled with dust,
        Her whole body abnormal,

1908   Like some low caste, a slave.
        And she walked along to the city
        Named Mattharat.[418]

1909   Throngs of people
        Came and went, back and forth,
        All the people from the village.

1910   She met one, an old woman,
        Who greeted her
        With gracious words:

1911   "O little one, where've you come from,
        Walking alone? Who abandoned you,
        You with no friends to travel with?

1912   From which city do you come?
        Please young one, speak.
        Don't keep silent, answer.

1913   Family, relations, relatives,
        A place or a city,
        Do you have one to stay at?"

1914   And the youthful lady answered the aged woman,
        "I left on a ship
        That sank midst the sea.

1915   Separated from my husband, I traveled alone
        Until I reached these borders.
        Here, this place, I have no relations."

193

Phintumadi Builds an Alms Hall

1916   The old woman
Heard the young moon speak
And invited her, the unfortunate one,

1917   To go and live, to reside
In her house and lighten her heart
Which ached from separation.

1918   Hearing that brought happiness
And she thanked the grandmother
Who had befriended her with compassion,

1919   "I'll reside in the house
Waiting and watching for my husband,
Separated, till I see his face again."

1920   And the Brahmin understood
And took the lady ahead
To her house, her residence.

1921   Almost dawn after the long night
The prince's lady thought
Of a plan to meet her prince.

1922   She'd take the demeanor of a nun
And give her excellent jewel,
Sparkling with its rays,

1923   To an old man to show it
To the rich merchants
Around the city in haste,

1924   To see how much money,
To guess the price,
A suitable and fitting price.

1925   And a rich man examined the jewel,
Saw the great value
Of this jewel, no two alike.

1926   So he bargained with gold,
Five hundred carts filled,
Loaded every cart filled to the top.

1927   "Do you agree? Are you still worried?
Will you disagree?
How much'll you add to be satisfied?"

1928   And so the woman quickly counted the gold,
The loaded swaying carts,
All five hundred filled with gold.

1929   She sent someone to carry it,
And so the aged woman
Gave it to the beloved lady,

1930   And she took it joyfully,
Gave it to the retinue,
The servants, the female slaves

1931   For all the ceremonial items,
For all the necessities
To build a golden hall.

1932   And then she ordered an artisan,[419]
Told him of her wish
To build an almsgiving hall.

1933   And the artisan engraved the story
With an elegant picture
On the beautiful wall:

1934   From first when the deity carried him,
The Solar dynasty noble,
To meet her in the prang,[420]

1935   To the time the two reached the water,
Grasped the log, arms embraced,
And swam in the currents.

1936   And a great gale they met,
Restless waves arose,
And striking, split the log.

1937   And the two grieved till near death,
The two on the waters,
The two separated.

Phintumadi Builds an Alms Hall

1938   And then she set out various things,[421]
            Numerous gifts,
            Of many different kinds:

1939   Silver, gold, treasures,
            Countless servants and a retinue
            With many kinds of food.

1940   Had a person as caretaker
            Divide and distribute the alms;
            Every day busy, never free.

1941   The throngs of people
            Received the alms,
            Then were taken to see the drawing.

1942   And whoever looked and was sad,
            He should bring the news
            And explain it with haste.

1943   Finished, he began the work,
            Distributing the wealth,
            Giving it to all the people.

1944   All the beggar groups,   *surangkhanang*
            Each begged for alms;
            Walked here and there,
            Poor, pitiful people,
            Maimed and lame people,
            Great throngs of people
            At the alms house.

1945   Some ate the food,
            Some received clothes,
            Some needed gold,
            Some desired silver,
            As they wanted, they asked,
            Told the caretaker
            To distribute well.

1946   Not deciding before,
They took as they pleased.
Everything was there,
No reprimands, no kneeling,
No one struck them,
No one forced to flee,
All were welcomed.

1947   Men, women, people without,
Received gifts he gave
With words of truth.
With great joy
These beggars noisily
Mumbled and spoke,
Calling out a blessing:

1948   "May you live long as heaven,
Your life long as earth,
Never knowing death,
Treasures and property
Only to increase.
We ask for merit
Throughout your life."

1949   All alms received
The throngs went in groups
To gaze at the walls,
Look at the drawings,
All in a group.
The guard waited, listened,
And watched their reaction.

1950   All looked at the drawing;
None showed surprise,
Talked back and forth,
No sorrow, no grief,
Happy and content
Not knowing the legend,
Nothing of the story

Samuttakote Swims Midst the Waves

1951   They only admired,
"Truly beautiful," they said,
"This legend, from where
Did it come? Who did it?"
Appreciating the beauty,
Praising, they passed on,
Showed no changes.

1952   At dusk he took the news
To the youthful beauty:
There were no results;
He looked and listened
To every person and group.
He neither saw nor heard
Strange reactions.

Samuttakote Swims Midst the Waves

1953   When the prince entered the great and wide sea,   sathun
he endured the tortures.

1954   Sea foam splashed and diminished his power as though to end
his life.

1955   Almost could stand it, the great grief, the great sighs,
more thinking, more great sorrows without end.

1956   "Strength gone, laments gone, thinking gone. Who to depend
on? Stamina gone," he reflected.

1957   A thousand sorrows, a thousand griefs, a thousand searches
for refuge, a thousand burning heats affected his heart.

1958   He sought a friend, sought one to give refuge, sought
the shore but saw only sky and foam.

1959   "Who'll help? There's no help. All there is, is great water.
I must survive. Will I? I want to survive, but I might not.

1960   Will my body and soul remain or be thrown into the water
and float down, not as one together.

1961   If I die, how'll my beauty hear about it or see me? O my
        unsullied queen, we'll never meet.

1962   Now, is my dear one in the water or on the land? Is her
        life destroyed or is she still with us?

1963   Oh when will I meet my loved one again? Death or saving my
        life are one and the same.

1964   To look for my lady, my ability's gone. Continually looking,
        staring, looking this way and that. Hidden from my eyes,
        she disappears."

1965   And he moaned in the water, seven days in
        the water.

1966   And then the young woman   sattharaa
        With the great power, the ruler,
        The jewel Mekala,[422]
        The woman deity,

1967   The keeper of the seas,
        The one who comes,
        Comes over the seas,
        Once every seven days,

1968   Came flying through the air,
        Came to the sea,
        And saw the Lord of Men
        Swimming.

1969   She cast her eyes down and saw
        This young man,
        "Who is he,
        Who suffers in the sea?

1970   Oh the skilled Samuttakote,
        Who met misfortune,
        When the outcast thief
        Stole the sword.

199

1971   The fierce-hearted phitthayathorn,
Wicked and ruthless,
Inflicted this harsh
Punishment."[423]

1972   Knowing this she flew to Indra's city,
Sutattani,[424]
And there paid
Obeisance.

1973   "For what reason does the prince
Swim midst the water with danger increasing,
Enduring pain and longing,
Sorrow building?"

1974   Hearing this, the King of Thunderbolts
Quickly commanded
The spotless woman,
Mekala,

1975   "You who guard the oceans,
Why do you fail to guard the Great One,
The Lord Buddha,
Protector of animals?[425]

1976   When you see noble men[426]
Who follow the precepts,
Who look for release alone
With independent knowledge;

1977   Or parents who guard moral habits,
Perfect in the precepts;
Or chaste women who follow
The perfect precepts;

1978   These three groups, if they fell
Into the water, you would
Help save them,
Save their lives,

1979   Carry them from the currents,
Their life in danger.
Rescue or they die.
Sustain them all.

1980   Why don't you help the prince?
        Why did you leave the Great Honest One
        Grieving in the water?
        You don't want to help?

1981   The phitthayathorn's robbery,
        Stealing the magic sword, is my duty,
        I'll force him
        To return it.

1982   Quickly go to the ocean, take him,
        This great one, the Buddha,
        From the water,
        And save him."

1983   And the noble lady received the order,
        Flew to the great ocean,
        Carried the Lord of the Land
        On to the shore.

1984   And the youthful ruler's grief
        Quickly diminshed and
        The unsullied one returned
        To the celestial palace.

The Magic Sword is Returned

1985   In an instant the immortal one,   todokka
        The great divinity,
        Went by magic
        To the phitthayathorn,

1986   The one to receive
        Severe punishment.
        And Indra grabbed his hand
        And ordered with pain,

1987   "Wicked thief
        Who brought strife,
        Why, without pity,
        Did you steal the sword?

201

The Magic Sword is Returned

1988   That wasn't your concern,
        You had no anger with him,
        There was no great reason,
        You did it with evil intent.

1989   If you fail to return it,
        Your life'll go fast,
        You'll no longer live,
        Ruined immediately."

1990   And then his hands swung
        The diamond thunderbolt,
        Rolling and shimmering,
        Swishes sounding like bees.

1991   Paying obeisance and bowing,
        Fearing punishment,
        He raised his two hands
        To Lord Indra:

1992   "O king, grant pity,
        Please forgive me,
        Don't pile up danger on me
        And destroy my life.

1993   I beg to return the sword,
        I must quickly offer it.
        I won't oppose you,
        The power of your words."

1994   So Indra forced him to make
        Truthful promises,
        And the immortal
        Returned to Phichayon palace.

1995   And the pitthayathorn sped
        To the spot the prince stayed,
        Quickly he arrived
        And returned the sword.

1996   And then he returned home,
        To Himawat,
        His former home
        Without losing his life.

Samuttakote Searches for Phintumadi

1997   When the prince awoke and saw   wasantadilok
        The lost sword returned,
        He was happy and content,
        His grief and obstacles checked:

1998   Now beyond the dangers:
        The arduous times in the sea,
        Hunger and bodily injuries,
        Emaciated without food.

1999   Many days he travelled over the waters,
        Among the hills of the sea,
        Not eating any food,
        For nearly seven full days,

2000   Planning to find the forest,
        The city's limit,
        And then to rest in content
        And to find food to eat.

2001   And with increased energy,
        He'd search, he'd look around
        For news if she still lived
        Of if she had died.

2002   And thinking thus he removed
        His regal raiments,
        Wrapped them up and hid them in a silk tree
        In the forest outside the city.

2003   And immediately he became a Brahmin,[427]
        Wandered through the forest,
        And reached a village
        Where people lived.

2004   He asked for food and provisions,
        A place to stay. And everywhere
        He asked for news of his bride,
        But found nothing of the flower.

203

2005   Alone and with hardship he reached
        Many people in many cities.
        But every place, land, region
        Knew nothing, and he failed to find her.

2006   Slowly, for over nine months,
        He went along his way
        Until he reached the site
        Of the city of Mattharat.

2007   He asked about the village, the area,
        And quickly learned the news
        Of the nun who gave alms,
        Usually in the pavilion.

2008   Whoever went to this place
        Could get food and provisions,
        Could get all sorts of things
        Divided and distributed.

2009   He decided to go to eat,
        To lose his great hunger at the early morning meal.
        He arrived and saw all happy and content,
        Every one of the groups.

2010   Men and women gave out the alms
        And many great things.
        He ate restraining his grief
        From passing along the onerous path

2011   One invited him to gaze at the lovely pictures,
        To admire the fine characters
        Inscribed on the wall;
        And then his heart leaped with joy.

2012   It started when the protecting spirit[428]
        Took the prince and his lady
        And flew to the city,
        Put him down in the celestial palace.

2013   And then enticed him to sleep together
        With the royal princess.
        He embraced and mounted her stomach,
        Rested on her breast, the two together.

2014   They indulged in the tastes of love,
        Sported in the games of love,
        Close in bed, slept in delight.
        Then returning, the spirit separated them.

2015   She awakened but missed the royal face;
        Her breast filled with heated pain;
        Thari consoled the lady
        But could not stop the agony at all.

2016   She drew every king, every heavenly deity
        In heaven and on earth.
        But the lady cried, "Not this one,
        A great king joined with me."

2017   She drew the prince's form,
        And this satisfied her heart.
        She honored the picture, hugged it
        Against her chest and moaned with love.

2018   She ordered her lady to fly off,
        To invite that prince there,
        To come, to stop quickly the confusion
        Raging in her youthful heart.

2019   And then Indra ordered in a celestial voice
        To ready the chariot Phichayan,
        For Matuli to take over,
        To drive through the air for the prince.

2020   And then the prince ordered his chief
        To march his soldiers
        To Romyaburi
        And all to wait in a resthouse.

2021   He mounted the celestial chariot,
        Flew through the air
        To the unsullied palace
        Where the two embraced.

2022   Ten nobles moved to the front
        In great numbers in Romyaburi,
        Set up scattered camps,
        Vying for the royal daughter.

2023   And the noble king, her father,
Invited them to lift the bow,
Place it before the kings
To raise it up and carry it forward.

2024   He'd give his noble daughter
To the famed one,
To the one successful
In following his wishes.

2025   And so the ten kings went forward
To raise it up,
That heavy bow, but all failed.
So they stopped unable to do more.

2026   And then the prince went to his unit,
Arrived at the site,
Carried the bow with magic power
And brandished it in the air.

2027   He pulled back the string, the earth echoed,
And the prince shot an arrow.
Echoes resounded over the earth
As he showed his incomparable power.

2028   And then the royal father
Bestowed his heavenly daughter
With a royal agreement
As he said he would.

2029   Ten warriors, their hearts broken, angered,
With evil intentions
Became great enemies
Planning to steal the beauty.

2030   And so the king sent his commander
To restrain them, their grief, their vexation;
And he told them not to fight,
Not to struggle and to fight.

2031   But the ten couldn't tolerate it
So showed their arrogance,
Not disheartened, but proud and arrogant;
Their fury increased without abate.

2032   They began to fight, every one, every king,
The ranks of soldiers ordered in place,
Ten kings, ten chariots, ten companies,
Companies one upon the other.

2033   And the prince in the chariot
Moved to the front
And fought every king from every place,
The enemies began to fight.

2034   And the prince asked his counselor Susangkan
Who the ten kings were,
And he answered with the name
Pointing to each enemy king.

2035   He pulled back the bow,
Shot the arrow and destroyed the enemy,
Destroyed every king from every city
And death covered the battlefield.

2036   And the great defender of the world
Gave his beautiful daughter
To be the sleeping partner
Through the wedding ceremony.

2037   And the noble lady told her story,
Went to pay respects to the great spirit,
The protecting spirit of the city,
In the royal pleasure garden.

2038   And the prince and his lady went to pay respects,
To make auspicious offerings,
To bid Sri Narakup farewell,
To return to the land of his noble father.

2039   Then they entered the wondrous forest,
The wondrous garden in the forest,
And there met a phitthayathorn
Lying sorely injured

2040   With numerous wounds
Spread all over his body,
With great grief and sorrow doubled,
His life about to expire.

2041   And the prince took him to a physician
To care and cure him.
And the phitthayathorn gave a great sword
With power to fly through the sky.

2042   And the prince took this jeweled weapon
Thanking and blessing him,
Then invited his beloved flower
To carry her around the area

2043   To admire the trees, admire the mountains
Around heavenly Himaphan
With its wondrous birds and animals,
A happy heart wherever the eye wandered.

2044   He embraced his love and flew
Into the heavenly halls,
Floated about Himawan
At glorious Mount Kaylat.

2045   They reached the golden palace
Of the King of Kinnarees,
Indulged in great joy and happiness
In that blissful heaven.

2046   From the immortal kinnaree city
To the gardens and mountains surrounding,
They went, and then played in Anodat
And Chattan, the lucid pools.

2047   They admired the countless elephant families,
Every different kind,
And then arrived at the jeweled dais,
The most excellent of beds.

2048   And while sleeping on the jeweled couch,
Slumbering for a long time,
A fierce phitthayathorn flew down
And stole their sword.

2049   They awoke and missed the powerful weapon;
A thousand pains struck their hearts,
With great agony and sorrow
They moaned in their grief.

2050   The two wandered about the forest,
        The great Himawet in sorrow;
        For days they followed the difficult path
        With grief as though ready to die.

2051   They reached the great wide water,
        The water swiftly flowing along
        With smashing waves breaking,
        Waves ready to destroy the bank.

2052   And the kapok log drifted to the sea,
        And the two dropped in,
        Grasped the bobbing log
        Midst the wind-blown foam.

2053   Smashing waves split the log,
        Broke it in two,
        And the pieces floated on the surface,
        Bringing endless troubles for the two.

2054   Each separated from the other,
        Each called out in sorrow,
        So finished the lengthy tale
        Samuttakote saw.

The Royal Couple is Reunited

2055   The whole story of the prince   *yaanii*/intharawichian
        With his princess
        He saw with sadness,
        With sorrow and with grief;

2056   "Who came to draw
        My whole story?
        O my delicate one,
        Where are you now?

2057   How'll I ever meet you,
        Your face gone for so long?
        Or, gentle noble one
        Are you close by? I'll look."

2058   His sorrow abated and he laughed
       Madly calling his beauty.
       But not seeing her, his sorrow returned,
       He cried with heart agitated.

2059   And then the almsgiver
       Looked at his changing condition,
       Each different, each surprising,
       As though he were mad, untrustworthy.

2060   So he took this story
       And explained it with haste
       To the noble beauty,
       So she knew every part.

2061   She listened and grew happy;
       Perhaps the prince had reached the hall;
       A joyful feeling arose,
       Extinguishing sorrow quickly.

2062   Thinking so, this royal angel
       Went quickly
       To the place they divided
       And distributed the provisions.

2063   She looked and met
       The face of the Lord of the Land
       Changed into a Brahmin;
       But it was clear, no confusion.

2064   Straight away she grasped his feet,
       Quickly she fell there,
       Her head and body dropped
       And she cried in sorrow.

2065   The prince gazed down
       At the sorrowing young nun.
       Looked at all the characteristics
       And instantly knew it was her.

2066   At the same time his arms
       Embraced the young beauty;
       His cries unrelenting
       As he lamented:

210

2067   "O dear one, when we separated[429]
        So fatigued midst the sea,
        I did not know
        If you had escaped or not."

2068   "O my husband, when you were pushed away,
        I resisted the rolling waves;
        I reached the shore still living,
        And there waited for you."

2069   "O dear one, I swam and swam
        In the sea for a long time,
        Counting at least seven days;
        A god helped me escape death."

2070   "O my husband, from the forest
        To this place, this village,
        For many days I wandered
        Remembering your heart."

2071   "O dear one, when Mekala
        Helped carry me beyond the waves,
        The swirling water, I sought you,
        But failed to see you. I despaired."

2072   "O my husband, when the old lady
        Sold my ring to the rich man,
        The gold allowed me to buy this place,
        This refuge, this home of rest."

2073   "O my dear one, when on the bank,
        That phitthayathorn
        Returned the sword in haste;
        So I changed to the wandering Brahmin."

2074   "O my husband, when they gave alms
        To the men and women,
        I hoped to meet you
        And so drew the story from the start."

2075   "O my dear one, I looked for you,
        Went to all the places, all the regions,
        Wandered about for many months
        With no news of you, my bride."

211

2076   "O my husband, waiting for news of you
I had people search in groups,
And so I met you
Here looking at the painting."

2077   "O my dear one, what sin
Forced us to separate for so long?
What goodness fulfilled,
Returned us together?"

2078   "O my husband, please let us go
To the golden pavilion
Where I, your servant,
Will receive the Lord of Men."

2079   Sorrow abated for the two
Who went to the palace;
She left the nun's order
And prepared him delicious foods.

2080   And then they fell asleep,
Their bodies content on the bed,
Their trials and troubles gone,
The journey's griefs over.

2081   Their rest completed,
All sorrows soothed away,
They sought sensual pleasures,
So long the two separated.

2082   For many nights their hearts found joy,
Close together in pleasant sleep;
Two happy, two delighted,
As desire embraced the two.

2083   And then they thought of the kings,
Their parents ruling
Both of the cities,
Their hearts waiting every day.

2084   So they sought the old woman,
Gave her the treasures
In all the great piles
At that pavilion of rest,

2085   Gave her half of everything
        And distributed the other,
        Inviting her to enjoy it,
        "I praise your goodness."

2086   To the great alms house
        Filled with goodness,
        She gave with the money
        To support all the helpers.

2087   Half the fortune she spent,
        Obtained all the gold,
        Divided it into piles
        To shovel out as alms.

2088   All the nuns and Brahmins[430]
        People from every place,
        Called out great praises,
        A great tumult offering blessings.

The Royal Couple Returns to Romyaburi

2089   And then the two nobles bid farewell
        To the old woman and left;
        She carried her ornaments
        And followed the prince.

2090   And the prince swung the shiny sword,
        Embraced his princess,
        Flew into the heavens
        And landed at the wide sea.

2091   He reached the silk tree
        Where his raiments were hidden,
        That shiny bright place
        Where the two nobles rested.

2092   With all the raiments and regalia
        The prince was adorned.
        And his first queen was decorated
        In luxurious ornaments.

213

2093   Then he carried his wife,
Flying into the heavens,
Drifting in the heavens,
And then reached Romyaburi.

2094   They stayed in the royal pleasure garden
At the edge of the city,
And there showed themselves
To the garden caretaker.

2095   And this gardner brought the news
To the king in haste.
And the king went to the garden
To greet the royal couple.

2096   Both paid homage and respect
At the feet of her father,
And he kissed their heads,
Touched the royal pair.

2097   And his two arms embraced them,
Hugged both bodies
And asked for the story
Of their separation, of their anger:

2098   "Please explain the story,
The lands you visited.
Son-in-law answer,
Hold not a word back."

2099   And he told the king, "I wasn't annoyed
With your royal order.
I went out to the forest,
To go and visit

2100   That great forest,
With hills all around,
And delightful caves
Abounding with gorges and streams."

2101   He told all from the beginning
Till the dangerous event,
A carefully detailed account
That explained everything.

2102   And the king listened to this
And then cried flowing tears,
Eyes filled with tears;
And both endured the grief.

2103   Now to the city they went
Content with cool hearts;
Every sorrow and adversity
Disappeared, no longer there.

2104   All his sorrows gone, Sri Narakup began to   sathun
ready his realm and life.

2105   He arrayed the capital city into a splendid site,
equal to Indra's eternal Sutat.[431]

2106   And he invited the two children to the city
decorated with ornaments

2107   To bestow upon them the kingdom's royal regalia
and the royal umbrella.

2108   And then he gave the kingdom and its treasure
to the Buddha of the Solar race, to rule in his stead.[432]

2109   Once finished he went into the forest area of Himaphan and
there became an ascetic, his hair twisted up like a crown.[433]

2110   And he advanced into the way of kasin, meditating upon earth,
gaining supernatural knowledge,[434]

2111   Destroying his old life, attaining fame in the lands of other
kings and nobles, knowing the chan, finding joy in his heart.[435]

2112   And when King Phintutat heard the story that his two children,
freed from their sorrow,

2113   Returned to rule Romyaburi, his melancholy and sorrow
disasppeared, all the danger gone.

2114   And he sent a messenger inviting the two noble ones to
return to his kingdom.

2115   And seeing that message Samuttakote desired to see his
        royal mother and father.

2116   And he readied the four divisions of chariots, elephants,
        horses, and infantry, organized into countless numbers,

2117   And all together the forces moved forward, flowing
        like water.

2118   Elephant forces in great numbers,[436]   maalinii
        Skilled in victory with tusks,
        Majestic, fearful.

2119   Elephant forces with noble signs,
        True fighters,
        Hindering enemies.

2120   Elephant forces smashing all to pieces,
        Fighting plunderers,
        Ruining, destroying.

2121   Elephant forces, highly skilled
        In shattering forces fleeing,
        Breaking them.

2122   Elephant forces, fearless;
        The enemy elephants,
        Subdued and destroyed.

2123   Elephant forces eliminating enemies,
        Proficient in victory,
        Skilled in fighting.

2124   Elephant forces praised
        In radiant raiments,
        Magnificent gold.

2125   Elephant forces, great bravery,
        Elephant pikemen
        Carrying hooks.

2126   Elephant forces, the color gray,
        Their sages on the neck,
        Mahouts on the end.

2127   Elephant forces spreading out,
Mahouts carrying leather whips
And beating.

2128   Elephant forces lining up,
Lances carried
In skilled hands.

2129   Elephant forces raising up,
Shields spread like fans
Glorious to see.

2130   Horse forces ready to subjugate;
The enemy in terror
Fears the power.

2131   Horse forces skilled
Fighting the enemy,
Destroying many.

2132   Horse forces arrayed
With ornaments
Of shining gold.

2133   Horse forces superior,
Troops raising wooden clubs,
Pulling back crossbows.

2134   Horse forces fearless,
They grasp swords
Swaying.

2135   Horse forces noble and powerful
Brandishing spears,
Swinging back and forth.

2136   Horse forces valiant,
Weapons catching rays
Spreading in the air.

2137   Horse forces ready to skirmish,
Charge in battle,
Spears stabbing.

2138   Horse forces shooting arrows
        That enter and split
        Bodies.

2139   Horse forces, great forces,
        Stepping like machines,
        Moving in rows.

2140   Horse forces moving quickly,
        Spreading like
        A windstorm.

2141   Horse forces in great lines
        Each checked
        And aligned.

2142   Chariot forces in great numbers,
        Bright and clear,
        Causing confusion.

2143   Chariot forces harnessing horses,
        Carved, handsome flags
        In tall lofty lines;

2144   Chariot forces decorated,
        Frames and axles curved
        Elegantly;

2145   Chariot forces, the best,
        Decorated with jewels,
        Much gold;

2146   Chariot forces glittering,
        Shimmering
        With shiny rays.

2147   Chariot forces in ranks;
        On a palanquin
        The leader sits.

2148   Chariot forces, glittering power,
        Slashing the enemy
        Dead.

2149   Chariot forces victorious,
        Wooden clubs swaying,
        Swinging about.

2150   Chariot forces carrying
        Handspears,
        Noble looking.

2151   Chariot forces with crossbows,
        Shooting the enemy
        Scattered around.

2152   Chariot forces with arrows and weapons,
        And countless bows
        To kill the enemy.

2153   Chariot forces with charioteers
        Brandishing spears
        Like whirlwinds.

2154   Infantry forces clamorous,
        Hands wielding
        Every kind of weapon.

2155   Infantry forces in countless numbers,
        Each brave,
        Terrible and strange.

2156   Infantry forces carrying
        Swords in hands
        Raised to strike.

2157   Infantry forces in gear,
        Beautiful breastplates,
        Brandishing spears.

2158   Infantry forces fearless,
        Marching in great numbers
        Beyond counting.

2159   Infantry forces in throngs,
        Grasping bows and arrows,
        Pulling back the strings.

The Royal Couple Returns to Phromburi

2160   Infantry forces carrying
Tasseled lances, flags,
Small knives.

2161   Infantry forces arrayed
With countless shields
Shimmering.

2162   Infantry forces twisting spears
Destroying the enemy
Fearing the power.

2163   Infantry forces destroying
Squads of foes
Fleeing in hair-raising fear.

2164   Infantry forces valiant,
All strong,
All brave in war.

2165   Infantry forces crying out,
Cries flattening the land,
The ground breaking up.

The Royal Couple Returns to Phromburi

2166   There were countless soldiers,   wasantadilok
Personnel divided up
Elephants, horses, chariots, and infantry,
Squads of valiant soldiers,

2167   Along with the two unsullied nobles
In their royal regalia,
Arrayed in shining jewels,
Beautiful with glittering rays,

2168   And they set forth on chariots,
Gleaming and glinting,
Arrayed with shining armaments
Like Indra's chariot Phaychayon.

2169   The forces marched forward
        On foot with great cries
        From the city to the forest,
        Along the perilous path.

2170   They marched in order,
        Passing many days,
        Till they reached Phromburi,
        That city of content.

2171   The two nobles quickly went forward,
        Paid obeisance, lifting their hands
        To their royal mother and father,
        Who asked what had gone before.

2172   They told reasons for sorrow,
        And the king listened,
        Pitying his royal son
        And daughter-in-law.

2173   And the two noble parents spoke;
        Tears covered their breasts,
        Grieving and agonizing
        For the sorrow created.

2174   Their sorrow gone they readied
        That noble ceremony
        To transfer the kingdom
        To the new king,

2175   To his dear, royal son,
        The great and noble deity,
        Who ruled the line in peace,
        Ruled the royal realm.

2176   Finished the king left his kingdom
        And journeyed to the forest,
        And there became an ascetic,
        In the forest of hardship and difficulty.

2177   He followed the four virtuous inclinations[437]
        And the four ways of knowledge,
        And then he died
        Entering the celestial palace.

2178 And then the head of the line, the Buddha,
   Ruled over the kingdoms,
   Both cities, in the ten paths for kings,[438]
   The royal duties of the king.

2179 And with a superior force
   He built an alms house
   To divide and distribute
   All things to the city.

2180 And he preached all aspects
   Of the five precepts of the Buddha,[439]
   And all the citizens were content
   When this Roller of the Wheel ruled.

2181 And the nobility progressed in the precepts,
   The noble way of Buddhism
   And after death were reborn
   Into another heaven.

2182 And so this story of the Buddha is complete,
   Ordered to show the way before,
   The story told from ancient records
   For the purpose of teaching.

The Tale is Explained

2183 A story was created to preserve   *yaanii*/intharawichian
   The Four Great Truths of the Buddha,[440]
   Ordered a collection of tales
   In the order they came.

2184 O noble monks,[441]
   Those of the Buddha's order,
   That phitthayathorn,
   The cruel one who stole the sword

2185 Was the god Devadatta
   With his cruel intent to destroy,
   Traits long inborn,
   His anger and hate never ceasing.

2186   The noble royal king
        Phintutat, Lord of the Land,
        Was Suddhodana, the father,
        Of the great and virtuous Buddha.

2187   The great queen, wife of the king,
        Was the mother of Buddha,
        And the soldier friend was
        Rahun, the son of the Gotama.

2188   And the Brahmin's son
        Was the younger brother Ananda,
        Caring for the family,
        His duty day after day.

2189   In Romyaburi the king
        Sri Narakup
        Was the monk of the right,[442]
        A disciple of great knowledge.

2190   And his queen was the aunt,
        The first female disciple,[443]
        That group of females,
        Disciples to the Great One.

2191   And the King of the Kinnarees,
        King Tummarat
        Was Moggallana
        Of great power and knowledge.

2192   And the peak of celestial Mount Meru[444]
        Was Thera Anuruddha
        With his celestial eyes
        And incomparable powers to see beyond.

2193   And the lady Mekala,
        That youthful deity
        Was that young lady,
        The noble Uppalavanna.[445]

2194   And the supreme woman,
        Phintumadi, the beautiful,
        Was the chief wife,
        The lovely Yasodhara.

2195   And the prince who praised the Bho spirit,
Samuttakote,
Was the Buddha, the Great Victor,
Powerful and virtuous.

2196   Bowing, take this ancient record,
Proceed and preach;
It's in the *Pannyatsachadok*[446]
Finished as the master taught it.

The History of the Composition

2197   To compose this verse, to speak in order,[447]   chabang
To compose and explain
Intricately the teaching,

2198   I offer this, I Krom Nuchit Chinorot,
Disciple of the Buddha,
The true line.

2199   Living at Wat Chetuphanaram,
I seek to be among the greatest in Siam,
The land of Ayutthaya.

2200   Then the patriarch Chinnabut
Saw the chan verse
Samuttakote was long incomplete.

2201   Left unfinished, this composition,
For ten kingdoms
And kings ruling the earth.

2202   Many years had passed and not one
Learned man
Had added to the composition.

2203   Krom Kraysorn Wichit, my younger brother,
And Phra Sombat Baan
Invited me to complete it.

2204   So I began to write but failed to finish
When the two died,
The plans then left incomplete.

2205   Disheartened, ability lost
        Through sorrow,
        I stopped, ceased trying.

2206   I stopped composing for a long time,
        Disillusioned with thinking and writing,
        I remained so for two rainy seasons.

2207   And then Krom Wongsasanit, my grandson,
        Invited me, wished me
        Success in the following compositon.

2208   Repeatedly, I tried the story,
        But stumbled, failed, doubted,
        Could not tell the tale without skill and fluency.

2209   Then with determination I started,
        Ashamed it was unfinished,
        Poets have not disappeared from Siam.

2210   I thought, wrote with perseverance,
        Added to the preceding,
        Followed my knowledge still like a child.

2211   I did not dare to compete with the others,
        To decry the old ones
        In their beauty. This I could not do.

2212   The first part Maharat interpreted,[448]
        But left unfinished
        Till Naray the Great continued.

2213   Two mouths made famous the story;
        Now three voices
        With my adding to that before.

2214   When finished this story
        Will praise the land
        And praise the king.

2215   A composition for the king,
        The highest in the capital
        Of Ayutthaya, the everlasting.

225

2216   May his life last in the world
With water, land, sky,
The shining sun and moon until the end.

2217   The chan composition created
Melodious, the greatest,
Completed the perfect collection.

Completion of the Composition

2218   We've reached the cunlasakarat,[449]   khlong 4
One thousand rainy seasons
And 211 others, it's said,
The year of the cock, the twelfth month,
Sunday, the fifth day of the waxing moon.

2219   The composition finished, the tale done,
Samuttakote continued, the story long unfinished,
An exemplary tale, a noble reason
To show the words of the Buddha, explaining the Law.

2220   May I attain for myself, in the future,
The status of great disciple, in every place,
My merit-making finished, my plan complete,
May I be among the most intelligent of poets.

2221   It's finished, the story of the Great Being,
An ancient story, that of the Buddha long before,
A legend of Buddha, before enlightenment,
Long ago, many kalpas long past.[450]

NOTES

1. Classical Thai poetry traditionally opens with an invocation (*kham namatsakan*) that praises the Buddha and deities incorporated into the Buddhist pantheon. Throughout the invocation and the poem, references to the Buddha frequently take the form of well-known epithets, in this case *satsada* (Glorious Teacher).

2. 'Ascetic fires' is used to translate the Sanskrit *tyagi* (one who has resigned, as an ascetic who abandons worldly objects). The sense of the line is that the Buddha first tried asceticism and then found it was not the way. Hence, he is beyond those attempts.

3. The *nagas* play an important role in Thai mythology, religion, and literature. Snake-like, these demi-gods live under the rivers and seas, where they guard vast wealth and treasures. Although they can be frightening and threatening, they are favorable toward Buddhism and its followers.

   The giants, *asura*, are demi-gods and enemies of the gods.

4. The Buddha is depicted as having circular decorations similar to the lotus on the bottoms of his feet. Legend holds that the lotus grew up to support the Buddha's feet.

5. Brahma is represented here as a deity who has yet to attain Enlightenment. The expression *baw don* is used to describe him. Typically, the Cambodian *don* means 'to reach a destination'. It can also mean 'to awaken or kindle as a correct sense of right and wrong' (McFarland, 319). With *baw*, a negative marker, the line suggests that Brahma has yet to be awakened or inspired by the Dhamma.

6. The Thai gesture of paying homage involves placing the hands palm to palm with the fingers touching and raising them above the head while bowing.

7. An epithet for Brahma, *thada*, meaning 'a creator or one who arranges and orders', appears here. Another for Siva, *sangkon*, is used and means 'the dispenser of happiness and welfare'. The text has misspelled the term.

8. Vishnu, the sustainer, is also praised. Invocations frequently include the Hindu triad of gods: Brahma, Siva, and Vishnu.

9. Ramathibodi is used as a general term to describe the king as all mighty and powerful. In invocations, kings are also praised.

10. Praises of kings normally describe their power and glory as extending through the three worlds of the Buddhist cosmology: heaven, earth, and hell.

11. Like the Buddha, the king is described as having lotus-like feet. Such a reference implies a Buddhist orientation toward the institution of the monarchy. Specifically, a Buddhist king should conduct his reign in accordance with the Dhamma and make manifest as much of the Dhamma as possible. In such a role, the king is the Dhammaraja (see Reynolds 1972). The description of the Buddhist king continues into the following stanza.

12. At this point, the poet describes the king's wish that leads to the present composition. That is, the king orders the retelling of the former life of the Buddha when he was Prince Samuttakote. Such an order would be entirely appropriate for a Dhammaraja to make. Tradition holds that the king is King Naray (1656-88), well-known as a patron of literature and the arts.

13. The composition will be a poem, poetry being the traditional form of literature.

14. The composition will be used as the text for a shadow puppet performance. While the shadow puppet theater is known to have existed during the Ayutthaya period (1351-1767), no extant evidence for this particular story remains. There is evidence, however, for performances of the *Ramakian*, which are still held today.

15. At this point, a plot summary of the entire composition begins and continues for the next forty-seven stanzas. Each salient section of the summary begins with the term *pang*, 'and then, at the time,' a structural device used to organize the text. Plot summaries of this nature frequently occur throughout classical poetry.

16. New items appearing in the summary will be explained as they occur in the story proper. For Phromburi, see notes 31 and 40.

17. See notes 98 and 202.

18. See note 41.

19. See note 31.

20. See note 231.

21. See note 55.

22. See note 209.

23. See note 55.

24. See note 38.

25. See note 418.

26. See note 11.

27. See note 433.

28. At this point, the poet recites the traditional invocation to the gods and former teachers, the *wai khru*, for the success of the shadow puppet performance.

29. Each of the cardinal directions has a guardian god: East—Indra; Southeast—Agni; South—Yama; Southwest—Nayrarit; West—Varuna; Northwest—Phayut (Varuna); North—Vaisravana; Northeast—Isana. Other gods may be associated with the directions. See note 207.

30. The poet implores the gods to enable him to create a magnificent performance.

31. The poet first sets the stage, as it were, by describing the setting and the characters from the first of the principal cities in the story, Romyaburi. These lengthy descriptive passages represent a hallmark of classical Thai poetry, each with its own internal organization (see Hudak 1988). This description and the one of Phromburi, the second major city, are spatially organized, the description beginning outside the city walls and moving to the center.

32. The seven annular walls of mountains with the intervening rings of oceans follow the traditional Hindu cosmography in which the heavens are surrounded by seven rings of mountains alternating with seven rings of oceans.

33. The rings of water are described as clean and pure, similar to the seven sacred rivers: Ganges, Jumma, Sarsuti, Satlej, Parushni, Marud-vriddha, and Arjikiya. The Parushni and Marud-vriddha are often identified as the Irrawaddy. In the *Ramayana*, the seven rivers are the streams into which the Ganges divides after falling from Siva's brow: Nalini, Hladini, Pavani, Chakshu, Sita, Sindhu, and the Ganges proper.

34. Generally, seven types of lotus are mentioned in literary compositions. The golden and white lotuses are the only two named here. See notes 347-49.

35. The level of lions probably refers to an architectural feature or level above which appear eaves and roofs. From a distance, the eaves and roofs form a continuous line suggestive of a line of mountain peaks. Typically, these edges are in the form of stylized *nagas*.

36. The porticos refer to large extensions or porches projecting from the main part of the palace. These porticos are characteristic of Thai temple and palace architecture.

37. Gardens and forests are important elements in classical Thai poetry. They function as sites for furthering the plot and as places for reflecting the characters' emotions.

38. The *kinnarees* are half-human and half-bird creatures that inhabit the celestial Himawan forest. They frequently appear as decorative figures in murals and sculpture groups.

39. The nine gems include the diamond, ruby, emerald, topaz, garnet, sapphire, moonstone or pearl, hyacinth or zircon, and cat's-eye (McFarland 1944, 440). Other sources list them as the pearl, ruby, topaz, diamond, emerald, lapis lazuli, coral, sapphire, and the unidentified go-met (Dowson 1972, 221). Reputed to have magical powers, each symbolizes one of the planets.

40. The description shifts to the second major setting, Phromburi, and its inhabitants. See note 31.

41. Indra, the King of Gods, resides in the Swarga heaven in the capital city Amaravati, renowned for its greatness and splendor. Legend places it near or on Mount Meru.

42. Like Romyaburi, Phromburi is surrounded by annular mountains and oceans. The comparison is to the *cakraphan*, the mythical range of mountains that encircle the earth.

43. Phaychayon—Indra's palace. Its Sanskrit name is Vaijayanta.

44. Recurring in Thai poetry, this simile compares the face to a full moon. Borrowed from Indic poetics, the comparison is frequently elaborated by equating attendants with stars surrounding the moon. See note 47.

45. The noble son is Samuttakote, who perfected his skill with the bow and arrow. This description prepares the audience for the bow and arrow competition in which the prince excels.

46. Unlike the *jataka* upon which it is based, the poem provides Samuttakote with a wife.

47. Here, the Indic simile comparing the face to a full moon is expanded to include the stars. See note 44.

48. The stanza suggests that the nobles and the prince are followers of the Dhamma and protectors of the righteous.

49. The invocation and descriptions completed, the poet shifts to an elaboration of the entertainments that precede a shadow puppet performance. Traditionally, performances begin with a variety of different short presentations or acts, known as *boek rong*. These acts may be actual short shadow puppet performances or live acts, which serve to attract the attention of the crowd and to prepare them for the main performance. Most critics regard those listed in the poem as shadow puppet performances and not necessarily live acts (see Pluang 1964, 83). However, the entertainments enumerated are typical of seventeenth-century Thailand and could very well be descriptions of intended actual occurrences. For an enlightening and in-depth discussion of seventeenth-century entertainments, see Reid (1988) 173-235.

50. Tradition maintains that King Naray ordered the composition for the shadow puppet performance.

51. Naray's capital was at Ayutthaya.

231

52. In the following stanzas, the poet describes the entertainments that will precede the shadow puppet performance.

53. See note 73.

54. The poet returns to a plot summary of the performance.

55. Indic cosmography, adopted and adapted by the Thai, places the abode of the gods in the region of the Himalaya mountains. The area is reputed to be filled with forests, gardens, and pleasure parks. At the center stands Mount Meru surrounded by seven rings of mountains alternating with seven rings of water. At the outer ring of mountains in each of the four directions lies a continent. To the south is Chomputhawip, the continent of human beings. It is called this because its shape resembles the shape of the jambu (chompu) leaf. In *Thai Buddhist Cosmology* (Reynolds and Reynolds 1982), this continent is referred to as the Jambu continent; the other three continents include: the Pubbavideha continent to the east; the Uttarakuru continent to the north; and the Aparagoyana continent to the west (Reynolds and Reynolds 1982, 124-35). The term Himaphan refers to the region in general. Other terms in use include Himawan, Himawat, and Himawet.

56. Emphasis is placed on the fact that the story is traditional and highly esteemed, not light and popular. Because of its high regard, the story carries an important message for the audience.

57. The first entertainment is a fight between two bald-headed men. Thai legend states that in one of their former lives, bald-headed men held cock fights. Because the cocks lost their feathers in these fights, the men lost their hair when they were reborn.

58. The term 'farmers' has been used to translate the Thai term chaw lum. Ambiguous, the term may refer to a city in the south.

59. Literally, Hua Khaeng means 'hard head': *hua* 'head' and *khaeng* 'hard'. Ay is a derogatory title often used before men's names; it is also a means of insult.

60. Literally, Hua Tan means 'heavy head': *hua* 'head' *tan* 'ton'. Hua Tan is a field farmer, *chaw ray*.

61. Here the poet plays with images suggesting that the bald heads look like melons.

62. Hua Khaeng, a *chaw lum* 'lowland farmer' in this translation, meets defeat. See note 58.

63. The second entertainment: sword fighting between a Lao and a Thai.

64. The exact location of this city or country, Phayao, remains in question. The name Krayhan suggests one who is bold and brave, *kray* 'powerful, superior'; *han* 'brave'.

65. Katay does not appear to have any secondary meaning.

66. The third entertainment: two Javanese fighting with spears.

67. The fourth entertainment: two rhinoceroses fighting. The second line of the stanza suggests that the rhinoceros was in some way associated with the God of Fire (Phra Phloeng). In Indic myths, however, the ram always appears with Agni, the God of Fire.

68. The Thai name Tuu Torn suggests that the animal has been castrated, *torn* means 'castrasted'.

69. 'Lasso' has been used to translate the Thai term *phraw*, which in central Thai means 'coconut'. However, in the northeastern dialect, the word can mean 'a kind of creeper' which may be used as a lasso or lariat.

70. The fifth entertainment: oxcart competition.

71. Literally, Luenam means 'a name spread around': *lue* 'rumor', *nam* 'name'.

72. In the name Kachaengboeng, *boeng* suggests the attitude assumed by surprised or angered cattle.

73. The sixth entertainment: crocodile combat. The name Nakleng means 'rascal'. Thaw Phanwang is the name of the fabled crocodile in the legend of Kraythong.

74. The dark-blue (*khram*) water refers to the water and dye used for the color of indigo. In the following stanza, the allusion is to water darkened by the insect *khrang* (*Coccus* or *Carteria lacca*), which produces the lac from which shellac is made. These insects suck sap from various barks and then excrete it. The excretion solidifies and forms a coating around their bodies. This is lac. In June and December, the tree branches with these insects are crushed with the

233

lac cleaned and melted into varnish, shellac, etc. (McFarland 1944, 179).

75. The seventh entertainment: boat races. Aśvina is the Sanskrit name for a month in the rainy season.

76. To assist in timing and to add a regal aura, music accompanied the races.

77. Reid 1988 (191) points out the need for the king's barge to have a victory, symbolic or otherwise.

78. It is at this point that the story of Samuttakote actually begins with the depiction of the forest and the forester's search for the elephants that Samuttakote will hunt.

79. *kliang*—a species of grass

80. The forest represents a place for entertainment, contentment, and pleasure-filled activities. It also holds terrors as the prince points out in the following conversation with his wife. See note 37.

81. Phintutat's description suggests that he too is a Dhammaraja. See note 11.

82. Flower-like means lotus-like.

83. Surasuda maintains it is the wife's duty to follow her husband wherever he may go. The five duties of the wife are (1) do all things necessary to satisfy the husband; (2) care for the husband; (3) follow tradition in all actions; (4) respect, honor, and obey the husband; and (5) praise the goodness of the husband.

84. The following stylized conversation between Samuttakote and Surasuda represents another common feature of classical Thai poetry. In this case, it is an interchange in which each addresses the other with stylized similes: a face like a full moon and a face like a lotus.

85. The Thai term *sangsong* is used to describe the elephants. While the exact meaning cannot be found, context suggests it means 'a group, herd'.

86. In Thailand, as in other Southeast Asian countries, the elephant held the greatest importance among the animals. Thai kings organized elaborate hunts for elephants with auspicious characteristics,

particularly albino elephants. In time, elephant hunting became a royal duty. King Naray, himself, is reputed to have been a great elephant hunter.

87. The four units of the ancient army were the horses, the chariots, the elephants, and the foot soldiers. The description of the army's preparation represents another feature of classical Thai poetry.

88. The Sindhu were a famed breed of horses from the Indus valley region.

89. A traditional Indic simile equates bustling groups of people to swarms of bees.

90. Besides the army, the prince's retinue includes those individuals necessary for the elephant hunt. The seer (*mawsit*) knows the required chants and rituals for appeasing the guardian spirits of the forest and the hunt. More commonly, he is referred to as *maw thaw*.

91. Pikemen seems to be the most appropriate meaning for the unidentified Thai term *phonsaw*.

92. Throughout the poem, the prince is compared to Indra, the King of Gods, comparisons that suggest not only his noble appearance but also his divine origin. The thirty-three deities refer to the number of deities in Indra's retinue.

93. The departure of the prince includes the usual musical accompaniment of stringed instruments, conches, bells, and drums.

94. The eight traditional weapons are the lance or spear, the sword, the trident, the discus, the sword with shield, the bow, the halbred, and the gun or cannon.

95. The jeweled mountain is probably Mount Meru, the mountain at the center of the world. See note 55.

96. Suriya, the god of the sun, has golden hair and arms and rides a chariot drawn by seven horses. In some representations, the chariot has one horse with seven heads. Throughout the poem, a number of different epithets refer to the sun, with Suriya being the most common. Using the Indic sun god's name helps to infuse the poem with a divine and magical aspect.

97. A traditional simile that equates the army and its movements to waves, streams, rivers, oceans, or seas.

98. The seer seeks a particular budding tree in which the forest spirit resides. (The tree identified is the Bho tree, the tree under which the Buddha attained enlightenment.) There, he requests permission to enter the forest. He tells the spirit the size of the hunting party and asks for protection. Not a simple affair, an elephant hunt requires a large number of rites and rituals to guarantee its success. See Indramontri (1930), Sodesiri (1975), and Rajadhon (1986).

99. As part of the ceremony, the spirit is offered adornments, chants, and scents in an area designated as sacred by flags and umbrellas.

100. After opening the forest, a second ceremony of propitiation is required. At the proper tree, the spirit is beseeched to allow the capture and training of the elephants at that spot.

101. Various texts list different offerings used in the rite. See Indramontri (1930), Sodesiri (1975), and Rajadhon (1986).

102. A sacred area is established with a representation of the protecting spirit of the tree. In some cases, this figure carries a large sacrificial knife.

103. Phra Uma or Parvati is the consort of Phra Isuan or Siva. Phra is an honorific.

104. The hawk's eyes (ta lew) are boundary markers made from plaited bamboo about six inches in diameter usually with six points (Davis 1984, 163). When set up, they designate a sacred area. Also see Rajadhon (1986).

105. The kraal method of capturing elephants is being used. With this method, elephants are driven into an enclosed space, lassoed, and then staked. Once tamed, they are then led back to the village.

106. The Thai classification and organization of elephants is based on two ancient Indic treatises: (1) *tamra kotchalak* which describes the physical characteristics of elephants that determine their auspiciousness and suitability for capture; and (2) *tamra khotchakam* which describes the way to train wild elephants, the way to ride elephants, and the chants and rituals necessary to capture them. Lists and descriptions of both the auspicious and inauspicious elephants appear in the *tamra kotchalak*. For a complete discussion of elephant classification, see Visuddhibedya 1979. See note 116.

107. The following elephants with their most salient characteristics are considered inauspicious and unsuitable for capture. See note 116.

Thuy—decayed tusks, short tail, small thin body; Tham—drooping stomach, slack ears, decayed tusks, sagging skin; Phamla—unsuitable for riding; Phahon—deep neck ridges, holds grass in the mouth; Salingkhankhon—(?); Chonkanloon—coarse right tusk, the rear higher than the head; upturned eyes; Ralomsangkay—bumpy head with no hair line.

108. Plubaek—tusks with split ends, shaky walk, deformed frame; Bangkin —bent tusks, one abnormal side, crooked tail, drooping ears; Thompluk—large cracked tusks, short crooked body; Thipasay —drooping back, bent knees; Kampotkamboon—spotted white body, drips saliva, feces drop over the hind legs; Yongyat—feet and trunk hit the body, high back, shifting eyes (?).

109. Prapluk—tapered tusks, crooked tail; Sukrip—large throat, large chin, crooked tail, causes a bumpy ride; Kattorani—high back legs, low front legs, long tail, trunk close to the tusks, curved nails; Bangbat—two crooked, upturned tusks, fails to walk straight; Nakphan—dull tusks, short trunk, low body, small eyes, arched back; Phinay—uneven tusks, uneven ears.

110. Landat—long hanging tongue, walks with mouth open; Yurayak —short and low body, large chin, short face, short tusks; Banlay—small testicles (?); Bidaw—projecting breasts, slack trunk; Kanawpluk—tusks with large base and small tip, sagging stomach, long trunk.

111. Rattan—red tusks, teeth, and nails; Thorahun—lame, sagging stomach, black throat, crooked bones; Tradokkanthuy—swollen face, crooked tail that drags; Chipsing—(?); Swamipote—flat face, uneven eyes.

112. Chonchalay—crooked back, low head, drips saliva, upturned eyes, drips milk, short tail; Kanaekkumkot—large and sagging ears, upturned eyes.

113. Tradungnak—high front and behind, weak back; Nakhornkat—tusks smaller than trunk, front and behind same size, trunk drapes around body when eating; Khaduansuk—bears young in the tenth year.

114. The list of unsuitable elephants corresponds to lists in various *kotchalak* treatises. Thirty-four types are listed, although the stanza reads thirty-three. The editors of the National Library edition of the poem (page 267) do not find Chipsing listed in the treatises and suggest that it may be the same as Tradokkanthuy.

237

115. Ayraphot or Airavata is Lord Indra's war elephant. In Thailand, it is depicted with thirty-three heads (equal to the thirty-three heavenly states). Indian mythology usually represents the elephant with one or three heads.

116. Following Hindu mythology, the ancient Thais divided all elephants into lineages. The highest and most important is the lineage of Brahma. The eight elephants in this group were transformed from the eight petals and twenty-four motes of pollen (or stamens in some texts) of the golden lotus that grew from Narayana's navel. These parts of the lotus Narayana gave to Siva who in turn gave them to Brahma. Owners of elephants from this lineage attain longevity and wisdom.

The lineage of Siva resulted from eight motes of pollen kept by Siva. Royal attributes and virtues characterize this group. Owners of these elephants are guaranteed wealth and power.

The lineage of Vishnu also resulted from eight motes of pollen from the original golden lotus. These elephants are characterized by love and mercy in the same degree as possessed by Vishnu. Owners are guaranteed victory over and freedom from want.

The last lineage, the lineage of Agni, resulted from the remaining 133 motes of pollen. These elephants were granted to Agni because he was in attendance upon Brahma, Siva, and Vishnu when the golden lotus was presented to Siva by Narayana. The elephants of this lineage have both good and bad characteristics.

The elephants descended from these four lineages are further sudivided according to attributes, form, and color.

In terms of the Hindu caste system, these lineages have the following equivalents: lineage of Brahma—Brahmins; lineage of Vishnu —Vaisayas; and lineage of Agni—Sudras. For more information, see Indramontri (1930).

This stanza and the preceding one suggest that these elephants are all auspicious, probably from the lineage of Brahma. In contrast, the thirty-four inauspicious ones listed earlier are probably descendents of the lineage of Agni. See notes 107-13.

117. Ancient Thai chariots had a long tapering end that terminated in a *naga*.

118. Besides those skilled in the elephant hunt, the prince's retinue includes Brahmins for conducting the rites and rituals necessary to an elephant hunt.

119. One of the most important rituals is the worship of fire during which Lord Agni is beseeched for blessings and success in capturing elephants. Agni functions as the mediator between men and the gods.

120. Another expert is the *hatsajan*, the sage skilled in training the elephants.

121. 'offered three leaves'—probably a reference to three special leaves (samit) used in ceremonies, especially those involving the king. These leaves include leaves of the mango, leaves of the flame of the forest, *Butea frondosa* (*Leguminosae*), and the leaves of the *takob*, *Flacourtia cataphracta* (*Flacourtiaceae*).

122. 'three teachers'—probably a reference to Brahma, Vishnu, and Siva.

123. The lasso used to catch the elephant is inhabited by a powerful spirit which must be propitiated separately.

124. Another ceremony is performed before the gates of the kraal.

125. A lasso on the end of a pole is used to snare the hind leg of the elephant.

126. With the elephant lassoed, the pole is dropped. Thereupon ensues a struggle to drag and secure the elephant to a tree.

127. The struggle to secure the elephant begins. A tame elephant is used to subdue the captured one.

128. The battle nearly finished, the elephant is staked and subdued.

129. Here, the poet does not differentiate among the different lineages. See note 116.

130. Kaylat—a mythological mountain made of silver and located in the Himalayas. It is said to be the home of Siva and Kuvera.

131. Chomlop belongs to the lineage of Vishnu. It is noted for its floppy ears.

132. Kobut belongs to the lineage of Vishnu: its skin is the same golden hue as a cow's; its tail is similar to a cow's; and its tusks are small.

Sihachongkat belongs to the lineage of Siva; its two hind legs are brown like a lion's.

133. The elephants listed in notes 133-135 belong to the lineage of Brahma. Ayraphot—skin color like the clouds, lotus-like feet, neat nails, high head, great strength, sparkling eyes, large tusks, back shaped like a bow.

Buntharuek—lotus white body, long golden tusks, copper colored nails, fragrant body.

Komut—red lotus colored body, large body, soft ears, tusks like the crescent moon, trumpets like a horn.

134. Anchan—purplish body, large tusks, short neck, trumpets like the wind blowing through bamboo.

Phamani—grey body, large tusks, trumpets like a clarion.

Butsapatan—colored like fresh betel, soft skin, freckled face, elegant body, trumpets like the thunder.

Sarawapom—(?).

135. Supradit—dusk colored body, white tusks, soft skin, long whiskers, trumpets with a rumbling sound.

136. With the hunt completed, the seer prepares another ceremony to leave the forest and to release the guardian spirits from their obligation to protect the hunting party. Although not stated, the seer beseeches the spirits to continue to protect the forest and its inhabitants.

137. Descriptive passages in classical Thai poetry appear in a variety of forms. In some cases, as in the descriptions of the cities Romyaburi and Phromburi, there is a tightly organized spatial organization, the description moving from outside the city walls to the inner palace of the city. Other passages are less consciously organized as in the following description of the forest and its animals.

138. The jamri is the bushy tailed yak. Its tail is used as a chowry and streamers on lances and halbreds. It is one of the royal insignia.

139. *khaem*—a species of tall grass sometimes used as fodder, *Sorghum halapense (Gramineae)*.

140. The *rabam* is a general term for a group style dance.

141. Frequently, the highlighted aspect of a description is meant to arouse specific emotions and feelings. In this forest description, the poet has emphasized the animals with their respective mates, which remind the prince of his wife and generate a longing and a sense of loneliness.

142. Within descriptive passages appear various kinds of catalogues. The simplest type involves the listing of flowers, trees, or the like in no particular order, although sound play helps to order the terms. A slightly more sophisticated list, as in this example, lists the terms in rhyming or alliterative sequences. No special patterns of rhyme or alliteration dominate the following catalogue. Since sound aesthetics are an important part of all catalogues, the listed items have been left in their Thai forms in this translation.

143. Du—a large, beautiful timber tree, *Pterocarpus macrocarpus (Leguminosae)*; pru—a scented hardwood used for medicinal purposes, *Alangium salviifolium*; prayong—a flowering tree, *Aglaia odorata*; yom (mayom)—the star gooseberry, used in purification rituals, *Phyllanthus distichus-euphobiaceae*; sarapi—sweet scented flowers, *Ochrocarpus siamensis*; phikun—small, star shaped, sweet smelling flowers, *Mimusops elengi (Sapotaceae)*; kanjanamuang —golden mangoes; monthan—a large leafed tree with yellow flowers believed to grow in heaven; kamyan—a tree yielding fragrant gum resin, *Styrax benzoides*.

144. Jambok—*Buchanania fastigiata, Amygdalicera stipulata*, or *Irvingia harmandii*; kannika—a tree with sweet-smelling white flowers, *Nyctanthes arbor-tristis*; kaew—a tree with fragrant white flowers, *Murraya paniculata*.

145. Karakate—the screwpine, *Pandanus furcatus (Pandanaceae)*; ket —palu, hardwood timber, *Mimusops hexandra*; kaew—see note 144; mali—jasmine, *Jasminum sambac (Oleaceae)*; maludi (maluli ?)—a type of tree; bunnak—Indian rose chestnut, *Mesua ferra (Ternstromiaceae)*; maliwan—jasmine; wannawan—hibiscus (?), *Hibiscus rosa-sinensis*.

146. As in the description of the animals, the poet has highlighted characteristics of the plants and anthropomorphized them.

147. Nangyaem—a shrub with fragrant flowers, literally the name means 'a woman slightly open', *nang* 'woman' and *yaem* 'slightly open', and therefore frequently appears as an image in erotic passages, *Cleredendron fragans*; khatueng—a tree with reddish brown bark, *Calophyllum inophyllum* (*Guttiferae*); lamduan—a tree with three-petaled strongly-scented flowers used as offerings to Buddhist monks, *Sphaerocoryne clavipes* (*Annonaceae*); jik—a tree or shrub with leaves used medicinally, *Barringtonia spicata* (*Myrtaceae*); jaeng—a type of tree, *Niebuhria decandra* (*Capparidaceae*); maeng (maenglak ?)— sweet basil, *Ocimum basilicum* (*Labiatae*); mongkhut—the mangosteen, *Garcinia mangostana*; khuy—a kind of creeper used as a red dye; khu—a small bush, *Pluchea indica* (*Compositae*); khlay—a type of tree.

148. Monnak (nakbut ?)—a moderate-sized tree with large white flowers, *Mesua ferra* (*Guttiferae*).

149. Elaborate interior monologues debating and analyzing problems represent another common literary device in classical poetry.

150. With royal characters, classical poetry highlights a variety of their activities, in this case, the royal bath, although no elaborate description follows.

151. The most sophisticated of the catalogues intermixes sound aesthetics, word play, and emotions. The following catalogue of birds and fish is just such a one, extending and expanding the emotion of longing and loneliness begun in the earlier descriptive passage of the forest animals.

152. Kungok—a peacock; kungan—a goose, Cygnus; kungon—white ibis, *Ibis milanocephala*; jip (krajip)—warblers or wrens; jap (krajap) weaver bird, *Ploceus Baya*. The word *jip* can also mean 'swallow a little at a time', and *jap* 'to rob or steal'. Hence, the line can also mean 'birds steal and then hide'.

153. Klingklong—black necked mynah, *Gracupica nigricollis*; jaw (krajaw) —a type of heron; the word *jaw* can also mean 'to sit quietly'. The line can therefore also be read as 'birds sit quietly', or 'the jaw bird sits quietly'. Krasa—common heron, *Ardea cinera*.

154. Rangnan—a species of bird; nangnuan—sea gull, sea terns, *Sterna sp.*; separated into two words, *nangnuan* means 'lady (*nang*) with creamy (*nuan*) skin'. Thus the sea gull is described as a 'lady with creamy white skin'.

242

155. Kanam—cormorant, *Phalocrocorax sp.*; this bird is symbolic of gluttony, but that interpretation is irrelevant to this passage. Petnam —whistling teal, *Dendrocygna javanica*. The repeated use of the word *nam* 'water' in the bird's name and in the description of their actions in the water helps to produce a rhyming effect in the Thai.

156. Ngua—*Anhinga melanogaster* (*Phalacrocoracidae*); khaw—Malay spotted dove, *Turtur tigrinus*; ten—kingfisher, *Alcedinidae*; kranay—a small bird similar to the woodpecker.

157. Huakhwan—scaly belly green woodpecker, *Gecinus vittatus eisenhoferi*. Huakhwan can also mean 'head (*hua*) of the axe (*khwan*)'.

158. Plaw—turtle dove, *Aenopopelia tranquebarica humilis*; sarika—mynah, *Acridotheres tristis*.

159. Prik—watercock, *Gallicrex cinereus*; iang—Thai mynah, *Acridotheres siamensis*; aen—ashy swallow, *Artamus fuscus*. The word *aen* can also mean 'to bend'.

160. Sangsaew—a common bird with black plumage, the king crow, *Buchanga atra*.

161. Phay—a species of bird; lang (kalang)—Siamese white—crested laughing thrush, *Garrnlax diardi*; pling—an unidentified species of bird.

162. Bawkhun—a species of bird; kangkhen—a species of magpie, *Copsychus saularis*. The first line of the stanza can also be translated as 'the young nobleman (*bawkhun*) held out a shield (*kangkhen*)'. Khwaek—night heron, *Nycticorax nycticoras*; ilum—watercock, *Gallicrex cinera*; khum—small quail.

163. Say—an unidentified species of bird.

164. Huahang—an unidentified species of bird; yung—Burmese peafowl, *Pavo muticus*.

165. Saek—collared pygmy owlet, *Glaucidium brodiei*; khwaek—see note 162; khaw—collared pygmy owlet, *Glaucidium brodiei*.

166. Khapkhae—cotton teal goose, *Nettapus coromandelianus*.

167. Yang—Indian pond heron, *Ardeola grayi*; plaw—see note 158.

168. Kwak—Chinese white-breasted water rail, *Amaurornis phoenicurus chinensis*. *Kwak* can also mean 'shake, wave' or represent the sound the bird makes.

169. Pharahit—an unidentified species of bird; jak (wak)—a mythological bird said to wail at night when separated from its mate; the name may also be translated as 'separated from'.

170. Topyung—*Caprimulgidae*; the name can also mean 'to slap (*top*) mosquitoes (*yung*)'; thungthong—an unidentified species of bird.

171. Nokkajok (jok)—common sparrow, *Passer sp.*; khonhooy—pelican ibis, *Tantalus leucocephalus*.

172. Phuradok—an unidentified species of bird; kokma—a species of bird; kot phloeng—black-necked stork, *Xsnorhynchus asiaticus*.

173. Changlek—Indian crimson-breasted barbet, *Xantholaema haemacephala indica*; krawan—an unidentified species of bird; krawaen—black racket-tailed magpie, *Crypsirhina varians*. The changlek bird makes sounds similar to its name, 'lek, lek'. The bird's name also means 'blacksmith', a person that makes similar sounds striking iron.

174. Lang—see note 161; khamin—babbler, *Mixornis rubicapella minor*.

175. The sight of the birds in loving pairs and their respective songs cause the prince to remember his beloved.

176. The cuckoo could also be translated as the karawik, a bird found in fairyland and whose songs have the power to enchant.

177. Kraho—giant carp, *Catlocarpio siamensis*; krahae—edible water fish, *Puntius schwanefield*; wua—perhaps the sea cow, *Halicore sp.*.

178. Krim—small fish similar to the fighting fish, *Ctenops vittatus*; kray—feather back, *Notopterus chitala*; saway—*Pangasius fowleri* (*Pangasiidae*).

179. Khangbuean—freshwater catfish, *Belodontichthys dinema* (*Siluridae*); khaw—catfish, *Wallago attu*; salit—*Trichopodus pectoralis* (*Anabantidae*); pho—freshwater fish, *Drepane punctatus, Tor stracheyi*; phruan—freshwater fish, *Labeo pruol*.

180. Khemakroy—a fish with a black back; namlang—*Amblyshynchichthys truncatus* (*Cyprinidae*); hualuang—an unidentified species of fish.

The last line could also read 'looked for the head of the village (*hualuang*)'.

181. Phram—a species of fish; salumphon—a fleshy fish; pluang—a carp, *Labeobarbus soro* (*Cyprinidae*); phrom—Osteocheilus melanopleura (Cyprinidae); pliaplen—an unidentified species of fish.

182. Thong—*Parasilurus*; kanthong—spear fish, *Istiophorus sp.* (*Istiophoridae*); henglen—an unidentified species of fish; kabork (krabork)—sea mullet, *Mugil tade*; kaben—ray or skate, *Raia*; khemakroy—see note 180; kray—freshwater fish, *Notopterus chitala* (*Notopteridae*).

183. Thepo—*Pangasius larnaudil* (*Pangasiidae*); chado—serpent-headed fish, *Ophicephalus micropeltes* (*Ophicephalidae*); kaemcham —freshwater fish with bright red cheeks, *Puntius orphoides* (*Cyprinidae*); maw—*Anabas testudineus* (*Anabantidae*). The second line can be read as 'cheeks (*kaem*) kissed/bruised (*cham*) by a boy (*chay*)'. The third line can be read as 'let the doctor (*maw*) see (*du*)' or 'give to the fortune teller (*mawdu*)'.

184. Maew—*Thryssa, Setipinna, Lycothrissa crocodilus*; linma—*Cynoglossus borneensis*; mu—*Acanthopsis choirorhynchus* (*Cobitidae*); kotchara— an unidentified species of fish; rahu—*Mobula Mobulidae*; janthamet—butter fish, *Stromateus*; thoramang—an unidentified species of fish. The second and third line also have the meaning 'the mythological monster (*rahu*) devoured the moon (*janthamet*)'. This is an allusion to the myth that a mythological monster devours the moon during a lunar eclipse.

185. Wan—a whale; tatum—small fish, *Puntius bulu* (*Cyprinidae*); chon —loach, *Lepidocephalus hasselti*. The name tatum can also mean 'protruding eyes'.

186. Kathing—spring eel, *Mastacembelus armatus*; aw—*Luciosoma harmandi* (*Cyprimidae*).

187. Ma—a seahorse (?); khlang—an unidentified species of fish.

188. Ka—a freshwater fish, *Morulius chrysophekadion*; hera—a fabulous marine creature; soy—*Dangila leptocheila* (*Cyprinidae*); saway—see note 178.

189. Fakphra—a bean, sword, a river fish, *Chelaoxygastroides* (*Cyprinidae*); sa—an unidentified species of fish; suea—*Toxotex*

jaculator; sup—freshwater fish, *Hampala macrolepidota*; khuea—goby fish, *Apocryptes serperaster*.

190. Rakkluay—bananas, *Gyrinocheilus koznokovi* (*Cyprinidae*); hangkiw —species of saltwater fish, *Caranx mate* (*Carangidae*); kuraw —thread-thin fish, *Eleutheronema tetradactylum*; kanaek—an unidentified species of fish; kot—catfish, *Mystus micracanthus*.

191. Mukham—*Boita cobitidae*; siw—small edible fish, *Rasbora retrodorsalis* (*Cyprinidae*).

192. Kradi—freshwater fish, *Trichopodus trichopterus*; kratrap—freshwater fish, *Pristolepis fasciatus* (*Nandidae*).

193. Chorn—serpent-headed fish, *Murrel*; chawat—an unidentified species of fish; chawaeng—an unidentified species of fish; hangkiw—see note 190; thukang—species of saltwater fish.

194. Phuang—*Gymocheilus kaznakovi*; chawaeng—see note 193; taphian —species of carp.

195. Paen—*Leiognathus dussumieri*; paep—*Paralaubuca typus* (*Cyprinidae*).

196. Juat—saltwater fish, *Johnius belengeri* (*Sciaenidae*); lot —*Mastacembelus circumcinctus* (*Mastacembelidae*).

197. Maew—see note 184; morm—an unidentified species of fish; chalamnu—shark, *Scoliodon palasorrah*.

198. Kralumphuk—shad, *Hilsa Alosa toli*; duk—freshwater catfish, *Clarias batracus* (*Clariidae*); daeng—white catfish; khayaeng—catfish; uk —*Hemipimilodus borneensis*; amphan—an unidentified species of fish.

199. Khuea—see note 189.

200. Naray or Narayana, an avatar of Vishnu. The milk sea refers to the ocean from which all life evolves. Vishnu is frequently represented as sleeping upon this ocean.

201. While not elaborated here, the dressing of the king is another royal activity frequently highlighted in classical poetry.

202. Large trees were said to be inhabited by guardian spirits that protected the forest trees and animals. To avoid misfortune, travelers in the forest propitiated those spirits. See notes 98 and 203.

203. The prince asks the guardian spirit for protection. See notes 98 and 202.

204. Ambrosia refers to the water of life produced by the churning of the oceans by the gods and demons. The gods having been defeated by the demons beseeched Vishnu for renewed strength and immortality. He ordered them to churn the ocean to produce the ambrosia (*amarit*). Mount Meru served as the churning stick and the *naga* Vasuki the rope. The demons shared in the work but did not benefit from the ambrosia.

205. The karawik was a melodious bird of fairyland whose song entranced the spirits and deities of the forest. The Indian cuckoo is referred to by this name. See note 176.

206. The poet uses the word *yak* for giant. Although of frightening aspect, these creatures were not totally malevolent. In temple architecture, they often appear as door guardians.

God of Love. In western mythology, this deity is Eros or Cupid. In Hindu mythology, his bow is made from sugarcane and the bowstring from a line of bees. Flowers tip each of the arrows.

Lord of the Discus—Vishnu

207. Trident Bearer—Siva with his consort Uma

208. Kuvera, the God of Wealth, was the guardian deity of the north. He is a white man, although deformed in body. Compare note 29.

209. The Garuda was the King of the Birds with the head, wings, and talons of an eagle, white face, red wings, and golden body. The vehicle of Vishnu, the Garuda, is a national symbol of modern Thailand.

The naga refers to the myth of the churning of the ocean. See note 204.

210. Possessed with magical powers, the supernatural phitthayathorn lived in the Himalayas and served Siva. The *khonthan* were heavenly deities, expert in music and song (the Indic Gandharvas).

211. The apsaras, celestial beings famed for their beauty, dwelled in Indra's heaven.

212. A reference to the composition *Anirut kham chan*, composed by Sri Prat during the reign of King Naray. The plot parallels that of *Samutthakhoot kham chan* with Anirut taken to the beauty Usa by the spirit Phra Phrom.

213. Finials refer to the characteristic architectural decorations for roofs of sacred buildings. A single finial resembles a gracefully curved finger pointing upwards. It is the final piece placed on the roof.

214. The Palace of Suriya is Phintutat's and the Palace of the Moon, his queen's. Phintumadi is evidently in the Palace of Suriya.

215. Based on a specific syllable number and order, the chan poetic meters had their origin in Pali and Sanskrit counterparts and reached their height of popularity during the Ayutthaya period. See Hudak (1990).

216. Mount Khanthamat—a mountain in the Himawan and famed for its fragrant forests (Gandhamadana).

217. In Thai, the first line reads 'he opened the *pathom*' with *pathom* meaning 'lotus, flower'. From this, it is conjectured that the doors or curtains were somehow similar to the lotus, perhaps resembling the petals of the flower.

    prang—a cone-shaped structure built to commemorate an event or spot revered by the Buddhists. Here it refers to the palace, which probably has a *prang* as part of its structure. See note 420.

218. Perhaps the most famous of the classical literary devices are the erotic passages, the *bot atsajan*. At times metaphoric, while at other times explicit, these passages always involve the lovemaking of two royal personages or deities. Structurally, catalogues of beauty based upon Indic metaphors and similes are almost always incorporated into these passages. Organizationally, the description moves from the top of the head, down the body, to the feet. The catalogue is only superficially dealt with here.

219. The night was divided into four watches or divisions of time, each three hours long (*yam*): the first from 6 to 9 P.M..; the second from 9 P.M.. to midnight; the third from midnight to 3 A.M.; and the last from 3 A.M. to 6 A.M.

220. The 'encircling mountain tops' (*yukunthorn*) refers to the closest of the seven concentric rings of mountains that surround Mount Meru.

221. The day-maker—an epithet for Suriya.

222. The great mountain—probably a reference to Mount Meru.

223. Descriptive passages of forests and forest animals are constructed so that they reflect the prince's feelings and emotions. See notes 37 and 80.

224. Formalized laments represent another characteristic device of classical poetry. These passages frequently include catalogues of beauty.

225. Buddhist themes appear in the poem at frequent intervals to remind the audience of the poem's true nature. In this case, the prince reflects upon the consequences of his past actions.

226. The Brahmins were an important component in ancient Thailand, officiating at royal rites and rituals.

227. Phintumadi's beauty is famous throughout the three worlds.

228. With this stanza begins an elaborate catalogue of beauty within a lament.

229. Eight desires—a reference to the physical attributes of a woman, although the poet enumerates more than eight. The number eight does not seem to refer to any specific list, but more likely to a general number.

230. Hook of love—a sharp, pointed object, often the fingernail, with which the God of Love catches people.

231. The term used, *sayomporn*, reflects the Indic custom of making a choice for marriage based upon one's own liking. Here, however, the chosen will be the one successful in the organized contests.

232. Phintumadi has been grinding her teeth and biting her cheeks in anguish. The teeth leave bite marks in the shape of a bow.

233. Siva draped with the naga king and astride his mount, the bull.

234. Vishnu astride his mount Garuda, the King of Birds.

235. Brahma astride his mount, the goose or swan.

236. Indra rides his mount Ayra, the elephant, and carries Vajra, a weapon of diamonds.

237. The God of Wind, Vayu, rides in a gold chariot drawn by red horses.

238. One of the four guardian deities of the world. Each presides over one of the points of the compass. See note 29.

239. Agni, the God of Fire, usually rides a ram. See note 67.

240. The Buddha-like characteristics of Samuttakote are repeatedly emphasized throughout the poem.

241. Matuli—Indra's charioteer.

242. Maker of Light—an epithet for Suriya. Suriya, the God of the Sun, was represented as driving a gold chariot with seven horses. Some representations depict a single horse with seven heads.

243. Opening flowers frequently suggest sexual intercourse in Thai poetry.

244. 'Blossoms' has been used to translate the Thai term *wanwet*, which in contemporary Thai means 'bedpan'. Context suggests the translation 'flower' or 'blossom'.

245. The contest for Phinthumadi does not appear in the jataka.

246. Stringing a bow to prove oneself is a traditional test of a hero. In the *Ramayana*, Rama won Sita in marriage by bending a bow.

247. Lists of warriors and their respective descriptions represent another type of catalogue. These warriors do not appear in the original jataka.

248. Kumphakan—in the *Ramayana*, a monster that slept for six months and remained awake for one day.

249. The Solar lineage arose from Ikshuaku, the grandson of the sun. Two branches sprang from this lineage, the elder ruling at Ayodhya. Rama belonged to this line. See note 246.

250. Saraphang—a reference to the *Sarabhanga jataka* (No. 522). In this jataka, the Bodhisatta was born as an archer. To demonstrate his skill as well as justify his position in the king's service, he performed

twelve acts of skill and art by shooting arrows through seven hard substances. Following this, he shot an arrow through a furlong of water and two of earth to pierce a hair at a half a furlong.

251. One *yoot* equals 9.94 statute miles.

252. Another catalogue begins with this stanza. Structurally, it is marked by the phrase "he sought...." Later it changes to "some nobles rode...."

253. In the catalogue of enemy kings, eleven, not ten, are actually listed.

254. Lord of Maces—Vishnu.

255. Phutchakaro refers to the naga, perhaps its name. It means roughly 'snake spirit'.

256. Kartikeya—son of Indra who became the God of War.

257. See note 253.

258. See notes 246 and 249.

259. Athit—the sun god, Suriya.

260. Phintumadi made offerings to the guardian spirit so that she could win Samuttakote in marriage.

261. Tradition holds that King Naray continued the composition from this point. The description of the hermit's kudi or residence represents another descriptive passage ordered spatially. In this case, the minute description begins at the top and moves downward.

262. See note 36.

263. Visanukam—the architect of the gods, famed for his glittering palaces and weapons.

264. The term *narayu* appears in the stanza as the next part of the kudi. It seems to mean 'some kind of door', although it cannot be found in any dictionary.

265. 'Flower' is used again to translate the Thai term *wanwet*. See note 244. Phuttan—hibiscus, *Hibiscus mutabilis* (*Malvaceae*).

266. Finial—see note 213.

267. Agni, the God of Fire, touched every part of human life and was therefore constantly invoked in rites and rituals. For a discussion of the word translated as fire ceremony, *kralaa*, see Jit Phumisak's article "Kralaaloom," 43-98.

268. The next four stanzas describe the decorations on the kudi's walls.

269. Jik—see note 147; jaeng—see note 147; maeng—see note 147; kannika—see note 144; karakate—see note 145; maludi—see note 145.

270. Phikun—see note 143; bunnak—see note 145; asok—the asoka tree, native to India, *Saraca indica* (*Leguminosae*); surapi (sarapi)—see note 143; ramduan (lamduan)—see note 147; maliwan—see note 145.

271. Krisana—a large tree with fragrant resin often used as incense, *Aguilaria agallocha* (*Thymelaeaceae*); krawan—cardamoms, *Amomum xanthioides* (*Zingiberaceae*); karabun—a low-blooming annual, *Sphaeranthus indicus* (*Compositae*); kun (kala ?)—a tree with white flowers found on banks of streams, *Hydnocarpus castanea* (*Bixaceae*); kraniat—*Adhatoda vasica Nees*; kanbun (karabun)—see above; kamkhun (kun ?)—plant with clusters of yellow flowers, *Cassia fistula* (*Leguminosae*).

272. Suphanka—*Cochlospermum Cochlospermacea*; pheka—a tree with large pods, *Oxoxylum indicum* (*Begoniaceae*).

273. Rang—small tree upon which a lac insect feeds, *Pentacme siamensis* (*Dipterocarpaceae*); rak—a tree from which laquer is obtained, *Melanorrhoea usitata* (*Anacardiaceae*); sakraw—a tree used for medicinal purposes; jaraling—*Averrhoa bilimbi*; kok—umbrella plant, *Cyperus alternifolius*; nangyaem—see note 147; ramyai (lumyai ?) —*Nephelium longana*; phai—type of tree used in building, *Adenanthera microsperma* (*Leguminosae*).

274. Pho—pipal tree, *Ficus religiosa* (*Urticaceae*); theptharu—a peppermint smelling pine, *Cinnamomum parthenoxylon*; lampu—tree with fruit for flavoring chutneys and curries, *Sonneratia caseolaris* (*Sonneratiaceae*); tongtaek—shrub, *Baliospermum axillare* (*Euphorbiaceae*); pradu (du)—see note 143; prayong—see note 143; yom—see note 143.

275. Tatum—small tree with milky juice, *Excoecaria agallocha* (*Euphorbiaceae*); rakam—a palm, *Zallacca wallichiana* (*Palmae*);

jambok—see note 144; ratchaphrik—laburnum, golden shower, *Cassia agnes Brenan.*

276. Khanang—*Homalium tomentosum.* Separated, the two syllables mean 'arms (*kha*) of the lady (*nang*)'.

277. Raksorn—shrub with double-petaled flowers, *Calotropis gigantea (Asclepiadaceae).* Separated, the syllables mean 'love (*rak*) increases (*sorn*)'. Laepnang—woody climber, *Quisqualis densiflora (Cembretaceae)*; also means 'fingernails (*laep*) of the lady (*nang*)'.

278. Lamjiak—species of screwpine, *Pandanus tectorius (Pandanaceae)*; jan—sandlewood, *Sirium myrtifolium*; malika—double jasmine; ket —see note 145; kaew—see note 144; kumari—an unidentified species of flower.

279. Phlap—evergreen, *Diospyros embryopteris (Ebenaceae)*; trakop—berry producing tree, *Flacourtia cataphracta (Flacourtiaceae)*; khanun— jackfruit, *Artocarpus integrifolia (Urticaceae)*; khanang—see note 276; chamchun—an unidentified species of fruit.

280. Khwit—wood apple, *Feronia elephantum (Rutaceae)*; khwat—evergreen tree, *Garcinia speciosa (Guttiferae)*.

281. Mayhiang—*Dipterocarpus intricatus (Dipterocarpaceae)*; charahan—n unidentified species of tree; mahat—large deciduous tree, *Artocarpus lakoocha.*

282. Bong—bamboo, *Bambusa tulda*; changyang—an unidentified species of bamboo.

283. Karawik—see note 176; nanwika—karawik(?); kronca—sarus crane, *Grus antigone*; kokin—cuckoo or coel, *Eudynamis malayana.*

284. Jip—see note 152; jap—see note 152; jok—see note 171; kangkhen —see note 162; ilum—see note 162; khum—see note 162; khaw—see note 156.

285. Iang—see note 159; aen—see note 159; karian—crane, Grus sharpi; phuradok—see note 172.

286. Yangthon—little egret, *Egretta garzetta garzetta*; krasa—see note 153; sarika—see note 158.

287. Say—see note 163; tranay (kranay)—see note 156.

288. Khapkhae—cotton teal goose, *Nettapus coromandelianus*.

289. Plaw—see note 158; khaektaw—a species of parrot; khaektaw could also mean 'guest (*khaek*) comes (*taw*)'.

290. Langling—a small medium-sized palm, *Pinanga*; separated, the word means 'kinds (*lang*) of monkies (*ling*)'.

291. Thengthut—a kind of bird. Separated, the word means 'to call out (*theng*) a message (*thut*)'.

292. Phaychayon was Indra's chariot. The name also refers to his banner or palace.

293. Nanthip, also Nandana, was Indra's garden north of Mount Meru.

294. Kaylat (Kailasa)—a mountain in the Himalayas said to be Siva's paradise and made of silver. It is also known as 'silver mountain'. It lies to the north of Manasa lake.

295. The mantra is a mystic or magic verse.

296. Tilottama was a Brahmin female condemned to be born as an apsara for bathing during the improper season. As an apsara, she brought about the destruction of the demons Sumpa (Sunda) and Nisumpa (Upasunda). Granted a boon by Siva, the demons warred against the gods, who sought help from Siva's wife. She in turn devised their destruction with Tilottama. Their story appears in the *Markandeya Purana*.

297. In the *Ramayana*, Phali (Balin) dethroned his brother, the monkey king Sukri (Sugriva). Reinstalled with the aid of Rama, Sukri became Rama's ally in his war against Ravenna.

298. 'Seven seas' refers to the seven great oceans of the world, the seven annular rings of water alternating with the seven rings of mountains that surround Mount Meru.

299. 'Shrunken' (*hu*) implies wrinkled, curled up, and contracted.

300. The phitthayathorn's lament includes one of the longest descriptive passages and catalogues in the whole poem.

301. The Thai word for 'scorch' (*dong*) refers to the blackened bottom of a pan used over an open fire.

302. The blue climber (anchan) has prominent blue flowers and is found throughout the tropics; *Clitoria ternatea* (*Leguminosae*).

Eight desires—see note 229.

303. The Thai describes the nose as a 'hook'. See note 230.

304. With this stanza begins the last section of the poem, composed by Prince Paramanuchit.

305. The Thai term used, *phutthangkun*, means 'one destined to be a Buddha'.

306. Sumali—a flower, a collection of flowers; surapi (sarapi)—see note 143.

307. The inclusion of the reference to sin, kamma, and their possible effects reminds the audience that even with the adventures and mythological characters, the story has a moralistic purpose.

308. An invitation to journey to the forest is a literary device that moves the plot forward as well as provides a reason for the inclusion of catalogues and descriptive passages.

309. Thai Buddhist cosmology describes the Himawan mountains as consisting of 84,000 peaks, each 500 *yojana* (*yoot*) high (Reynolds and Reynolds 1982, 290).

310. The five peaks (mountain ranges in Reynolds and Reynolds 1982) surround Anodat lake.

311. Sutat (Sudassana) mountain is replete with gold and bends toward Anodat lake like a crow's beak (Reynolds and Reynolds 1982, 293).

Kaylat—see note 294.

312. Kan (Kala) is dark blue-green like the anchan flower (Reynolds and Reynolds 1982, 293).

Jit (Citta) has seven kinds of jewels. It is inhabited by golden swans. The Bodhisatta lived there when he was Dhatarattha, the king of swans (Reynolds and Reynolds 1982, 293).

313. Khanthamat (Gandhamadana) is replete with emeralds and covered with trees and vines. It is also referred to as 'Intoxicating Fragrance' (Reynolds and Reynolds 1982, 293).

314. The five peaks bend over the pool. The streams and rivers that feed the lake are never dry. The sun and moon can penetrate the pool with their rays only from the side, never from above. Hence, the waters are always cool, which explains the pool's name, Anodat 'unheated' (Reynolds and Reynolds 1982, 294).

Seven large lakes lie in the Himawan: Anodat (Anotatta), Kannamunda, Rathakara, Mandakini, Chattan (Chaddanta), Kinala, and Sihapapata (Reynolds and Reynolds 1982, 292).

315. Hongsa—a goose or swan; suwa—a species of parrot; kukkut—jungle cock; konca (kronca)—see note 283; sari (salika ?)—mynah, *Acridotheres tristis*; kungan—see note 152; karawik—see note 176; kunan (kunala)—Malayan coel, *Eudynamis malayana*.

316. See note 314.

317. Kung—shrimp; kang—mantis shrimp; kumapin—long-nosed alligator; makorn—a mythical fish; kot—catfish; ka—catfish, *Mystus micracanthus*; krim—see note 178; kray—see note 178; kratrap—see note 192.

318. Kralumphuk—see note 198; duk—see note 198; salat—featherback, *Notopterus notopterus*; salit—see note 179; lot—see note 196.

319. Ma—see note 187; maw—see note 183; mu—see note 184; bu —gobies, *Glossogobius giuris* (*Gobiidae*); ba—*Leptobarbus hoeveni* (*Cyprinidae*); paen—see note 195; paep—see note 195.

320. Khaw—see note 179; khuea—see note 189; chorn—see note 193; sangkhawat—*Pangasius pangasius* (*Pangasiidae*); saway—see note 178.

321. Malaengphu—a type of mollusk; chanak—sawfish, *Pristis perotteti*; chalam (chalamnu)—see note 197; thepo—see note 183; thepa —freshwater catfish, *Pangasius santiwongsei* (*Pangasiidae*); trapak—*Puntius daruphani*.

322. Krapaep (paep)—see note 195; krabork (kabork)—see note 182; chado—serpent-headed fish, *Ophicephalus micropeltes* (*Ophicephalidae*); kraho—see note 177; krahae—see note 177; khangbuean—see note 179.

323. Soy—see note 188; say (saway)—see note 188; suea—see note 189; kradi—see note 192; kradong—an unidentified species of fish.

324. Karakot—crab; katchaba—tortise; jariew—turtle; jaraw—sea turtle; aw—see note 186; uk—see note 198.

325. Nuanjan—*Chanos chanos* (*Chanidae*); hangkiw—see note 190; kukkura—a kind of fish—see note 191.

326. Surapi (sarapi)—see note 143.

327. With this section, Prince Paramanuchit began the final section of the poem.

328. Nantawan—another name for Indra's garden.

329. Rama belonged to the Solar dynasty. See preceding stanza and note 249.

330. Indra is often referred to as "The One-Thousand Eyed."

331. Phra Naray was another manifestation of Vishnu.

332. Siva—'great king of the noble trident'.

333. Indra's celestial city—Amaravati.

334. Kammalasontani is Phromburi. Literally, the term means 'the city of the one who has the lotus flower as a seat'. Phromburi means 'the city of Brahma', and Brahma is depicted as sitting on a lotus.

335. Another reference to merit and its consequences emphasizes the moralistic nature of the story.

336. The Anodat pool consists of four landings for bathing. The first is for male devata (Reynolds and Reynolds 1982, 295).

337. The second landing is for female devata (Reynolds and Reynolds 1982, 295).

338. In Reynolds and Reynolds 1982 (295), this is the fourth landing, the one for "hermits, sages, and those with occult knowledge."

339. In Reynolds and Reynolds 1982 (295), this is the third landing, the one for the Pacceka Buddhas, those who have gained the knowledge to attain Nibanna but do not preach it.

340. Chattan lake is one of the seven lakes found in the Himawan (see note 314). It is surrounded by seven mountains or mountain ranges.

In this place, the Chattan elephant king, who was the Bodhisatta, was born.

341. Seven ranges of mountains surround Chattan lake.

342. Suphanbat (Suvannaratna)—the innermost range of mountains surrounding Chattan lake; it is made of solid gold.

343. Manibat (Sabbamani)—the jeweled mountains surrounding the lake. Suriyabat is not listed in Reynolds and Reynolds 1982, although there is mention of Culasuvanna, the mountains of vermillion, and Cula-udaka, the mountains of emeralds (Reynolds and Reynolds 1982, 297).

344. Janthabat, the gleaming silver mountains, is not mentioned in Reynolds and Reynolds 1982, although there is mention of Culasuvanna, the mountains of vermillion, and Cula-udaka, the mountains of emerald (Reynolds and Reynolds 1982, 297).

    Uthokbat (Maha-udaka) are the mountains of crystal.

345. The Mahakanbat mountains (Mahakala) are those of sapphire, colored like the blue-green anchan flower.

    The Julakan mountains (Culakala) are ink-dark, like the anchan flower according to Reynolds and Reynolds 1982 (297).

346. The center of the pool is said never to dry up or to become dull and cloudy (Reynolds and Reynolds 1982, 299).

347. Jongkonni—a lotus that bears multiple white blossoms per stem.

348. Ubon—a white lotus; nin—a blue lotus; lohito—a red lotus.

349. Patthama—a lotus; sawet—a white lotus; kamut—a long-stemmed white lotus.

350. Mitsakawan—Indra's pleasure garden.

351. The rice does not need to be grown or cultivated (Reynolds and Reynolds 1982, 300).

352. Here, the nine forests of flowers include the seven types of lotuses, the flowers of Mitsakawan, and probably the forest of rice.

353. The description of the vegetation beyond the pond follows fairly closely the description found in the Reynolds and Reynolds 1982, 296-97.

354. The forest seems to be the same as the one described in Reynolds and Reynolds 1982 (301). Indra's park, Mitsaka (Mitsakawan), includes both flowers and trees. See note 350.

355. This group of elephants belongs to the lineage of Brahma. See note 116.

356. The Chattan elephant has the following characteristics: large body, tall, white skin comparable to a polished conch shell, red foot pads, trunk the color of a white banana, tusks that emit six colors. It also has supernatural powers (Reynolds and Reynolds 1982, 298).

357. The Ubosot elephants are colored gold like the sunshine; they can walk around the annular mountainous rings from morning to noon.

358. The Hemahatthi elephants have skin colored like natural gold.

359. The Mongkonayra elephants are blue like the anchan flower. They are also referred to as Mongkonhatthi.

360. The Khanthakhot elephants have skin like the bark of the kritsana tree, body and feces fragrant like the kritsana flower.

361. The Bingkhon elephants have skin like the sunshine.

362. Tallest of all the elephants, the Damop elephants have copper-colored skin.

363. The Banthon elephants have skin the color of silver-pure Mount Kaylat.

364. Born on the Ganges, the Khangkhay elephants have bodies the color of flowing water.

365. The Kalawaka elephants have a totally black body like the wings of a crow.

366. The prince tells the story when he, the Bodhisatta, was the elephant Chattan.

367. The ground around Chattan pool is pure gold with a slab of cat's eye. Nearby are two gold pools, one clear and the other fragrant (Reynolds and Reynolds 1982, 298).

368. Sawk—an ancient unit of measure that extends from the tip of the middle finger to the elbow joint; two spans, half of a meter.

369. Indra was often referred to as the King of Thunderbolts.

370. Another reference to the consequences of merit.

371. This stanza begins the literary device of analyzing a problem through a dialogue.

372. The five great rivers include Ganga, Yamuna, Aciravati, Mahi, and Sarabhu (Reynolds and Reynolds 1982, 296). These rivers originate in one of the rivers that flows out from Anodat pool.

373. The accumulated merit based on their past deeds will determine their present fate.

374. Traditionally, before death, one asks for forgiveness for any sins committed towards others.

375. Sins have three sources: actions, words, and thoughts.

376. See note 373.

377. Unmarried women or widows were looked down upon, seen as not having any means of support.

378. The following catalogue takes the form "The...reminds me of/is/tells of...." The name of a tree, flower, or animal fills the first blank while the same word with a secondary meaning or a homonym fills the second and completes the pun. Sawat—*Caesalpinia crista*; a homonym meaning 'to love, join in, pleasure' completes the pun.

Rak—*Calotropis gigantea* (*Asclepiadeae*); the word also means 'love'.

379. Sala—short-stemmed palm, *Zalacca wallichiana* (*Palmae*); the word also means 'to relinguish, renounce'.

Rakam—*Calotropis gigantea* (*Asclepiadeae*); the word also means 'sorrow, grief'.

380. Kratum—a species of evergreen, *Excoecaria agalloch* (*Euphorbiaceae*); a modification of the first syllable *kra* to *kara* produces the meaning 'hands' with the whole word meaning 'to beat the chest with the hands'.

381. Tum—bael fruit tree, *Aegle marmelos* (*Rutaceae*); onomatopoeia for the sound of beating.

Sok—tree under which Buddha was born, *Saracaindica* (*Leguminosae*); the word also means 'sorrow'.

382. Phanlawk—a tree that probably produces a fire—red flower.

383. Sayyut—fragrant climber, *Desmos chinensis* (*Annonaceae*); reversing the syllables produces *yut* 'to stop' and *say* 'evening'.

384. Sukkrom—tree with red fruit used for medicine; reversing these syllables produces a homonym *krom* 'to be melancholoy' and *suk* 'happiness' which is negated in the Thai.

385. Sathorn—*Millettia buteoides* (*Leguminosae*); the word also means 'to recoil'.

386. Thingthorn—*Albizia procera*. The first syllable, *thing*, means 'to throw away'.

387. Rok—probably a woody sprawler, *Terminalia alata* (*Combretaceae*); a homonym means 'disease'.

388. Kanphay—*Afgekia sericea Carib*; split into two syllables, the two syllables mean 'to protect against (*kan*) danger (*phay*)'.

389. Marum—horseradish tree, *Moringa oleifera* (*Moringaceae*). The second syllable, rum, means 'to gather, flock together'.

390. Kamjat—*Zanthoxylum budrunga* (*Rutaceae*); the word also means 'to limit'.

391. Makawk—hog plum, wild olive, *Spondias pinnata* (*Anacardiaceae*); the second syllable, *kawk*, means 'to suck'.

392. Jak—nipa palm, *Nipa fruticans*; the word also means 'to be separated from'.

393. Teng—a large forest tree, *Shorea obtusa* (*Dipterocarpaceae*); the word also refers to a type of Chinese scales with a horizontal bar.

394. Mafaw—*Trewia nudiflora*; the second syllable, *faw*, means 'to be withered or wilted'.

395. Saba—elephant creeper, *Entada phaseoloides*; the second syllable, *ba*, means 'to be crazy'.

396. Ramngap—*Mimosa pudica* (*Leguminosae*); the word also means 'to curb or lessen'.

397. Nat—camphor plant, *Blumea balsamifera* (*Compositae*); a homonym, *anat*, means 'to be destitute'.

398. Suramarit—ambrosia, heavenly elixir.

399. Wannam—creepers; the first syllable, *wan*, has a homonym meaning 'day' while *nam* means 'water'.

400. Dapphit—phitsanat—*Mimosa sirissa*, used as an antidote against poisoning; separately, the syllables mean 'to stop, extinguish (*dap*) poison (*phit*)'.

401. Jak phrak—mythological bird with a wailing sound at night when separated from its mate; the word also means 'to be separated from'.

402. Phirap—a kind of dove, *Columbidae*; a rhyming syllable, *philap*, means 'to lament'.

403. Thengthut—a kind of bird; separately, the syllables mean 'to throw out (*theng*) a message (*thut*)'.

404. Khokma—a species of bird; *ma* means 'horse'.

405. Krawaen—black racket-tailed magpie, *Crypsithina varians*; the word also means 'to keep watch'.

406. Khawmong—owl, *Glaucidium cuculoides*; the second syllabe, *mong*, means 'time'.

407. Khawkun—a type of owl; the second syllable, *kun*, means 'to call out'.

408. Saek—a type of owl, *Tyto alba*; the word also means 'to make clear'.

409. Khwaekkhwan—a heron; *khwan* also means 'ax'.

410. Ragnan—a species of bird; *nan* means 'a long time'.

411. Lang—Siamese white-crested laughing thrush, *Garrulax diardi*; *lang* also means 'a sign of destiny, an omen'.

412. See note 176.

413. Nori—a parrot-like bird, *Loriidae*.

414. Khaektaw—species of parrot, *Psittacidae alexandre* (*Psittacidae*); the syllables also mean 'a guest (*khaek*) comes (*taw*)'.

415. Benjawan—a multi-colored parrot.

416. Kayfa—silver pheasant, *Euplocamus lineatus*; *fa* also means 'sky, heaven'.

417. Phintumadi questions the cause of their separation, but does not attempt to identify it.

418. Mattharat—perhaps Mathura, an ancient and famous city on the right bank of the Yamuna, the birthplace of Krishna.

419. Reading the story carved on the wall represents a variation on the technique of including summaries in the poem.

420. Prang—a cone-shaped structure built to commemorate an event or spot revered by the Buddhists. Here it refers to the palace where Phintumadi and Samuttakote met. See note 217.

421. The items to be distributed were those she bought from the gold she received from her ring.

422. Mekala was the female deity who guarded the seas. She passes over the seas once every seven days.

423. The prince has been punished because of some cruel act he performed in a former life.

424. Sutattani—a name for Indra's city.

425. Samuttakote is identified as the Buddha.

426. The reference seems to be to the parents and wives of those who seek knowledge on their own.

427. Samuttakote disguises himself as a Brahmin.

428. The reading of the frieze functions as a summary.

429. A summary within a stylized dialogue.

430. All those at the alms house celebrate the reunion of Samuttakhote and Phintumadi.

431. Sutat—Sutattani, Indra's city.

432. Buddha of the Solar Race refers to Samuttakote.

433. Ascetics often twisted and piled their hair on top of their heads, giving the impression of a crown or at least in this case mirroring the crown that Sri Narakup wore. The original Thai reads that he became a Brahmin (*phram*); however, the nature of the actions suggest that 'ascetic' is the more appropriate translation. Earlier, Narakup is described as an ascetic. See note 27.

434. Kasin—one of the ten objects of meditation as laid down by Buddhism. These objects include earth, water, fire, wind, blue, yellow, red, white, light, and the sky as seen through a narrow opening (McFarland, 66).

435. Chan (jhana)—meditative absorption consisting of four grades of abstract trances in which the believer has all bodily emotions removed. Stage One has the believer sit cross-legged in a secluded spot concentrating on a single thought. The soul fills with ecstasy and serenity while the mind still reasons upon the object of concentration. In Stage Two, the mind removes the reason while the ecstasy and serenity remain. Following this occurs Stage Three during which ecstasy is removed leaving a state of tranquility. Finally, in Stage Four, the mind becomes indifferent to all emotions, whether pleasurable or painful (McFarland 1944, 313).

436. This description of the army's departure is the most elaborate in the poem and representative of classical literary devices.

437. The four virtuous inclinations are (1) metta—goodwill toward all living things; (2) karuna—compassionate interest in all living things; (3) mutthita—love for all living things; and (4) ubekkha—impartiality, showing no preference or prejudice.

Four ways of knowledge—see note 435.

438. The ten kingly virtues are almsgiving, morality, liberality, rectitude, gentleness, self-restriction, non-anger, non-violence, forebearance, and non-obstruction.

439. The five precepts of the Buddha forbid killing, stealing, taking two wives, lying, and taking intoxicants.

The Roller of the Wheel (or Cakkavatti) is a Great Being who has attained his high status from the accumulation of merit in previous lives. At his birth, a series of miracles occur, and then at a later age, his being causes the wheel to roll from the bottom of the ocean. With the wheel is associated the Dhamma and the solar disc, and with the wheel, the Great Being conquers the four continents and becomes the universal ruler. Ruling with Dhamma, he brings prosperity and happiness to all. At his death, the wheel returns to the ocean until another Cakkavatti appears. See Reynolds, 20.

440. The Four Great Truths are (1) sorrow is always a part of existence; (2) sorrow results from desire and passion; (3) sorrow ceases with extinction of desire; and (4) desire can be extinguished by following the right path.

441. Following the format of the jataka stories, Prince Paramanuchit completes the composition by providing the traditional frame, addressing the monks who are listening to the tale and explaining to them who the characters represent.

442. Sariputta—the monk of the right.

443. Visakha—the chief female disciple.

444. The peak of the celestial mountain refers to Indra.

445. Uppalavanna—one of the two chief female disciples of the Buddha. See note 443.

446. The *Pannyatsachadok* consists of fifty extra-cannonical jataka tales popular in Southeast Asian countries. The story of Samuttakote is one of these stories. See Introduction for more details.

447. See Introduction for the circumstances under which Prince Paramanuchit came to finish the composition.

448. Maharat—Maharatchakhru

449. Cunlasakarat—the Thai minor era, beginning March 21, 638 A.D. Legend holds that Laochakarat established a kingdom in Chieng Lao by virtue of this new calendrical system. Known as Cunlasakarat (The Lesser Era), this system was devised by a Burmese king who wanted the surrounding countries to accept it. When only Lanna Thai adopted the system, Laochakarat was made king of Lanna Thai. If this story is true, then this episode would be the first recorded appearance of the Thai in local history. See Kasetsiri 1976, 48, n. 12. Kasetsiri records the date as 639 A.D.

The date recorded in the stanza is equivalent to 21 October 1849.

450. *Kalpa*—a vast period of time equal to 4,320,000,000 solar years.

In the Thai stanza, the first word or syllable of each line can be read vertically to produce a meaning separate from the stanza as a whole. In the English version, the first phrase in each line, separated by commas, translates the Thai.

APPENDIXES

Appendix A

For each of the forty-seven manuscripts, the following table provides the National Library Number (NL), the lem number, the stanzas recorded in each lem, the stanzas missing, the acquisition date if available, and miscellaneous information. A series of numbers separated by commas appears under miscellaneous notes: 113,1/2,32. These numbers refer to the location of the manuscript. The first number records the cabinet in which the manuscript is found (113); the second its position on the shelf (1/2); and the third the bundle in which it is tied (32). The term *wak* indicates one line of a stanza.

Table 1

NL No.	LEM No.	Stanzas Recorded	Acquisition Missing	Acquisition Date	Miscellaneous Notes
NL1	1	1-640	-	Jan. 12, 1913	Yellow writing on black paper; National Library purchase; 113,1/2,32
NL2	2	641-1298	-	Jan. 12, 1913	Yellow writing on black paper; National Library purchase; 113,1/2,32
NL3	3	1299-1849	-	Jan. 12, 1913	Yellow writing on black paper; National Library purchase; 113,1/2,32
NL4	4	1850-2221	-	Jan. 12, 1913	Yellow writing on black paper; National Library purchase; 113,1/2,32
NL5	1	1-517	-	n.d.	Yellow writing on black paper; 113,1/2,32
NL6	2	518-997	-	n.d.	Yellow writing on black paper; 113,1/2,32
NL7	3	998-1456	-	n.d.	Yellow writing on black paper; 113,1/2,32
NL8	3	998-1456	-	n.d.	Yellow writing on black paper; 113,1/2,33
NL9	4	1457-1813	1635; 1686-93	1930	Yellow writing on black paper; Gift of 1686-93 Caw Phraya Mukmontri (Uap Bawrohit); 113,1/2,33
NL10	1	1-305	-	n.d.	Yellow writing on black paper; 113,1/2,33
NL11	2	306-668	659; 660, wak 3	n.d.	Yellow writing on black paper; 113,1/2,33

268

NL No.	LEM No.	Stanzas Recorded	Acquisition Missing	Acquisition Date	Miscellaneous Notes
NL12	3	669-994	-	n.d.	Yellow writing on black paper; 113,1/2,33
NL13	1	1-365	-	1900	Yellow writing on black paper; Gift of Phimsen Caw Krom Phuttharatnasathan; 113,1/2,33
NL14	2	366-653	-	1900	Yellow writing on black paper; Gift of Caw Krom Phuttharatnasathan; 113,1/2,33
NL15	3	654-988	-	1900	Yellow writing on black paper; Gift of Caw Krom Phuttharatnasathan; 113,1/2,34
NL16	4	989-1277	-	1900	Yellow writing on black paper; stanza 1252 marked as start of maharatchaniphon; Gift of Caw Krom Phuttharatnasathan; 113,1/2,34
NL17	1	1-368	-	Oct. 29, 1932	White writing on black paper; lem marked as Maharatchakhru composition, copied by Naay Ruang Camlong; Gift of Phrayaratchasena; 113,1/2,34
NL18	3	369-747	520; 542; 543, wak 3	1907	White writing on black paper; Gift of 543, wak 3 Phrarachaphirom (Cem Burananon); 113,1/2,34
NL19	3	1090-1456	1346	n.d.	White writing on black paper; 113,1/2,34
NL20	4	1456-1855	1547	n.d.	White writing on black paper; 113,1/2,34
NL21	5	1857-2221	-	n.d.	White writing on black paper; illegible stanzas: 2199-2200; 2220-2221; 113,1/2,34
NL22	1	1-355	-	n.d.	Yellow writing on black paper; lem marked as Maharatchakhru composition; Gift of Naay Ket Camlong; 113,1/2,34
NL23	2	356-721	-	n.d.	Yellow writing on black paper; lem marked as Maharatchakhru composition; Gift of Naay Ket Camlong; 113,1/2,34
NL24	3	721-1089	-	n.d.	Yellow writing on black paper; Gift of Naay Ket Camlong; 113,1/2,35
NL25	4	1457-1910	1856, wak 4 1857, wak 1	May 12, 1916	Yellow writing on black paper; marked 1857, wak 1 as a new lem written; Gift of Phra Ong Caw Ying Wongcan; 113,1/2,35
NL26	4	1094-1456	-	n.d.	Yellow writing on black paper; stanza 1252 marked as start of phraratchaniphon; 113,1/2,35
NL27	3	833-1251	-	Oct. 29, 1953	Yellow writing on black paper; marked as used for the 3rd printing, 1950, pp. 94-141; Purchase from William J. Gedney; 113,1/3,35

NL No.	LEM No.	Stanzas Recorded	Acquisition Missing	Acquisition Date	Miscellaneous Notes
NL28	4	1252-1456	-	Oct. 29, 1953	Yellow writing on black paper; stanza 1252 marked as start of maharatchaniphon; marked as used for Karusapa 3rd printing, 1950, pp. 141-163; Purchase from William J. Gedney; 113,1/3,35
NL29	2	518-997	853; 854, wak 1,2, and 4	n.d. n.d.	Yellow writing on black paper; 854, wak 1,2n.d. stanzas 853, wak 3 replaced with and 4 stanza 854, wak 3; 113,1/3,35
NL30	3	998-1156	1145, wak 1	1914	Yellow writing on black paper; stanza 1144, wak 3 and 4 replaced with stanza 1145, wak 3 and 4; Gift of Caw Com Manda Chum R. 4; 113,1/3,35
NL31	4	1147-1855	1199, wak 1,2, and 3	n.d.	Yellow writing on black paper; and 3 stanza 1198, wak 3 and 4 replaced with stanza 1119, wak 3 and 4; stanza 1252 marked as start of maharatchaniphon; 113,1/3,35
NL32	1	1-377	-	n.d.	Yellow writing on black paper; 113,1/3,36
NL33	1	1-392	-	n.d.	Yellow writing on black paper; 113,1/3,36
NL34	1	1-355	-	n.d.	Yellow writing on black paper; stanza 89, wak 3 and 4 are replaced with stanza 90, wak 2 and 3 stanza 4 remains; Gift of Krom Lekhatikan Kana Ratthamontri (Sutipho); 113,1/3,36
NL35	1	1-374	366	n.d.	Yellow writing on black paper; Gift of Sutipho; 113,1/3,36
NL36	1	1-335	-	Dec. 16, 1925	White writing on black paper; Gift of Krom Phranarewaranit; 113,1/3,36
NL37	1	1-368	-	Sept. 5, 1925	Yellow writing on black paper; Gift of Phraratchaprasit (Thian Chuto); 113,1/3,36
NL38	1	1-370	100-106; 155-156	n.d.	Yellow writing on black paper; stanza 155-156 123, wak 1 and 2 replaced with stanza 122, wak 3 and 4; stanza 123 repeated; 113,1/3,36
NL39	1	1-411	-	1908	Yellow writing on black paper; Gift of Phra Ong Caw Ying Praphat; 113,1/3,37
NL40	1	1-334	-	1909	Yellow writing on black paper; Gift of Phrasuwanphakdi (Um); 113,1/3,37
NL41	1	1-464	-	Sept. 27, 1932	Yellow writing on black paper; Gift of Nang Khriawan Thephatsadin; 113,1/3,37

NL No.	LEM No.	Stanzas Recorded	Acquisition Missing	Acquisition Date	Miscellaneous Notes
NL42	1	67-817	1-66; 817, wak 3, 4	1916	Yellow writing on black paper; Gift of 817, wak 3, 4 Caw Phraya Mukmontri (Uap Pawrohit); 113,1/3,37
NL43	2	366-653	-	1908	Yellow writing on black paper; Gift of Caw Ying Prapak; 113,1/3,37
NL44	1	104-180	-	n.d.	Yellow writing on black paper; cover and back torn; 113,1/3,37
NL45	-	1662-1874	1874, wak 3 and 4	n.d.	Yellow writing on black paper; and 4 113,1/3,37
NL46	-	1180-1243	-	n.d.	White writing on black paper; 113,1/3,37
NL47	-	566, wak 3-904	635, wak 2,3, 4-700, wak 1; 788-861, wak 4	n.d.	Yellow writing on black paper; from Wat 904 4-700, wak 1; Bowaniwet; 113/1/3,37

Appendix B

Table 1

List of Thai Meters and Stanzas in the Poem

Meter	Stanzas
chabang	1-66, 138-140, 146-153, 161-250, 263-305, 312-418, 455-522, 531-544, 549-668, 675-687, 713-721, 727-743, 757-801, 807-854, 861-976, 986-988, 1024-1177, 1185-1187, 1192-1195, 1232-1238, 1247-1251, 1332-1344, 1355-1396, 1457-1463, 1533-1549, 1655-1689, 1814-1845, 1893-1943, 2197-2217
khlong 4	2218-2221
maalinii	1798-1813, 2118-2165
sathun	722-726, 1188-1191, 1345-1354, 1412-1456, 1518-1532, 1617-1654, 1777-1797, 1953-1965, 2104-2117
sattharaa	1690-1705, 1966-1984
surangkhanang	122-137, 141-145, 154-160, 1944-1952
todokka	1485-1489, 1706-1721, 1985-1996
wasantadilok	88-90, 251-262, 545-548, 688-712, 955-1023, 1179-1184, 1210-1231, 1397-1411, 1490-1517, 1550-1580, 1722-1741, 1846-1892, 1997-2054, 2166-2182
yaanii/intharawichian	67-87, 91-121, 306-311, 419-454, 523-530, 669-674, 744-756, 802-806, 855-860, 977-985, 989-994, 1178, 1196-1209, 1239-1246, 1252-1331, 1468-1484, 1581-1616, 1742-1776, 2055-2103, 2183-2196

BIBLIOGRAPHY

Buck, William. 1976. *Ramayana*. Berkeley: University of California Press.

Chakrabongse, Chula, Prince. 1967. *Lords of Life: A History of the Kings of Thailand*. 2nd Revised Edition. London: Alvin Redman.

Cowell, E.B. ed. 1978a. "Chaddanta-jataka (No. 514)." In *The Jatakas or Stories of Buddha's Former Births*. Vol. 5. Reprinted. Delhi: Cosmo Publications, 20-31.

_____. 1978b. "Sarabhanga-jataka (No. 522)." In *The Jatakas or Stories of Buddha's Former Births*. Vol. 5. Reprinted. Delhi: Cosmo Publications, 64-79.

Davis, Richard. 1984. *Muang Metaphysics: A Study of Northern Thai Myth and Ritual*. Bangkok: Pandora.

Dhaninivat, H.H. Prince. 1965. "Hide Figures of the Ramakien." *Journal of the Siam Society* 53:61-66.

_____. 1959. "Notes: Nang Talung." *Journal of the Siam Society* 47(2):181.

_____. 1948. "The Shadow-Play as a Possible Origin of the Masked-Play." *Journal of the Siam Society* 37(1):26-32.

Dowson, John. 1972. *A Classical Dictionary of Hindu Mythology and Religion, Geography, History and Literature*. 12th ed. London: Routledge & Kegan Paul.

Gedney, William J. 1989. "Siamese Verse Forms in Historical Perspective." In *Selected Papers on Comparative Tai Studies*, ed. Robert J. Bickner, John Hartmann, Thomas John Hudak, and Patcharin Peyasantiwong. Michigan Papers on South and Southeast Asia, Number 29. Ann Arbor: The University of Michigan, 489-544.

Horner, I.B., and Padmanabh S. Jaini. 1985. *Apocryphal Birth-Stories* (Pannasa-Jataka). Vol. 1. London: The Pali Text Society.

273

Hudak, Thomas John. 1990. *The Indigenization of Pali Meters in Thai Poetry*. Monographs in International Studies, Southeast Asia Series, No. 87. Athens, Ohio: Ohio University Press.

_____. 1988. "Organizational Principles in Thai *phannanaa* Passages." *Bulletin of the School of Oriental and African Studies* 51(1):95-117.

_____. 1987. "Internal Rhyme Patterns in Classical Thai Poetry." *Crossroads* 3(2-3):94-103.

Intramontri, Phya (Giles, F.H.). 1930. "Adversaria of Elephant Hunting." *Journal of the Siam Society* 23(2):61-96.

Jaini, Padmanabh S. 1986. *Apocryphal Birth-Stories (Pannasa-Jataka)*. Vol. 2. London: The Pali Text Society.

_____. 1981. *Pannasa-Jataka or Zimme Pannasa (in the Burmese Recension)*. Vol. 1. London: The Pali Text Society.

_____. 1983. *Pannasa-Jataka or Zimme Pannasa (in the Burmese Recension)*. Vol. 2. London: The Pali Text Society.

Jones, John Garrett. 1979. *Tales and Teachings of the Buddha: The Jataka Stories in Relation to the Pali Canon*. London: George Allen & Unwin.

Kasetsiri, Charnvit. 1976. *The Rise of Ayudhya: A History of Siam in the Fourteenth and Fifteenth Centuries*. New York: Oxford University Press.

Kerdchouay, Eurayporn, and Michael Smithies. 1973. "Great Shadow Play of Thailand." *Orientations* 4(8):47-50.

Kieyakul, Sumalie, Lieutenant. 1982. "Samutthakhoot kham chan suan thii taeng samay krung sri ayutthaya: kaanwikraw lae wijaan ching prawat" [The Ayutthaya portions of Samutthakhoot kham chan: A Historical Analysis and Criticism]. In *Aksornsaat niphon 2: ruam botkhwaam thaang phaasaa lae wannakhadii thay* [Arts Theses 2: Collected Essays on Language and Literature], ed. Trisin Bunkhacorn, Chanda Roengraklikhit, and Porntip Phukphasuk. Bangkok: Faculty of Arts, Chulalongkorn University, 220-61.

Maharatchakhru, Phra, King Naray, and Prince Paramanuchit Chinorot. 1980. *Samutthakhoot kham chan*. 3rd printing. Bangkok: Ministry of Fine Arts.

_____. n.d. *Samutthakhoot kham chan.* Manuscripts 1-47. Bangkok: Aksornsaat Division, National Library.

McFarland, George Bradley, M.D. 1944. *Thai-English Dictionary.* Stanford: Stanford University Press.

Nicholas, René. 1927. "Le théâtre dòmbres au Siam." *Journal of the Siam Society* 21:37-51.

Phillips, Herbert P. 1987. *Modern Thai Literature: With an Ethnographic Interpretation.* Honolulu: University of Hawaii Press.

Phumisak, Jit. 1986. "Kralaahom." In *Ruam botkhwaam thaang phaasaa lae niruksaat* [Essays on Language and Philology]. 2nd ed. Bangkok: Dokyaa, 43-93.

Pluang na nakhorn. 1964. *Prawat wannakhadii thay samrap naksiksaa* [History of Thai Literature for Students]. 8th Edition. Bangkok: Thay Watthana Phanit.

Posakritsana, Phaop. 1977. *Wannakam prakop kaanlen nang yay wat kanon* [Literary works on the giant shadow play at Kanon temple]. Bangkok: Samnak Naay Ratthamontri Toratat and Witthayut.

Prat, Sri. 1979. *Anirut kham chan.* 4th printing. Bangkok: Ministry of Fine Arts.

Rajadhon, Anuman, Phya. 1986. "Notes on the Thread Square." In *Popular Buddhism in Siam and other Essays on Thai Studies.* Bangkok: Thai Inter-Religious Commission for Development and Sathirakoses Nagapradipa Foundation, 145-67.

Rajanupab, Damrong, H.R.H. Prince. 1967. *Nitaan Boraannakhadii* [Ancient Tales]. Bangkok: Khurusapa Press.

Reid, Anthony. 1988. *Southeast Asia in the Age of Commerce, 1450-1680: The Lands Below the Winds.* New Haven: Yale University Press.

Reynolds, Frank. 1972. "The Two Wheels of Dhamma: A Study of Early Buddhism." In *The Two Wheels of Dhamma,* ed. Gananath Obeyesekere, Frank Reynolds, and Bardwell L. Smith, AAR Studies in Religion no. 3. Chambersburg, PA: American Academy of Religion, 6-30.

Reynolds, Frank E., and Mani B. Reynolds (trans.). 1982. *Three Worlds According to King Ruang: A Thai Buddhist Cosmology*. Berkeley: Berkeley Buddhist Studies Series 4.

Rosenburg, Klaus. 1976. Die Epischen Chan-Dichtungen in der Literatur Thailands mit einer Vollstandingen Ubersetzung des Anirut Kham Chan [The Epic chan Poetry in the Literature of Thailand with a Detailed Translation of Anirut kham chan]. Hamburg: Gesellschaft fur Natur und Volkerkunde Ostasiens.

Soedesiri, Rote. 1975. "Elephant Hunting." *Muang Boran Journal* 2(1):38-48.

Smithies, Michael, and Eurayporn Kerdchouay. 1972. "Nang Talung: The Shadow Theater of Southern Thailand." *Journal of the Siam Society* 60(1):379-90.

Terral, G. 1956. "Samuddaghosajataka: Conte Pali Tire du Pannasajataka." *Bulletin de l'Ecole Francaise d'Extreme-Orient* 48(1):249-351.

Visuddhibedya, La-iad. 1979. *Chang nay wannakhadii sansakrit lae wannakhadii pali* [Elephants in Sanskrit and Pali Literature]. M.A. thesis, Department of Eastern Languages, Chulalongkorn University, Bangkok.

Yuden, Wannaw. 1984. *Prawat wannakhadii samay sukhothai lae ayutthaya* [History of the Literature from the Sukhothai and Ayutthaya Periods]. Bangkok: Thai Watthana Phanit.

MONOGRAPHS IN INTERNATIONAL STUDIES

Africa Series

ISBN Prefix 0-89680-

38. Wright, Donald R. *Oral Traditions From the Gambia: Volume II, Family Elders.* 1980. 200pp.
     084-9 $15.00

43. Harik, Elsa M. and Donald G. Schilling. *The Politics of Education in Colonial Algeria and Kenya.* 1984. 102pp.
     117-9 $12.50

45. Keto, C. Tsehloane. *American-South African Relations 1784–1980: Review and Select Bibliography.* 1985. 159pp.
     128-4 $11.00

46. Burness, Don, and Mary-Lou Burness, eds. *Wanasema: Conversations with African Writers.* 1985. 95pp.
     129-2 $11.00

47. Switzer, Les. *Media and Dependency in South Africa: A Case Study of the Press and the Ciskei "Homeland."* 1985. 80pp.
     130-6 $10.00

48. Heggoy, Alf Andrew. *The French Conquest of Algiers, 1830: An Algerian Oral Tradition.* 1986. 101pp.
     131-4 $11.00

49. Hart, Ursula Kingsmill. *Two Ladies of Colonial Algeria: The Lives and Times of Aurelie Picard and Isabelle Eberhardt.* 1987. 156pp.
     143-8 $11.00

51. Clayton, Anthony, and David Killingray. *Khaki and Blue: Military and Police in British Colonial Africa.* 1989. 235pp.
     147-0 $18.00

52. Northrup, David. *Beyond the Bend in the River: African Labor in Eastern Zaire, 1864-1940.* 1988. 195pp.
     151-9 $15.00

53. Makinde, M. Akin. *African Philosophy, Culture, and Traditional Medicine.* 1988. 175pp.
152-7 $13.00

54. Parson, Jack ed. *Succession to High Office in Botswana. Three Case Studies.* 1990. 443pp.
157-8 $20.00

55. Burness, Don. *A Horse of White Clouds.* 1989. 193pp.
158-6 $12.00

56. Staudinger, Paul. *In the Heart of the Hausa States.* Tr. by Johanna Moody. 1990. 2 vols. 653pp.
160-8 $35.00

57. Sikainga, Ahmad Alawad. *The Western Bahr Al-Ghazal Under British Rule: 1898-1956.* 1991. 183pp.
161-6 $15.00

58. Wilson, Louis E. *The Krobo People of Ghana to 1892: A Political and Social History.* 1991. 254pp.
164-0 $20.00

59. du Toit, Brian M. *Cannabis, Alcohol, and the South African Student: Adolescent Drug Use 1974-1985.* 1991. 166pp.
166-7 $17.00

60. Falola, Toyin, ed. *The Political Economy of Health in Africa.* 1992. 254pp.
168-3 $17.00

61. Kiros, Tedros. *Moral Philosophy and Development: The Human Condition in Africa.* 1992. 178pp.
171-3 $18.00

62. Burness, Don. *Echoes of the Sunbird: An Anthology of Contemporary African Poetry.* 1993. 198pp.
173-X $17.00

63. Glew, Robert S., and Chaibou Babalé. *Hausa Folktales from Niger.* 1993. 136pp.
176-4 $15.00

Latin America Series

9. Tata, Robert J. *Structural Changes in Puerto Rico's Economy: 1947-1976.* 1981. xiv, 104pp.
107-1 $11.00

11. O'Shaughnessy, Laura N., and Louis H. Serra. *Church and Revolution in Nicaragua.* 1986. 118pp.
126-8 $11.00

12. Wallace, Brian. *Ownership and Development: A comparison of Domestic and Foreign Investment in Colombian Manufacturing.* 1987. 186pp.
145-4 $10.00

13. Henderson, James D. *Conservative Thought in Latin America: The Ideas of Laureano Gomez.* 1988. 150pp.
148-9 $13.00

14. Summ, G. Harvey, and Tom Kelly. *The Good Neighbors: America, Panama, and the 1977 Canal Treaties.* 1988. 135pp.
149-7 $13.00

15. Peritore, Patrick. *Socialism, Communism, and Liberation Theology in Brazil: An Opinion Survey Using Q-Methodology.* 1990. 245pp.
156-X $15.00

16. Alexander, Robert J. *Juscelino Kubitschek and the Development of Brazil.* 1991. 429pp.
163-2 $25.00

17. Mijeski, Kenneth J., ed. *The Nicaraguan Constitution of 1987: English Translation and Commentary.* 1990. 355pp.
165-9 $25.00

18. Finnegan, Pamela May. *The Tension of Paradox: José Donoso's The Obscene Bird of Night as Spiritual Exercises.* 1992. 179pp.
169-1 $15.00

19. Sung Ho Kim and Thomas W. Walker, eds., *Perspectives on War and Peace in Central America*. 1992. 150pp.
172-1 $14.00

Southeast Asia Series

47. Wessing, Robert. *Cosmology and Social Behavior in a West Javanese Settlement*. 1978. 200pp.
072-5 $12.00

56A. Duiker, William J. *Vietnam Since the Fall of Saigon*. Updated edition. 1989. 383pp.
162-4 $17.00

64. Dardjowidjojo, Soenjono. *Vocabulary Building in Indonesian: An Advanced Reader*. 1984. xviii, 256pp.
118-7 $26.00

65. Errington, J. Joseph. *Language and Social Change in Java: Linguistic Reflexes of Modernization in a Traditional Royal Polity*. 1985. xiv, 211pp.
120-9 $20.00

66. Binh, Tran Tu. *The Red Earth: A Vietnamese Memoir of Life on a Colonial Rubber Plantation*. Tr. by John Spragens. Ed. by David Marr. 1985. xii, 98pp.
119-5 $11.00

68. Syukri, Ibrahim. *History of the Malay Kingdom of Patani*. Tr. by Connor Bailey and John N. Miksic. 1985. xix, 113pp.
123-3 $12.00

69. Keeler, Ward. *Javanese: A Cultural Approach*. 1984. xxxvi, 522pp., Third printing 1992.
121-7 $25.00

70. Wilson, Constance M., and Lucien M. Hanks. *Burma-Thailand Frontier Over Sixteen Decades: Three Descriptive Documents*. 1985. x, 128pp.
124-1 $11.00

71.   Thomas, Lynn L., and Franz von Benda-Beckmann, eds. *Change and Continuity in Minangkabau: Local, Regional, and Historical Perspectives on West Sumatra.* 1986. 363pp.
127-6 $16.00

72.   Reid, Anthony, and Oki Akira, eds. *The Japanese Experience in Indonesia: Selected Memoirs of 1942-1945.* 1986. 411pp., 20 illus.
132-2 $20.00

73.   Smirenskaia, Zhanna D. *Peasants in Asia: Social Consciousness and Social Struggle.* Tr. by Michael J. Buckley. 1987. 248pp.
134-9 $14.00

74.   McArthur, M.S.H. *Report on Brunei in 1904.* Ed. by A.V.M. Horton. 1987. 304pp.
135-7 $15.00

75.   Lockard, Craig Alan. *From Kampung to City. A Social History of Kuching Malaysia 1820-1970.* 1987. 311pp.
136-5 $16.00

76.   McGinn, Richard. *Studies in Austronesian Linguistics.* 1988. 492pp.
137-3 $20.00

77.   Muego, Benjamin N. *Spectator Society: The Philippines Under Martial Rule.* 1988. 232pp.
138-1 $15.00

79.   Walton, Susan Pratt. *Mode in Javanese Music.* 1987. 279pp.
144-6 $15.00

80.   Nguyen Anh Tuan. *South Vietnam Trial and Experience: A Challenge for Development.* 1987. 482pp.
141-1 $18.00

81.   Van der Veur, Paul W., ed. *Toward a Glorious Indonesia: Reminiscences and Observations of Dr. Soetomo.* 1987. 367pp.
142-X $16.00

82. Spores, John C. *Running Amok: An Historical Inquiry.* 1988. 190pp.
140-3 $13.00

83. Malaka. *From Jail to Jail.* Tr. and ed. by Helen Jarvis. 1990. 3 vols. 1,226pp.
150-0 $55.00

84. Devas, Nick. *Financing Local Government in Indonesia.* 1989. 344pp.
153-5 $16.00

85. Suryadinata, Leo. *Military Ascendancy and Political Culture: A Study of Indonesia's Golkar.* 1989. 250pp.
154-3 $18.00

86. Williams, Michael. *Communism, Religion, and Revolt in Banten.* 1990. 356pp.
155-1 $14.00

87. Hudak, Thomas John. *The Indigenization of Pali Meters in Thai Poetry.* 1990. 237pp.
159-4 $15.00

88. Lay, Ma Ma. *Not Out of Hate: A Novel of Burma.* Tr. by Margaret Aung-Thwin. Ed. by William Frederick. 1991. 222pp.
167-5 $20.00

89. Anwar, Chairil. *The Voice of the Night: Complete Poetry and Prose of Anwar Chairil.* 1993. Revised Edition. Tr. by Burton Raffel. 180pp.
                                                                         $17.00

90. Hudak, Thomas John, tr. *The Tale of Prince Samuttakote: A Buddhist Epic from Thailand.* 1993. 275pp.
174-8 $20.00

91. Roskies, D. M., ed. *Text/Politics in Island Southeast Asia: Essays in Interpretation.* 1993. 321pp.
175-6 $25.00

ORDERING INFORMATION

Orders for titles in the Monographs in International Studies series may be placed through the Ohio University Press, Scott Quadrangle, Athens, Ohio 45701-2979 or through any local bookstore. Individuals should remit payment by check, VISA, or MasterCard.* People ordering from the United Kingdom, Continental Europe, the Middle East, and Africa should order through Academic and University Publishers Group, 1 Gower Street, London WC1E, England. Orders from the Pacific Region, Asia, Australia, and New Zealand should be sent to East-West Export Books, c/o the University of Hawaii Press, 2840 Kolowalu Street, Honolulu, Hawaii 96822, USA.

Other individuals ordering from outside of the U.S. should remit in U.S. funds to Ohio University Press either by International Money Order or by a check drawn on a U.S. bank.** Most out-of-print titles may be ordered from University Microfilms, Inc., 300 North Zeeb Road, Ann Arbor, Michigan 48106, USA.

Prices are subject to change without notice.

* Please include $3.00 for the first book and 75¢ for each additional book for shipping and handling.

** Please include $4.00 for the first book and 75¢ for each additional book for foreign shipping and handling.

Lightning Source UK Ltd.
Milton Keynes UK
UKHW010031091022
410021UK00011B/306